UP IN THE AIR

A Pilot's Journey

PRAISE FOR

Up in the Air, a pilot's journey

If Robert Fulton flies a jet or helicopter as good as he writes and tells the story of his aviation career, he must be one heck of a pilot. The lessons learned and experiences related in this book are a worthwhile read for anyone in aviation from a student pilot to the senior airline captain flying all over the world.

Captain Brian Will
777 & 737 Captain, American Airlines, retired
Former US Air Force F-15 pilot

Rob Fulton's book Up in the Air allowed me to have a virtual copilot seat next to him. I felt his fears as if I had been there. I was around to watch him work through a variety of life-threatening flight challenges.

This book reinforced my belief that difficult challenges provide the opportunities to grow and to become better from life's lessons. This is not a book about flying, it is a book about navigating through life.

Jack Kane
Audit Committee Chairman
Health Catalyst

UP IN THE AIR: A Pilot's Journey is one of those books that is hard to put down especially if you like adventure stories that are true. It is a book about facing and overcoming challenges as well as a superb example of how it is possible to reinvent yourself if you want to. It's a must-read.

Marianne Oehser, retirement expert and author of
Your Happiness Portfolio® for Retirement:
It's Not About the Money.

Robert Fulton has had an amazing aviation adventure and career. He has captured the excitement of flying and shares the traumas and close calls he has experienced and the satisfaction he has enjoyed over decades flying helicopters and fixed wing aircraft in combat and civil aviation.

Howard Putnam
Former CEO Southwest Airlines & Braniff International
Author: The Winds of Turbulence
Speaker Hall of Fame

Up In the Air is a tale that captures the awe and wonder of flight that many appreciate but so few actually experience. This story not only captures the delicate balance between life and death experienced by aviators everywhere, no matter whether you fly a Cessna, an Apache, or an F-16, where every exciting moment and in every story there is a split-second difference between disaster and mission completion. Reading about Rob's life in the cockpit brings these moments and stories to life and leaves the reader with the deep appreciation of the calling to the air that captures the dreams of us all.

Jeff Valenzia
F-16 Pilot

I know Robbie Fulton personally and he is my friend, but believe me my thumb is not on the scale when I tell you this is a GREAT book!

We are both experienced pilots although our careers took different turns. He went to war and flew a gunship in Vietnam. He has an ATP rating in both fixed wing and helicopters. Well you get the idea. If you love flying, you will love reading this book.

Captain C.E. Chapman
Eastern Airlines, retired

UP IN THE AIR

A Pilot's Journey

ROBERT FULTON

Up in the Air, A Pilot's Journey

Copyright © 2020 Robert Fulton

Cover and Interior Design: Indigo Design, Inc.

designbyindigo.com

ISBN: 978-1-7347014-0-1

Printed in the U.S.A.

DEDICATION

Ernest Gann, Antoine de Saint-Exuperty, and Pierre Clostermann were flyers and authors that inspired me from a young age to not only go up in the air, but to live an adventurous aerial life full of variety while accumulating valuable experiences. This I seem to have accomplished through their influence. Although these men became legends and I am not, I would like to humbly offer this book as a tribute to their lasting ability to inspire us all.

ACKNOWLEDGMENTS

Editor: Linda Campbell

Linda worked double duty throughout the editing challenge as she taught her classes at a college in Arizona and faithfully offered up insightful and marvelous edits that contributed so much to the quality of the narrative in the book.

Cover Design: Audria Wooster

Audria created a unique and unusual design for my book using tools and talents others in the industry struggled to embrace. She "got it!"

Interior Design: Audria Wooster

SUPPORT AND GUIDANCE

Debra, my good wife who without complaint and with generous encouragement urged me forward to the completion of the project.

Marianne Oehser, my dear friend and point man (woman) who tirelessly offered guidance, helpful suggestions, read the manuscript early, supplied plentiful and relevant articles and digital instruction, and involved friends and associates of hers who willingly wrote reviews after having read the book.

Thank You!

TABLE OF CONTENTS

FOREWORD

Dear Reader,

When you open the pages of this book, there are some facts about the author that you should keep in mind. No, he isn't crazy, and, yes, he really did encounter all of these scenarios. And that's why I am so proud to call him my father. We have taken very different career paths, he as a career pilot and I as a Communications Executive at a Fortune 50 company, but writing is one place where our paths have crossed. I do not know of anyone fuller of stories to tell than my father. The art of storytelling is truly that—an art—and Robert Fulton has finally told his stories—and we are finally allowed to listen.

I also want to call attention to the word Journey in the book title. We are all on some kind of journey at each point in our lives, and some parts of that journey are more difficult than others. Sometimes our path is smooth, straight, and easy, while other times, it is full of rocks, thorns, and a seemingly endless incline. But that's really what a journey is, isn't it? A journey has both a start and an end, but what I think we really learn from this exciting read, is that the middle of the journey—when we're really in the thick of it—is where it matters the most because it transforms us into the person we need to be.

You will treasure every tale in this work; each one is different, yet all experienced by the same person. My father has had an adventurous spirit for as long as I can remember. He has taken me aboard helicopters and boats ever since I was born, and I fondly look back at pictures and videos from our adventures. As I recall those times, some insights about my father stand out to me the most: how he is always up for "finding a way," and no matter what challenge he faces—and there have been some serious ones—he just figures it out. That mindset takes resilience, strength, and faith in yourself, traits that are hard to find these days.

A great example of this "We will find a way" attitude happened one morning in Utah during a visit to my grandmother's house. My father quietly walked down to the basement where I was sleeping on the couch and gently whispered, "Wake up. I saw this waterfall when I was flying the other day. We're going to find it."

I awoke excited but couldn't help wondering "How does he know how to get there?" He saw the waterfall from an aerial view. There was no path or trail, just something he happened to see below while in-flight. But that kind of detail doesn't matter to my dad. Now, don't confuse his thirst for adventure with carelessness; Rob was always incredibly prepared. That day, he had packed food as well as a weapon in case we encountered a panther (a risk I was unaware of at the time). He just knew that with his sense of direction, we would find it.

And that we did. After trekking through thick brush with pathless twists and turns, we rounded a corner onto the most beautiful display of waterfalls I had ever seen. Four crystal-clear falls crashing down slate-gray rocks into a pristine pool of water. We left with a few scratches from our hike through uncleared forest, and later heard of panthers in the area, but we had found our waterfall. And not many people can say that.

Even twenty-five years later, when my husband, Sean, and I were staying with my father and lovely stepmother, Debbie, in Estero, Florida, I was not surprised when my father woke us and said, "I heard about this place in the Everglades called the Ten Thousand Islands. Let's pack up the sailboat and go camping there. And don't worry, we'll find it." So with a big grin on my face, we got up, packed the boat, and found it. And, boy, was it worth it!

I am excited for you to read this book and hear the actual stories from such an interesting perspective. Even more, I hope they inspire you with a similar courage to navigate your own path in life. As you read these pages, not only will you be immersed in countless adventures and unimaginable flight scenarios, but you will also see how the reinvention of one's self and ongoing adaptability remain critical skills in today's ever-evolving world. Whether your journey is up in the air or down on the ground, everyone has something to gain from these adventure-filled stories brimming with wit and useful life-lessons.

Enjoy every moment,
Elise Fulton

GLOSSARY

A/C .... Stands for Aircraft Commander

ADF .... The most basic navigation device, its single needle points or homes on an AM radio signal, including your local AM radio station.

Adit .... A nearly horizontal passage leading into a mine.

ATC .... Air Traffic Control

Autorotation .... When a helicopter loses engine power, the collective lever (power) is placed down (no pitch in main rotor blades). As it glides downward, the aircrafts design enables the air coming up through the main rotor blade to spin them at an RPM adequate for controlled flight.

Avionics .... Refers to the radio package in an aircraft that contains both communication and navigation radios.

Azimuth .... An angle of horizontal deviation.

Cedar Bolt .... Like split firewood, a bundle of cedar blocks is secured by a rope into a pile of wood, weighing approximately a thousand pounds. Each bolt is then attached to a hook suspended by a cable from the helicopter and then transported from the forest to a loading zone.

Chicken Plate .... The front ceramic plate of a bullet- proof vest that can be removed and rested on the lap of a pilot to cover his chest while secured in his aircraft by a three-point harness. The plate is secured between the pilot's chest and the harness.

Chinook .... A large double-rotor helicopter (one rotor over the tail, one above the cock pit), capable of lifting 20,000 pounds or carrying up to 40 troops.

Cobra .... The name applied to the AH-1G two-man gunship. Also referred to as a "Snake" or "Huey Cobra."

Collective .... The pilot-operated lever that controls the amount of pitch in the main rotor blades. On turbine engines, a governor adjusts the power requirements, but on a piston engine, the pilot must manually adjust the throttle (attached to the collective) to match the load requirements. Increased main rotor pitch requires an increase in throttle, etc.

Control Friction .... An adjustable friction attached to each helicopter control enabling the pilot to regulate the amount of pull needed to move that specific control (such as the collective) or to lock it to prevent further motion.

Control Rods .... Vertical rods that the cyclic and collective in the cockpit move up and down through mechanical linkage to a rotating swash-plate that changes the pitch in the main rotor blades to control helicopter flight.

Core Drill .... A small portable drill that penetrates rock strata to accumulate a continuous rock sample in its hollow pipe. Also referred to as a Diamond Drill.

Crabbed .... If the prevailing wind is not directly on the aircraft's nose the aircraft must be partially angled into the wind so it can maintain its desired course, thus "crabbed into the wind."

Cyclic .... The vertical stick control between the pilot's legs used to control the helicopter's direction or speed by changing the pitch of the main rotor blades at different locations within their rotation. Also referred to as "stick" or "joy stick."

EMS .... Emergency Medical Services

FBO .... Fixed Base Operation (providing fuel and other aviation-related services at an airport)

Ferry Flight .... Flying an aircraft minus passengers from one location to another in order to reposition it geographically.

Fixed Landing Gear... Aircraft with landing gear that does not retract for flight.

Fixed-Wing .... A defining term that distinguishes an airplane from a rotary wing (helicopter).

Flare .... Bringing the nose up gradually or steeply to lose forward speed. Also can be done sideways by tipping the helicopter fuselage upward on either side.

Flight Idle .... A throttle position on a jet turbine engine that means the engine is at full RPM for flight.

Fuselage .... The basic structure of an aircraft to which the wings or rotors are attached.

GCA .... A ground controller gives flight corrections to the flying pilot until the pilot has the runway environment in sight. This is done by reference to radar, thus Ground Controlled Approach.

Grunt .... Reference to ground soldiers in Vietnam, not derogatory.

Hand Prop .... A method of starting a piston airplane engine when no electrical power is available (i.e. dead battery). Limited to small aircrafts only.

Hospital Transfer .... When a patient in critical condition is transferred by EMS helicopter from one hospital to another offering a higher level of care.

Huey .... A nickname for the helicopter "work horse" of the Vietnam War. Used as a Medevac, troop transport, resupply transport, and gunship. Eight feet wide by forty-eight feet long; top speed 115 mph.

IFR .... Instrument Flight Rules. Regulations that govern flights conducted during weather-related visibility restrictions less than three miles.

ILS .... A ground station that transmits both an azimuth and a glide slope, which are combined to provide a precision approach for incoming aircraft down to 200 feet.

Incoming .... Refers to enemy artillery in the form of mortar shells, rockets, and small artillery rounds.

Mag Check .... A pre-takeoff piston-engine check that tests the two magnetos suppling electrical voltage to the engine spark plugs. Both mags must be working for a safe flight.

Mini-gun .... A Gatling-style-rotating barrel (six) assembly, firing 6,000 rounds per minute of 7.62 ammunition. Mounted in the swiveling, nose turret of the Cobra gunship.

NCO .... Military Non Commissioned Officer. (i.e. sergeant).

NOMAX .... A fire-retardant material used in jackets, flight suits, and flight gloves for increased flight safety.

OD .... Olive Drab—a color.

Open Tail Boom ...... Refers to the structure on a helicopter that connects the tail to the fuselage and is constructed from metal tubing without a metal or fabric covering.

Passenger Manifest.. The list of specific passengers loaded aboard an aircraft for transport to a distant destination. One copy is held at the departure location.

PBY .... A type of large amphibious airplane used for long-range patrol during WWII. Used as passenger aircraft after the war in remote areas. Rumored to never exceed 100mph, landing, taking off, or at cruise.

Pedals .... Reference to the left and right foot pedals on the floor of an aircraft. In an airplane, they move the rudder. In a helicopter, they control the tail rotor's pitch. In a helicopter, the left pedal is pushed when power (collective is pulled up) is increased to the main rotor. The right pedal is pushed (collective is lowered) when power to the main rotor is decreased. Used for turning during a hover, but not in flight.

Prop Plane .... Referring to an airplane with a propeller as opposed to one that has jet engines for propulsion.

PSP .... Pierced Steel Planking (Marston Mat). An interlocking steel mat that measures ten feet by fifteen inches with a total of 29 holes that reduces each piece's weight during shipping. Used in WWII for building runway surfaces. Used in Vietnam to construct landing surfaces or barriers of any length or height in remote areas of of operation.

Revetment .... Also referred to as a "berm." Wall of sandbags to protect aircraft, encampments, equipment, etc. Built up on two or three sides of parked aircraft as protection from enemy artillery. Often held in place in Vietnam by PSP.

Rotor Disc .... When the main rotor of a helicopter spins so that individual blades can no longer be distinguished and the resulting blur appears as a disc.

Rotor Wash .... The huge volume of wind displaced by rotor blades gusting at initial speeds of up to 100 mph. The greater the pitch angle in the main rotor blades, the greater the down wash below or behind the helicopter.

Slipping .... A flight maneuver which allows an aircraft to lose altitude rapidly by crossing the flight controls (i.e. making a left turn, but pushing the opposite rudder).

Slip Tank .... A mounted fuel tank externally mounted to the belly of an aircraft.

Snake .... The nickname for the Bell AH-1G, designated the Cobra by its manufacture.

Tail Boom .... The structure on the helicopter that connects the tail to the fuselage. The tail rotor drive shaft is attached on top of its length and is most often covered, but easily accessible.

Torque Gage .... A primary instrument on the aircraft panel that measures the amount of power available on a jet engine. Commonly used on turbine engine applications.

Transitional Lift ...... An aeronautical term that identifies the point in helicopter flight (12-18 mph) when the main rotor is no longer the only source of lift and is aided by clean air moving across the rotor disc during forward flight. When reached, the engine power can be reduced with no loss of performance.

Transponder .... A radio that automatically transmits an identifying return signal when an inquiry is directed at it electronically.

VC .... Viet Cong

Venturi Effect .... The increased speed and lowering of air pressure as air passes through a restricted opening.

VFR .... Visual Flight Rules. Regulations that are used when operating an aircraft in unrestricted visibility or during sustained visual contact with the ground.

VOR .... A ground-based, radio navigation device, which transmits an azimuth for each of the 365 degrees of compass heading.

Walk Around .... A term referring to an inspection that the pilot conducts briefly prior to flight, checking for the obvious: doors latched, vital controls connected, and fluid levels acceptable. A quick procedure compared to an initial preflight inspection.

WOC .... Warrant Officer Candidate. A term referring to a flight school student. Upon graduation, the Army promoted a successful candidate from the rank of E5 to Warrant Officer.

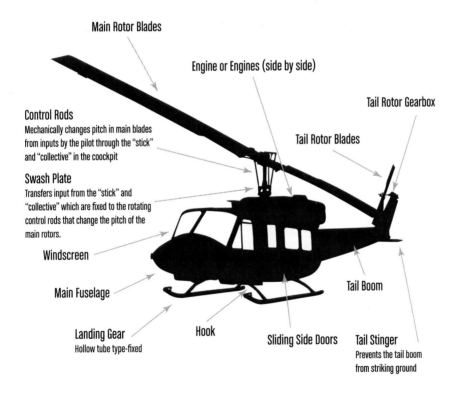

Main Rotor Blades

Engine or Engines (side by side)

Tail Rotor Gearbox

Control Rods
Mechanically changes pitch in main blades from inputs by the pilot through the "stick" and "collective" in the coockpit

Tail Rotor Blades

Swash Plate
Transfers input from the "stick" and "collective" which are fixed to the rotating control rods that change the pitch of the main rotors.

Windscreen

Tail Boom

Main Fuselage

Landing Gear
Hollow tube type-fixed

Hook

Sliding Side Doors

Tail Stinger
Prevents the tail boom from striking ground

Rudder
Steers aircraft during ground operations

Elevator
Controls nose-up, nose downin flight

Engine

Cockpit

Single Wing
Trailing edge holds Flaps
(for landing).
Ailerons (for turning)

Tail Wheel
Rolls on the ground during taxi and initial
take-off, blocking forward visibility over
the nose that is canted upward

Main Gear (2)

INTRODUCTION

It took me thirty years to come to grips with the emotions that were churned up by an event in the chapter "Snakes and Rockets." During those years, I desperately needed to turn the trauma of that experience into words and help myself forward. I thought about it often but was never able to find the voice to form the phrases that would release me from that profound sadness.

Only after all those years of composting that particular event, and with help from the VA, who identified me in a survey regarding PTSD issues and offered me treatment, did I manage to free myself with eleven pages of words I put onto a computer screen.

I had other memories, not as dramatic, but also memorable, why not record them also? I began to appreciate, at this point, that after almost fifty years of non-stop employment as a pilot I had many experiences that would be of interest to others. As these tales unfolded, I became aware of their variety and their compelling circumstances. I was startled to realize just how often I had reinvented myself to stay employed and viable. I kept writing. All these stories are real. I was there.

The helicopter was reinvented in the course of the Vietnam War where it functioned as an aerial jeep, ambulance, truck, and rocket launcher. The use of reliable and much lighter jet-powered engines instead of the heavy steel internal combustion engines finally made the helicopter feasible to operate continuously day and night.

On the home front, a new industry, supplied with a constant stream of veteran Vietnam helicopter pilots, developed and began to expand its opportunities, finding new applications for helicopters of any size.

I joined in this outbreak of evolving ideas relatively early. Companies and owners constantly expanded their fleets and techniques to master the next "big idea." Logging, supporting off-shore oil drilling, building power lines and ski lifts, hunting for tuna off a ship at sea, and moving trauma patients from a car wreck on the highway to the emergency room of a hospital all came out of that period of rapid expansion and new utilizations for the helicopter.

For helicopter pilots, it meant a lot of choices for work, but when you got to the new job, which was usually a relatively new concept in helicopter operations, few of the pilots there had any in-depth experience of how it all worked or where the idea was headed. Did the new concept work economically? How long would it last? How you managed your flight task in the new endeavor would eventually produce the answers. Crashes and high expense were the killers of some of these new notions. Many concepts, however, survived the early years and established themselves as vital and beneficial applications of vertical flight.

Sometimes the ideas were great, but due to the abundance of helicopter pilots, the pay was terrible, and you may be gone six weeks or more and only home for just a couple of days. If you didn't like that routine, the company knew there were a dozen pilots standing outside the door who would say yes to the job. It got better later—much later. Someone like me had to find a way to navigate through all this and get to the "much later" part when the pay would be better and more frequent rotations back to civilization meant you could finally have a home life.

I have always thought as an aviator that I was never smarter, braver, or luckier than my last flight. To leave the earth in any mechanical device takes grit. Working in an aerial world where you put whatever machine you are flying up against fate, weather, unforeseen obstacles, and a long list of variables to accomplish a specific task reminds you of your forward-leaning self back on earth, pushing into the headwinds presented to you in that world of chaos. You will find in these chapters not unlike your life on the ground—challenges, dangers, and demands for urgent action. No doubt there are parallels here, and I intend to uncover them.

I loved flying from the very beginning and never lost my passion for it. It never occurred to me that I had any special gifts in that regard. I just knew after the first flight that being a pilot was all I wanted to do.

Wanting to fly replaced my determination to grow up and be a Royal Canadian Mounted Policeman. I lay in front of the console radio cabinet every week listening intently to "Sergeant Preston of the Yukon." About age eleven, I switched to "Sky King," and I never looked back.

I have used simplified technical explanations in these stories only because the events cannot be fully appreciated without some explanation of how things work or what is going on aerodynamical and mechanically. I have included a glossary and diagrams to help you unwind these tales. Hopefully, these aids will provide the insight needed to understand and appreciate the action in each chapter.

More than any other time in history, events and the rapid expansion of technology challenge workers to somehow reinvent themselves many times over in order to advance financially, professionally, and personally. You will see in the course of reading this book that although I was a pilot, the challenges of each new task was often drastically different in application whether in a fixed-wing or a helicopter. There wasn't much time to get yourself up to speed in the assignment you were given. The tools and objectives kept changing as you worked. Most assuredly, you will find it the same in your own efforts to stay relevant.

There are other stories, of course, many of them. I selected these stories to illustrate the variety of my experiences and my constant challenge to reinvent myself. I hope that readers who are not fliers or are not necessarily experienced in this field will also have the interest to pick up the book. My wish is that in a meaningful way, it will be entertaining, informative, and helpful to all readers.

I have always loved a good "hangar story," listening to other pilots—young or old—demonstrating with both hands in the air their diving, hovering, and twisting as they describe their favorite adventure in the sky. My wish is that you will find similar enjoyment in these pages.

My earliest flight-related memory, most likely at the age of four, was of standing with my little sister in our backyard near the wooden swing my father had built for us and painted green from leftover house paint.

Mom had joined us there, still in her apron after fixing breakfast. With a faded red hose, she watered her flowerbeds, the smell of the freshly watered plants mixing with the precipitating dust we had kicked up from around the swing producing the perfume of fresh rain. The cool morning air beginning to warm into summer heat enveloped my sister and me with the promise of a new day.

Suddenly, Mom gestured toward the sky. "Look Robbie," she said, a touch of amusement in her voice, "your Dad is waving down at you!"

I followed the direction of her hand and saw, hanging in the air above us, a silver blimp slowly making its way across the sky. The longer I stared at the curious phenomenon, the more I could imagine my dad leaning out a window of the little house beneath it and waving down at me. It became very real.

My baby sister, a toe head, dressed in a short white smocked dress, squinted into the morning sun as we jumped up and down, fully embracing the idea of waving up at our Father waving down at us!

"Look Mom," I cried, "he's up in the air!"

Of course, my Mom knew that my Father was working at the sawmill, but she obviously enjoyed producing this fantasy for her two young children.

That particular morning launched a fascination with flight that has never died. The limits of my small mind were suddenly expanded as I was introduced, although in a fairy tale way, to the concept of flying across the vastness of the blue sky that was everywhere you looked. It may have been the first seed planted in my youthful imagination that later produced my life, up in the air.

Chapter 1

THIRTY SECONDS OVER TOKYO

Have you ever been immersed in absolute darkness at least once in your life, the kind of blackness that hides your hand in front of your face? Perhaps deep in a cave or in a room with no windows and the lights are out. Impenetrable. A little scary? Afraid to take a step forward?

Substitute bright white for darkness. The same effect, but now your world is white, and your senses are confused in the same way—there is no direction, there is nothing. Not the white that brings light and clarity, but the white that is draped over you like a thick sheet. Consider impenetrable whiteness, so blinding that visibility ends at your fingertips.

In the Arctic, they call this a "whiteout." There are no shadows. There is no contrast. There is only white. The deep chill of arctic cold and high wind are present, but neither wind nor cold can give you a sense of your location, direction, or movement. There is only white, and then there is fear.

The Arctic latitudes at the top of North America are considered semi-arid, however, snow still blankets the surface during the long winter due to the extreme temperatures. Fierce winds regularly sweep the landscape and blowing snow, torn by the wind from its tentative attachment to the surface ice and tundra, generates a whiteout that could last for days and extend as high as 1000 feet or more. Snow drifts accumulate but remain invisible to the eye.

During the winter months when night lasts almost twenty-four hours, mounted ropes interconnect all of the important destinations in each village. Lanyards of frozen cord—like a giant web—attach each home to the life-sustaining lines throughout the town. Each resident grips these lifelines leading from their dwellings to the Post Office or store when walking there and back during the total blindness of a whiteout. Letting go for even a moment and stepping away a foot or two can lead to a cold death.

I had never before heard the term whiteout, but now I was in one on Melville Island in the high Arctic islands of Canada. I was struggling through my first civilian flying job, virtually ignorant of these conditions or their dangers. I had learned and honed my helicopter flying skills where there was no snow: in both the American South and Southeast Asia. A single, long airplane flight had taken me from the known into the unknown. I just didn't know it yet.

Less than a month earlier, I had received an "early out" and an honorable discharge from the Army at Fort Rucker, Alabama, deep in the heart of Dixie. My wife and two small children were left behind and living in our recently purchased house trailer. I took our Volkswagen Super Beetle north to Calgary,

Alberta, Canada, where I knew there were lots of helicopters and hopefully, a flying job. My family would join me as soon as I started getting a regular paycheck. If that sounds somewhat daring or even a bit too optimistic, it was a fitting prelude for what was about to unfold.

As I stepped from a just-landed Boeing 737 onto the top end of an up-sloping "pea gravel" runway in Resolute Bay, Northwest Territories, 600 miles above the Arctic Circle, about fifty yards to my right was an idling red and white helicopter. Since the U.S. Military had none of these types of aircraft in its inventory, I had no idea that they even existed, given my limited knowledge of the civilian helicopter industry.

The Chief Pilot of Klondike Helicopters out of Calgary, Alberta, stood near the helicopter. He was a stocky man. He stood with his feet apart. His bright red ball cap, the word "Klondike" scrolled in white across the front, was pulled down snuggly on his round head. Strands of blondish hair protruded from its edge and fluttered rapidly in the rotor wash from the running helicopter.

He walked up, shook my hand firmly, gave me a quick once-over, and grabbed my bags. He walked deliberately to the rear door of the helicopter, opened it, and threw them onto the bench seat with a thud.

I stared at the unfamiliar helicopter. The sides of its yellow floats rippled like wavelets on a small pond on a windy day. Its bubble nose flowed back to a smooth cowling, which dropped abruptly to a long, low tail boom that ended with a spinning tail rotor. I hadn't known that helicopters even came with floats.

Fairchild FH 1100—Over Arctic Seas

The chief pilot motioned me to the copilot's seat on the left. As soon as I climbed up over the float and managed to get seated and strapped in, he handed me a headset that immediately poured a steady stream of instructions into my ears.

We flew down the runway to the south and crossed the beach where the runway began its upward slope. Wrecks of broken aircraft, including a Lancaster bomber, littered the approach end of the runway. The wreckage of half a dozen other aircraft littered the beach down to the edge of the lapping waves. The strange world I was entering was just beginning to show itself.

We climbed to 1000 feet and looked out over the harbor where several large freighters were at anchor. I was unsure which ship we were flying to, but it looked like any one of them would be easy to land on given their size. But to my amazement, we stayed at altitude and flew right over them. Farther offshore and just a speck in the distance, a small ship was underway. We began our letdown, the chief pilot talking all the way. Between what I was seeing and what I was hearing, I had no idea what I was retaining or even understood.

The Theta was 180 feet long. Believe me, as ships go, that is tiny when seen from an approaching helicopter, especially with the ship underway. The ship steamed at about 12 knots. As we approached, it turned slightly to give us the relative wind over its starboard quarter. The chief pilot circled once and came to a hover at the height of the helipad built atop a group of industrial mobile homes squeezed together on the low-cut, center portion of the ship. From a steel mast to our right, perhaps twenty feet from our rotor tip, cables and wires ran from thirty feet above the helipad to the bridge to our left, just beyond the spinning main rotor blades. The landing area was within the box of air created by these four obstacles.

The pilot said something about fastening my eyes on the heli-deck and not EVER looking at the side of the moving ship or the water below. But he fought the controls roughly, the helicopter bucking and jumping under his hands and feet in our sideways hover. I learned later that he had been flown in as a replacement just four days earlier, so there was no telling if he had done this just once before—or never.

By concentrating solely on the speed of the passing heli-deck, a helicopter pilot would find himself coming to a steady hover just short of the pad, relative to the moving ship. In reality, though, the helicopter would actually be hovering sideways at 12 knots, the same speed as the ship wallowing side to side in the moderate sea. This relatively equal relationship would enable the pilot to approach the landing deck at a 90 degree angle and land normally as if on a section of runway. Well, not exactly, but kind of!

This landing sequence was required on the Theta since her mission required that she tow an array of large cables behind her as part of the seismic process we were executing. Thus, she could not slow down or turn sharply while dragging cables with ends that held sophisticated, compressed-air discharge ports.

Each time you were landing under the overhead cables and between the towering bridge and the mast, onto the helipad secured atop the trailers. No guardrails or obstructions were allowed on the landing pad for obvious reasons. Even a brief downward glance at the water rushing past the ship while landing would cause you to lose your sense of motionlessness with the helipad in front of you, causing you to slide immediately into the superstructure of the bridge. This could only end one way: Disaster!

On that first day, we literally crashed onto the helipad. Bang! It jarred my teeth!

"Hold the controls," blurted the chief pilot over the intercom.

He twisted the throttle to idle and jumped out his side door, heading for the stairs down to the main boat deck.

He returned shortly afterwards with a couple of bags of his own, opened the aft passenger door, and threw them in on top of mine. With his short legs flailing, he threw himself up onto the float and into the pilot seat. Without a word, he rolled the throttle swiftly to flight RPM and then ripped the poor aircraft off the deck into the air. We were quickly clear of the moving ship.

I understood from all this that he had left the ship while it was underway at sea to meet my plane and see if I had shown up. That same plane was his ticket home. In this part of the world, you were lucky to see a scheduled flight from the south once every 24 hours. There was a reason for his rush.

The trip back to the plane was my "checkout" in this particular aircraft. Besides all the chatter out and back, he cut the throttle once to demonstrate an autorotation. After the recovery from the autorotation, he gave me the controls and told me to fly him to the plane at Resolute Bay. That was my introduction to civilian flying and that model helicopter. That is all the training there was.

When we landed at the ramp again, we shook hands, and he wished me luck, grabbed his bags from the still-running helicopter, and disappeared into the 737 not long before it started its engines for the return trip to Calgary. By the time I returned to the Theta, they had anchored, and the ship sat quietly with only a gentle, rocking motion. That worked for me for a first landing onboard.

I had learned before I left Calgary that the previous mechanic (called an engineer in Canada) in a drunken fit had tried to throw the captain overboard from the bridge, and the pilot (Canadian Navy) had walked off in a dispute over his living quarters and the job in general. At that particular moment, I had walked into the company office in Calgary when all this had fallen on management. The company had been desperate not to lose the contract, so I think they would have taken a chance on anyone with a license.

It had been an odyssey of memorable and curious events leading up to this point. How it would end was still in question; there were no crystal balls even in these mysterious latitudes.

I was now flying off of and onto a 180-foot ship sailing in the Arctic Sea amid icebergs and snow-covered islands. The vessel held forty-five men, a helicopter, and trailers full of seismic equipment. It was a little ship, considering the space required to accommodate a landing and departing helicopter amidships, enough bunks for the crew, a working laboratory/office, and some place to eat and clean up.

Under normal circumstances, it would be manned by a crew of eight, but it had been chartered and fitted out for this expedition by a large Canadian oil company. Transformed from the mission, it had ordinarily been designed for harvest at sea, but it was now a Noah's Ark with forty-five men assigned to dozens of different tasks and technically complicated functions.

The purpose for a helicopter on board, besides moving personnel and supplies, was to assist with the ship's mission of pinpointing oil drilling opportunities on the ocean floor. This was accomplished by dispatching the helicopter to a nearby island where a technician set up and activated a transponder on shore. Using a continuous electronic signal, the transponder identified its exact position to the equipment back onboard so the ship could triangulate its correct geographical position at sea.

Long black air hoses that the ship trailed behind it 24/7 led to huge, compressed air valves underwater that would discharge a great explosion of air on demand. This colossal noise would send strong sound waves beyond the ocean floor into the layers of the earth's crust. Those seismic waves were recorded electronically on the ship's data equipment and then turned into paper maps. The sound waves created anomalies on the maps, geological patterns that identified possible oil pockets for future drilling.

This whole procedure would be conducted on land using dynamite and movable metal houses, called "Dog Houses" carried by helicopter across mountains and through deep swamps. The seismic waves generated by an explosion would travel back to the Dog House, full of subterranean mapping equipment, and create similar anomalies that could be tapped for the black gold. Plotting your position on land, however, was much easier than at sea. The transponder requirement was a key component to the success of our nautical exploration effort.

The remaining transponder was the last one to be retrieved. The mission would then be over. The Theta and its pirate crew, good captain, and teams of geologists would return to port after six weeks on an icy, summer sea searching for oil deposits deep below the sea floor.

The transponders cost six thousand dollars each. We had had to abandon two of them over the last several days because of weather issues. With a military urgency honed in me by my very recent service in Southeast Asia, I was determined to make the attempt rather than abandon yet another transponder. We had placed it within the last week, so I was sure I could find it quickly.

Watching from the deck of the slightly rolling ship, the helicopter mechanic looked out at the slightly misty shoreline in the distance and the odd whitecap splashing white and foamy across the dark sea.

Tall and lean with a weathered ball cap on his head, he had twenty years on me, a veteran of his craft. Most days, he had a two or three-day shadow of stubble and almost always looked stern, despite laughing out loud harder than anyone I ever knew. "Stretch" was a knowledgeable and experienced "bush" engineer with the morals of an eighteenth century pirate. A veteran drinker, he could down a large bottle of over-proof rum in a single night with a mate, and he did so more than once during our voyage.

Before he went below for an afternoon nap in our submarine-like cabin, he turned to gruffly warn me against flying out to pick up the last navigation transponder on shore.

I looked at the warning tilt of his head that expected an acknowledgment on the spot. To avoid his direct stare, I looked down at the slow rolling deck and nodded. He took the nod as a yes, turned on this heel, and grasped the handrail leading down to the main deck. He paused momentarily on the upper stair, and then the top of his battered cap quickly disappeared below.

I stayed behind, squinting at the far horizon. I could clearly see the black shoreline, the low, snow-covered hills, and the solid cloud deck that thickly covered the whole scene. Maybe I could make it.

I gave the technician who would travel with me a heads-up. Hal was a happy fellow, short, with a black ski cap and dressed in a heavy, dark purple jacket with frayed cuffs and a missing button. He joked constantly, but was good at his job of setting up and activating navigation devices.

I looked over the helicopter for any unfastened latches, checked the inflation of the floats, double-checked the fuel and added two, five-gallon jugs of gas to the side racks, and untied the helicopter. Hal then clambered on board, and we lifted off into the unsettled weather. It had been a good twenty minutes since the engineer had left me at the ship's railing. I was sure we would be back before he woke up.

The cloud deck was still solid, but the distant shoreline seemed a little less distinct due to a slowly creeping mist. However, the wind had not increased, and the odd whitecap still broke the surface of the dark, almost black, sea below us.

Snatching up the transponder on the run still seemed doable. I was convinced we could get back before anything serious changed with the weather. What I didn't yet understand was that it seldom worked that way in the Arctic. Severe, localized conditions are not only possible, but probable.

We flew inland. As I hovered close to the ground in terrain filled with small gullies, both of us searched earnestly for the anchored tripod with varnished, wooden legs and topped off with a solid black, electronics box the size of a basketball. The entire contraption stood about six feet.

Overall, visibility was falling. We were hovering nearer and nearer to the ground in order to move around at all. The possibility of absolute zero visibility didn't occur to me. Abruptly, everything disappeared in blowing snow hurled by what we would learn later were 50mph winds.

I pushed the collective (power lever) of the helicopter all the way down. The aircraft struck the surface with a solid bang. We did not stop moving! It felt like I was still flying, even though the collective was fully down. I moved the stick to compensate for what seemed like flight as the aircraft shot down an unseen hill, sliding on its pair of yellow floats. The metal tubes that constituted the landing gear thankfully were enclosed by the attached floats. Without the floats, the metal tubes would have sunk into the snow in which case we would have no doubt flipped with catastrophic consequences. Helicopter floats were used to land on water, but they did a helluva job keeping you on the surface of snow as well.

All at once, we stopped without warning. The view through the bubble of the helicopter was opaque. The SSB (long-range radio) antenna, protruding unicorn-like from the nose of the aircraft, drooped where it had been broken in half. To have stopped so abruptly, we must have hit something we couldn't see as we coasted onto level ground. The engine was running, the blades were turning, but we were suspended in a cloud of impenetrable white.

Gathering my jangled senses, I struggled to take in the circumstances and regain control of piloting the running machine amid an environment I did not, at the moment, comprehend. Was this immediate danger or temporary disorientation? Would things get better soon, or must I act? The fact that the movement had stopped and we were sitting on something solid was helpful, as I soon recognized one direction at least: down.

I held firmly to the pilot's door and cracked the latch with caution as I pushed into the new world I had somehow entered without intent. But this was not OZ. The wind howled with an ungodly fury, tearing at everything I could see and feel. Despite noise and force, no sense of direction was apparent, just wild racket and hard pushes one way or another.

I stepped onto the float, gripped with my fingertips the rain gutter above the door, and pressed myself against the fuselage. Looking down, I had no idea if it was 1000 feet or two feet to something solid. I closed and latched the door behind me and stepped off the float cautiously, my boots sinking into crusty snow. I was still beside the helicopter, I felt deeply relieved that it had not disappeared above me as I plummeted out of sight. Some of my distress eased.

Suspended in a world of white was not as silent as one might imagine. The wind coursing and bubbling over the metal frame of the helicopter fuselage and through the spinning blades produced high-pitched whistles and unearthly groans. Only an arm's length away, the red and white form of the helicopter was all that kept me oriented.

How far could I see ahead of the helicopter? Could we get out of here? Could I hover forward? These were the most pressing questions. I moved to the front of the aircraft and put my back against the bubble. Then, I took a pace forward. My legs sank up to my knees in the blowing snow. I took a second step and looked back at the machine. The outline was still clear as a bell. I took another step and again looked back. Still good.

About four steps later, the image of the machine blurred. With one more footstep, the aircraft began to disappear. Each additional step erased some other detail of the vessel I had somehow landed safely on this strange planet. At last, good sense kicked in, or else I ran out of nerve.

I returned to the ship. This was summer in the Arctic. When I had left the lower forty-eight, I thought that my Army field jacket would do; it was all I owned that was warm.

Now, I pulled it tighter around me. I tried to close openings that were channeling the frigid air beneath the olive-drab cloth. Brushing the accumulating snow from my coat, I noticed my name tag, FULTON, faded but still sewn above the right breast pocket. Would this name tag later confirm my identity when they found my frozen body? A sudden thought. Push it out, forget it! Not helpful.

Obviously, I understood little about this latitude. Thinking that this field jacket had protective value against such icy temperatures was downright foolish. The thought of wind as a danger had not been on my mind when I packed the coat in the duffel bag at home. That jacket was all the protection I wore besides a stocking cap and gloves.

Clambering over the float, I opened the cabin door and dropped into the pilot seat. Being back in the cockpit felt surprisingly warm, despite a malfunctioning heater. It was actually calming to be free of the howling air outside and its dangerous chill. Back on the ship, the mechanic hadn't worried about the heater. After all, it was summer. Nevertheless, the cabin temperature minus the wind chill outside was adequate for now.

As I reached back and latched the pilot door, I looked over at my companion in the copilot's seat. The expression on his face was unchanged. He looked unperturbed, not fearful, not perplexed. He was sure I had figured it out. It was momentarily comforting to know only one of us was grasping for an idea of how to proceed. He was bundled up and had extra layers of body weight for added insulation. A veteran of these latitudes for some time, he was better prepared than I was.

I glanced at the panel. The single ADF navigation needle flickered slightly in its round gauge pointing to the ship at sea. Unaffected by our dilemma, it pointed home, which seemed far away at this particular moment. How long would this last? Could we stay warm? Was there enough fuel? What was next?

As I welcomed and grew accustomed to the calming stillness inside the aircraft, I glanced outside once more. With some amazement, I noticed that despite the blinding whiteness, my recent footsteps were still visible, small impressions in the wind-streaked snow.

If I could still see my footsteps, then perhaps someone walking ahead of the helicopter could provide a reference as I flew forward. I could hover forward slowly, following Hal as he pushed into the whiteness. A reference was all I needed to control the ship. He was a brave fellow and a good sport to boot. He nodded as I explained the plan, confident that I knew how to extract us from this torment of white and noise.

He bundled out of his side of the helicopter and proceeded to walk slowly ahead of the machine as instructed. His body leaned into the gale, his head lowered to avoid the pricks of blowing snow. There had been no argument, no protest, just a walk in a blizzard requested of a perfectly willing man.

We made some forward progress, at least. I believed it was forward. But to where? I had not thought that far ahead, but was still solely focused on the "one step at a time" strategy, submerged in blind faith and hope.

This effort—man walking, followed closely by helicopter—seemed to go smoothly for the first five minutes or so, then I started to lose my man! Up to his knees at first. Then nothing below the waist. By the time only his chest and head were visible, a horrific thought screamed out a clear warning.

If he disappears, I will never see him again!

The helicopter skipped briefly across the snow as I pushed the power off and cranked the throttle to idle. I flung the door open and threw myself outside, lurching forward to get a hand on my friend. He was almost buried in the whiteness. It was like reaching into thick steam for something that had disappeared. As my hand closed on Hal's sleeve, I looked back. The machine was still there, but barely. The wind was bitter and so strong, but we made it back. Touching the still running helicopter was one of the greatest reliefs of my life.

Back in the machine, waiting for my heart to slow, my mind flashed back to how I had first become entangled on a path leading to this nearly impossible predicament.

Helicopters weren't what I had in mind when I joined the U.S. Army three years earlier. I knew what a helicopter was, but if you wanted to fly for a living, I thought airplanes were what you did. My original goal had been Air Force or Navy flight training through college programs, but sporadic income had limited my progress.

Time was passing, so I jumped at the Army Warrant Officer Program as the last "learn to fly" train leaving the station. But the Army put me in helicopters, not planes. In my mind, it didn't seem worth the fight for a change of schools, so I let go of the idea of flying Beavers; it didn't sound exciting anyway. I would take my chances with the rotary wing challenge, and there were plenty.

In fact, here I was three years later, facing one of them in a rising Arctic wind in the center of a blizzard. Was it an exciting enough mission? Yes, but not quite what I had had in mind at the start of my career. This was not an A to B type of work; you had to put it together as you went, a lot of variables in this game of "keep the helicopter flying."

Glancing at my companion, I noticed a slight blur of confusion in his eyes. More solemn now, he searched my face for the real solution, the one that would take us home. I glanced at the ADF needle. The slight wagging of the pointer showed that the ship was still there, waiting for us to figure this out, to come back aboard.

Outside our bubbled craft, the world showed no mercy. No footsteps, no landmark, no sky. Still wrapped in the whitest of cloaks, we stared into nothing.

The helicopter mechanic had been right. I was wrong. Was he still sleeping? How much time had it been since we had left the ship? When would we be back? Would we get back? Fuel—how much, how long? Next step? Think about it, and get it right if you can.

With the SSB antenna broken, we had no radio contact with the ship. Our line of sight VHF was useless down in these gullies. Help and advice were unavailable at the moment, but I tried. After repeated attempts to reach out on the radio, its only response was to sit silently in the panel and stare back at us. We were both silent. We were very alone, and we were both feeling it.

Somewhere, out of my concern, a thought began forming. Someone back in Calgary, speaking of the vastness of the territory I would be flying in, had said to shut down the aircraft to save fuel if I got stuck away from base and wasn't sure what to do next. Made sense. However, he hadn't mentioned the getting it started again part. That could be the real challenge, or so it was with us a short time later.

Even above the steady roar of the wind against the airframe, we could hear the engine go silent. The gauges in front of us unwound toward their zero marks. Blown by the high wind, the rotors did not slow when deprived of power. They windmilled for the longest time before they began to dip and bang against the mast in their last throws of rotation.

I switched off the battery. Warning lights flickered and went off on the panel. It was now devoid of animation. The vibration was gone, the whine of the turbine was gone, and the swish of the blades was now absent; I had taken life from the machine. The reassuring vibrations of potential capability were gone. It was now only a chunk of heavy metal and hard seats. The term alone carried a heavier weight than I had ever imagined. And it was colder.

Hope slowly seeped out of the helicopter, exiting our solitary world into the fury outside. Without sound and vibration to offer some assurance of an option for life and rescue, the air grew colder, the white whiter still, and despair began its steely creep sooner than later. We were saving fuel, but what difference would it make if we were never able to move again?

After twenty minutes, I decided that shutting down the engine had been a bad idea, and in just about two minutes, it was going to seem like a terrible idea. We had to keep the helicopter running and find some way to move—there was hope in that. Silently staring into nothing we could measure had replaced hope with pointless fear, always a bad tradeoff.

I reviewed the start-up sequence: switches off, battery on, throttle set, pull the trigger, and add the fuel at 15% of engine rotation. The norm for a jet turbine engine should be a smooth rise to a warm peak EGT(engine air/gas temperature), followed by a slight dip in engine temperature. Then a second surge of EGT would approach a peak gas temperature below the red line (temperature limit) before dropping to a stabilized idle temperature. After this sequence, release the trigger at 58% of engine rotation. Rotors are now turning rapidly, and the engine is stable at idle.

These were the steps I anticipated for a normal start. It didn't go like that. Instead, like hearing fingernails on a blackboard, I cringed as I watched a dangerously high spike of temperature, followed by a heart-stopping plunge of the needle towards zero.

What the hell was that? my brain screamed as I abruptly closed the throttle and stared at the gauges.

Thankfully, I hadn't spoken it. Hal had no part in this procedure and just stared out of the bubble trying to ignore the strange noises coming from the engine during my efforts to get it started. He had never witnessed such an animated engine start-up, I was sure of that. He made a concerted effort to avoid what might be happening, obviously leaving his comfort zone very unwillingly.

I, too, was struggling at the edge of my very limited Arctic experience. I had weathered situations in Vietnam and survived, but none of those had been in the same bucket as this one. I didn't understand this environment nor did I appreciate its true perils. Such hazards of engine start up hadn't been discussed before I had left Calgary. I thought I was a veteran pilot, but no, here in the Arctic, I was still green, and this was a crash course in getting it right. Even more, the time factor was going to cap it all shortly. I would never become seasoned if I couldn't figure this out.

Throttle off, battery off. For a third time, I climbed out into the gale. I leaned hard into the wind walking back along the airframe to open the cowling and check the engine for any defects. Only much later did it occur to me what was actually happening. At this moment though, the engine was going to start, if only from sheer desperation. You know the attitude when you determine, "I have to do this, no matter what!" Even if I had known the reason, it wouldn't have changed a thing. We were where we were, and the wind was what it was.

Nothing found, cowling secured, fingers freezing. Clamber back onto the floats, squeeze into the cockpit, latch the door. And start a second time. Switches off, battery on, throttle set, trigger; oh, that amazing trigger, it got everything rolling. It excited the starter that turned the compressor—a powerful air pump—drawing unbelievable amounts of air into the front of the engine. Throttle on, here comes the fuel to expand the hurricane of compressed air, that turns the gears and makes everything work together. Simple? Not really, not this time.

What I didn't understand was that the jet engine reached peak power only when it was fully running. During start-up, the air pulled into the front of the engine where it was combined with fuel was actually colliding with and being pushed back by the howling gale that blasted into the rear of the engine, pushing hard in the wrong direction.

As soon as I introduced fuel at 15% capacity, the needle on the temperature gauge became hypersensitive. If I tried to advance the throttle just an eighth of an inch, the needle spiked and fell in a crazily erratic pattern. I gripped the throttle hard enough to get blood out of a stone as I attempted to freeze the slightest movement of my wrist. Moving it at the wrong moment could spell the end of this precarious dance between no chance to stay running and the ultimate goal of a stabilized engine. If only I could just get through this tricky rock and roll maneuver that I had never practiced. Time limits and sequencing patterns were all exceeded as I urged the engine to cooperate, or at least not fizzle into silence. Let me get to the end of the start-up at a tranquil 58%, and we will have a chance! I believe God understands all technical aspects of prayers as they come to him, or at least He reads between the lines.

At last! Through pure grit, I finally reached 58%. I have no idea how long it took although one minute is the normal limit. Two frozen men and a lost helicopter against an expanded engine start-up envelope balanced the scales just fine with me. I can't fully explain my feelings from that moment, but I knew that although we were still facing the whiteness outside, we had somehow scaled a new and very steep hill. We were definitely back in the game.

Hazy sunlight was beginning to blur through the blowing snow that was at least 500 feet thick. The faint light would come and go, but when I looked straight at it, I could see areas where the high wind had scrubbed the ridges clear of snow. Small, black pebbles, frozen to the ground, appeared in the dim light as if marching along in a serendipitous line. They were perhaps six inches to a foot apart. Single stones, black, directional, a gift from nature's fury. This is what we desperately needed to energize us with renewed determination.

The black stones, bound solidly to the earth by the frozen temperatures, were a good reference. Anchored well, they could not be moved by the rotor wash of the hovering helicopter. Each time they became visible, I could count on them for needed reference to judge movement in any direction.

The gale blew perpendicular to the ridge that aligned with the feeble sunlight. And the sun's descent was roughly in the direction of the shoreline, as well as on the same side of the island as the ship at sea. All this we could use, and we did.

For forty-five minutes, as the fuel gauge dropped towards its lower markings, we struggled along our Hansel and Gretel path of stones. Whenever the sun disappeared behind a cloud of blowing snow, we dropped to the thinly crusted ground and waited for the next flood of light to bring our small trail back into sight. Over and over, we stopped and started, moving roughly forward, snaking along the ridge.

Each time the white curtain fell completely, I lowered the collective and hoped for level enough ground to avoid the dreaded rollover as I bumped to a stop. It wasn't like there was a choice in the matter. Yo-yo like, we stayed with our track. The sirens of false shadows, silhouettes, and clearing spaces nearby that came and went like mirages did not tempt me. I did not abandon our chosen trail nor did I lose faith in our stumbling progress.

Sometime during this renewed journey to the shoreline, the radio crackled to life with a scratchy voice that seemed far off. They did not hear my reply, filled with an urgent need to contact anyone on planet Earth. It was the Canadian Coast Guard, called by our ship to conduct a search. Broadcasting in the blind, they told us that the wind was above forty knots and they were stuck over blowing snow hundreds of feet thick, unable to descend in zero visibility. One more call out, and the voice disappeared into constant static. Hal looked over at me, the brief shine of hope on his face had quickly faded. He pulled at his gloves and looked up at the sky, then sighed. He was still in the fight. Only a brief utterance, "shit," came over the intercom.

We were still very alone, but more hopeful as the trail of stones stretched farther ahead and my sudden landings became less frequent. Although we tipped and rocked slightly when we dropped to the ground each time, Hal did not grasp at the door post, but moved his body with the machine and stared straight ahead.

"Bull riding, in the snow," I declared, attempting to lessen the strain we were both feeling with weak humor. Hal managed the weakest of smiles.

The light seemed to shine stronger through the snow-filled air. As we gradually descended toward broader patches of barren ground—still very white in spots but blown clear of loose snow—the stones were larger and more scattered. Brief glimpses of the shoreline also raised our spirits, and the curtain of white opened and closed more frequently as we dropped out of the low, snow covered hills we had navigated at such a snail's pace. Relief flooded Hal's face. I wondered if the absolute glee I felt showed on mine.

I landed the aircraft near the water's edge where we could look through the falling snow at the heaving, dark gray sea. Such relief, such promise! Briefly, Hal moved both his gloved hands to his face, covered it, and leaned forward against his seatbelt.

The waves were white-capped, every one of them. It was not the same sea we had crossed hours earlier. It was now much darker, the clouds low and gray and the waves high and steep. Except for the wet, inky black stones along the barren beach, our world was dull, the light from our recent friend, the sun, now fading.

We sat amid the endless Arctic, earth and sea stretching in all directions, uninhabited, empty of life or aid. Only the unseen ship called to me, the haven we must reach regardless of the surrounding view.

I always carried extra fuel on the helicopter in red, five-gallon jugs strapped to side baskets outside of the cabin. The aircraft's fuel gauge indicated that we were low on fuel. I knew the direction of the ship, but not how far out she floundered in heavy seas, awaiting our return.

Before we left the ship, I briefed Hal. "Look man, I am not sure how far out there she is. We'll empty everything we have into the tank. Watch your step on these rocks."

With the helicopter running, we struggled out onto the slippery shore, undid the fuel jugs, brought them around to the fuel port on the side of the aircraft, and emptied them into the tank. Drops of fuel sprayed onto Hal's dark purple coat, but he stayed focused on the task at hand and ignored the jet fuel delivered by the stiff wind. Hal gripped the rear door firmly as I secured the empty jugs in the back cabin. The wind was deafening; we could only shout at each other outside the aircraft.

Buckled in, we both looked at the fuel gauge. Without exchanging a word, we looked at each other with some disappointment. We had hoped it would indicate a more robust level of fuel. We understood this would be a one-way trip; there wasn't enough gas to get back to shore.

I can still hear that final winding up of the main rotor as we prepared for a flight we hoped would end well. We knew it was a gamble; success depended on the timing, headwind, and conditions around the ship at sea, as well as the gray clouds not touching the water's surface. None of these conditions were in our control, but their sum needed to total up in our favor.

The floats slid over the wet rocks of the shore as the metal landing gear lost its spread and the aircraft's weight transferred to the rotor, lifting us away. The view through the bubble below my feet changed from a black, rocky shore to white-capped waves. I kept the ADF needle at 12 o'clock. It pointed to salvation.

Hal's facial expression deepened into anxiety as the height of the waves increased below us.

We didn't talk. We both strained our eyes, looking as far ahead as we could for the red and white ship. Ironically, despite the red and white of both airship and sea vessel, only gray was present in both sea and sky or for that matter in the entire world as it seemed. As grim as it appeared, it was pure gold to us when compared to the all-white world we had just left.

Even before we left shore, I could not have imagined the tossing, rolling, and near vanishing of the ship behind steep waves that appeared at our first sighting. I can still see that certain angle of the ship, only one end visible behind a heaving wall of sea etched indelibly on the canvas of my mind.

We did not have the fuel to return to shore, but we did have enough to circle and stare and wonder just how to land on that plunging ship.

When the mind squeezes in concentration over a pressing need, it will discard most faulty ideas early on and replace them with long-forgotten solutions you would never have remembered in an entire day of trying. At this moment, one of those pearls of memory was offered up.

When I was a kid, we didn't have a TV, but my Mom loved the movies. One Saturday afternoon I saw Thirty Seconds Over Tokyo in a theater with her and my sister. Now all these years later, as I stared at the ship being tossed in the sea 300 feet below us, what came back to me was the black and white picture of the lifting bow of the Hornet as the B-25 launches at the very apex of that rise. Right now, my main problem was the rising and falling deck of our ship below, specifically how to catch it at the brief moment it became level and stationary between swells.

Faced with a similar issue, in reverse, the film's Lt. Col. Doolittle (Spencer Tracy) decides to send his B-25s rolling as the bow of the carrier pitches down so they will reach the end of the deck just as it lifts skyward, perfectly positioning the departing aircraft in a climbing attitude.

Unlike those B-25s, I was already flying, but I needed the helicopter to meet the deck at the very moment the ship stopped coming up and I stopped coming down. I had never been in the Navy, so that film version was the only picture in my mind comparable to the ship I now saw below me, tossing in a similar sea. At this moment, I was never so glad that my Mom had loved the movies.

I had the theory in my head of how to proceed, but now came the hard part. I could see some of the crew holding lines while standing on the icy and windswept stairs leading to the helipad, looking at us in the same way we were looking at them. What was next, and when? Their bodies were ducked into the wind and spray from the heaving bow. They looked soaked.

I watched the ship rise and fall; it seemed more rhythmic than staggering. I tried to be a metronome, click, click, measuring the rhythm of the ship up and down, up and down. I could do nothing about the roll. I quickly looked at Hal—he was holding on now—we didn't have life jackets.

I picked my best position for the wind. The captain seemed to sense what I needed and heeled the ship slightly to a new heading. My eyes and senses fastened onto the rolling and plunging deck. I fought to bring the aircraft to a relative standstill in relation to the constantly moving helipad. I ignored the waves and the tearing of the white caps just out the side windows. We were low above the swirling sea.

I made my move when the ship seemed at its highest point. I crossed over the deck as it fell away, trying to follow it down at the same rate while staying centered at the same time. The cables and wires strung from the mast to the bridge swayed wildly just above the main rotors. As the ship bottomed out, we slid onto the icy deck but could not stop the helicopter from skating sideways. I fought to keep it on the deck without lifting off again. The rotors were turning at 100%, I was ready to fly off if we slid off the pitching deck.

The men waiting on the stairs suddenly raced forward and surrounded the helicopter, winding ropes and various lines around any solid part of the landing gear or airframe they could find, straining and tying off the ends to the edges of the deck. A running helicopter is a bad place for men with loose ropes. But they had no choice. They had to address the roll of the deck that threatened to chuck all of us over the side. Without them, nothing I could have done would have brought the aircraft to a standstill.

Once the first line was secured, the helicopter became part of the ship. Sliding off the deck would only mean hanging inverted against the ship's side, not flying off for another try. Only when the last line was secured did the machine seem to sigh and settle into one spot, give a foot or two.

Hal pulled at his wool cap and slid it onto his lap. He pulled off his gloves and ran both his hands through his thinning hair— he looked sideways at me with a combination of reprieve and satisfaction. A slight smile moved his lips. In his eyes, admiration twinkled. I said nothing, but patted him sharply on the shoulder.

By the next day, the helicopter was covered with three to four inches of ice from the spray thrown up by the plunging and rising bow. No one could approach it without taking the chance of sliding overboard from the ice-covered landing pad. Two days later, when the storm had passed and the warmer air had melted the ice, a close inspection of the aircraft showed no damage except for the SSB antenna.

After the landing, I went to my bunk, which was located under the steering gear and over the propeller of the ship, which together caused a lot of loud commotion. When underway, we could barely hear one another talk. That was lucky for me because the mechanic had the lower bunk. I believe he gave up on chewing me out because of all the energy needed to make himself heard. I didn't mind; after all he had been the one that lead the charge to secure the sliding aircraft.

The steering gears were overworked from the stormy seas, and the whirling propeller coming out of the water—*bunkity, bunkity, bunkity*—sang a duet with the steering gear three times as loud as before, but it was heaven to me. I was down, and someone else somewhere in the ship was worrying about the passage and navigation to our next destination. I was just a gratified passenger with an assigned seat.

Aboard the Theta

Chapter 2

IN THE BEGINNING

Imagine four hundred orange helicopters converging from all points of the compass at least twice a day on a single landmark— the Parker County Courthouse—in Weatherford, Texas, a small town just fifty miles west of Fort Worth. They were joining what could be considered, even temporarily, a site ranking among one of the eight wonders of the modern world: A twenty-five-mile lineup of small helicopters queueing up to land.

It was a miracle that pillars of smoke and falling aircraft parts did not punctuate its snaking course more often. On the days that one of them suddenly fell out of line and descended out of sight to land or crash behind scattered trees or in the tall grass having run out of gas or losing an engine—or striking another helicopter—the line simply closed up and pressed on toward its destination. Don't look! Someone would help out your fellow aviator, but not you. Stay in line, keep moving, watch the spacing, how's the fuel holding out? Watch out for the guy ahead of you!

The courthouse's red roof and white brick structure stood out starkly against the rocky, rolling hills of northeast Texas. Unusual and almost exotic, its single, three-story tower rose above its supporting four-story structure, making it a beacon for struggling novice pilots buzzing above and looking for the way home. This giant dance of bobbing machines resembled swarming bees approaching their hive. As they neared the vicinity of the courthouse, each one would somehow manage to detach from the swarm to join the vector that began at the courthouse and led to the landing ramp at Fort Wolters.

In daytime, if you kept your head on a swivel, other helicopters could be identified and avoided, however at night, the whole area for several miles around the courthouse would be transformed into a red, green, and white medley of blinking lights. Like lighted ships on a turbulent sea, they would disappear and then reappear from behind a ghostly wave as they turned or passed behind other helicopters. At night or in the daytime, judging the distance, rate of closure, and the airspeed of others when joining the growing line of oscillating helicopters was, at first, downright terrifying.

Like gathering spilled marbles into a straight line the helicopters assembled into a single, nose-to-tail trail that paralleled Texas Highway 180 leading to Mineral Wells, twenty-seven miles away and the end of the return flight. The bright orange copters held just two pilots. At times, one pilot was an instructor, but more often than not, two beginners sat side by side with only twenty hours, plus or minus, of total helicopter time between them.

As soon as two novice pilots had learned to hover, they were paired and then launched into the surrounding countryside to practice what they had learned up to that point in the syllabus. Most often, the destination was a satellite training field, but later in the training, a solo flight to any cow pasture with a prearranged ring of old tires served as the terminus.

These training fields lay scattered across the empty Texas plain, each one named for a Vietnamese base or town to replicate the future destinations of the pilots currently training. Each field had a small building, a wind sock, and a single, paved runway with helicopter parking ramps on either side. They were uncomplicated on purpose.

Joining the tail end of the wildly oscillating row of helicopters was always a challenge. It required careful timing to join the snaking train of helicopters that began over the courthouse, *careful* being the key word. Coming to a five-hundred foot hover was out of the question, and there was no leaning out the door to wave the next helicopter forward as a courtesy. And no tower issued helpful instructions: "Orange helicopter behind orange helicopter, you are too slow. Speed up!" No, that would never have worked! You were on your own.

Wildly displacing the aircraft controls was common in pilots with so few hours. Pulling back on the stick would pitch the nose up like a rearing stallion, instantly climbing the helicopter which also caused it to slow. On the other hand, pushing the stick forward not only increased airspeed for catching up, but it also positioned the helicopter for a dive with its tail in the air while rapidly closing the space between you and the machine ahead.

Pity the aircraft behind you trying to stay clear of your tail rotor as you attempted to maintain correct altitude and spacing behind a plunging or climbing aircraft in a space that narrowed or widened constantly. Such gyrations continued unabated all the way down the aerial pathway until the first three helicopters turned to land three abreast on the giant ramp at Fort Wolters, followed by the next three, and so on until all had landed.

That part of the Texas hill country had only one towering landmark: the Baker Hotel. Constructed in 1929 to accommodate world travelers seeking the healing waters of the nearby hot springs, it was gigantic and too much to pull down when its usefulness was over. Now mostly shuttered, it rose fourteen stories into the Texas sky, a beacon for low-flying pilots. Its vertical sandy-colored walls and bell tower sat stoically awaiting its final deterioration from blowing Texas winds, hot sun, drenching rain, and eventually a wrecking ball sometime in the distant future. For now, it marked the center of the universe for every Army helicopter pilot qualifying for his wings. The town surrounding it lay just miles from the base that pumped out neophyte helicopter pilots for the war in Vietnam at the rate of six hundred a month following nine months of training.

My instructors were ex-Vietnam pilots who had finished their tours and were now assigned to train pilot candidates who would soon find themselves flying low over the same jungle themselves. These crusty veterans of the war zone knew exactly what they were doing. You couldn't fluster them, not outwardly anyway.

Our helicopters were the civilian Hughes 269A model, unmodified and coated in bright orange paint. The Army designated them as TH-55 Osages. Under each one's aluminum floor, a 180hp Lycoming engine turned a drive shaft connected by pulleys and rubber fan belts to the main transmission input shaft containing the sprag clutch (engine disengagement from the rotor).

The belts were slack after you started the engine. To get the main rotor turning, the tensioner, connected by a cable, would be activated either by a hand brake style lever or an electric switch located between the pilots' seats. This was a simple arrangement with no mechanical linkage between engine and transmission to consume labor and parts. Rubber fan belts, who would have thought?

The helicopter's throttle, located on the collective (pitch lever), looked similar to the throttle on a motorcycle, which many of these young Warrant Officer Candidates (WOCs) had been driving before entering the flight program, but it turned the opposite direction. Quickly twisting this throttle in the wrong direction would result in a serious engine overspeed.

Many nights at the barracks, mechanics would wander down the hallways in search of a novice pilot whose name they read off a battered clipboard. When the new candidate was located, the mechanic challenged him with the potentially embarrassing question, "How many rpm did it go to?" The reluctant answer, usually muttered from the middle of a deep red face, would result in the mechanic having to return to the hangar to replace the engine that same night.

When helicopter candidates arrived at Fort Wolters, the first thing the Staff Sergeants did was line them up left to right by height. Those below a certain height were assigned the smaller TH-55, but those around six feet were assigned the OH-23 Raven built by Hiller, the standard training helicopter before Vietnam. They were no longer as numerous since a fair number of Hillers had been lost to crashes during the early days of stepped-up helicopter training.

The TH-55 had hypersensitive controls, but pilots could move the controls in a Raven, change their mind, and move them back to where they had been, and the helicopter wouldn't have moved at all. Looking back and having flown a Hiller later in civilian life, I was very happy to have been 5'10" at Fort Wolters.

Helicopters had never been part of my hoped-for aviation future. I didn't even know how they worked. I had always wanted to be a pilot, and to me, that meant an aircraft with wings, period.

As a kid, I had been buckled into the rear seat of a fabric covered PA-20 built by Piper Aircraft, forest green with yellow stripes. My mom had arranged for a family friend who had flown in Korea—as a Navy carrier pilot—to take her and me up in his plane on a Saturday afternoon. From then on, I was hooked, and I never looked back. I built airplane models, subscribed to "Air Progress Magazine," and generally immersed myself in all things aviation.

Both of my parents had been in the Royal Canadian Air Force during WWII. Neither had been aircrew, but they had the uniforms, insignias, old magazines, and scrapbooks loaded with pictures, letters, and articles that I devoured over and over as a young boy growing up in the States, where they had moved after the war.

Terry and the Pirates was my favorite comic strip in the Sunday paper, and I eagerly awaited its delivery every weekend. I would flop down on the living room floor and turn straight to *Terry* before reading anything else, including *Prince Valiant*.

I also went through a lot of rubber-band-powered airplane kits. They came in a small cellophane package and could be purchased at the grocery or drug store for a dime, assembly required. Whenever I could earn ten cents, I opted for a wind-up airplane over a dime comic book.

I was only seven when my parents divorced, which was not as common then. It seemed like my Dad had gone very far away—Northern Canada. He got work building a remote dam in coastal British Columbia. When I was a little older, I flew up there in the summers. The last leg of the trip was on a float plane—usually a civilian PBY (a surplus WWII amphibious aircraft that had the fuselage of a boat and large blisters protruding from each side of its slender fuselage for wartime observation). I was always thrilled when the stewardess put me on the cushioned seat in the giant dome of plexiglass, a unique view designed to obscure nothing. Landing on broad saltwater inlets, the aircraft would plow through the green water to shore where my father was always there to greet me. I loved my Dad.

But with my Dad up in Canada, no one was around to guide me through my fairly challenging model projects. My only little sister had no interest at all.

I eventually tackled mounting a tiny gas glow-plug engine to a plane I had built that was controlled from the ground by two fifteen foot wires coming out of the right wing tip and leading to a plastic U-shaped handle in my hand. It was not free flight. The aircraft simply went around and around, but in my mind, I would be controlling the flight of a plane through the air above me. I remember never managing the trick of getting the model engine to run for more than ten seconds. I had probably let my ambition outrun my age and ability, but it always seemed like a thrilling procedure to try to master. And although my model plane stayed grounded with its tiny engine attached, I never quite gave up on the "dream."

My life hit serious turbulence when I turned sixteen. I didn't *crash and burn* as seemed likely at times, but my dreams of working in the sky had to be packed away into the farthest recesses of an imaginary plane and grounded for several years while I grappled with the fallout from my mother's short-lived remarriage, which left the three of us penniless. I went to work for a local dairy to support us and hold on to what we had. My mother enrolled in a junior college, and when she married again, almost three years later, I left home.

During my summers in high school, I had worked on a ranch in Calgary, Alberta, Canada, owned by Ernie Young, a good friend of my uncle. Again, I contacted my uncle, who had another friend who owned a helicopter company. I got a job there, working high in the Canadian Rockies as an apprentice mechanic, where I had to wash the machine, gas it, load it, wait for it to come back, and wipe off the grease. I lived with the pilot's family in the small town of Golden, British Columbia, next to the Trans-Canada Highway. The pilot was a great father and husband, and the comfort of a normal family life, though brief, was a healing balm.

The single helicopter supported a mining operation on a mountainside some distance from Golden, and it was the mine's only connection to civilization. It was a Bell 47, a turbocharged machine with a large plexiglass bubble. I never rode in it, nor did it inspire a career in rotary wing at the time, but it did fly.

A couple of years later, I got married. we moved to Calgary where we lived downtown in a small first apartment, located on the second floor of a six story, faded brick building in the center of the city. I sold pots and pans door to door initially. My wife worked as a bank teller and then I got a new job with a large finance company, HFC--goodbye to soar knuckles. We didn't own a car, so we took the city bus to work.

I hung out at the airport on weekends and eventually found a job there, but we would have to cut expenses. To accomplish, that we moved to Ernie's ranch setting up housekeeping in an old war surplus bunkhouse with no hot water and an outhouse for a privy, but it was rent-free. Because there was no rent or utilities to pay, I could get the low-paying job I found pumping gas at the Fixed Base Operation. We bought a small Morris convertible and drove the fifteen miles to Calgary every morning. The only bathtub we had was the largest metal tub ("What size is your dog, madam?") we could buy. Every Saturday night, we took turns bathing in that contraption which demanded a certain proclivity for contortion. One bathed while the other heated water on the stove and poured the rinse water.

I was working around airplanes, but it hurt to watch while others soared off and on the giant concrete runways and I stayed feet planted on the ground with a rag and glass cleaner in my hand. However, I had arrived at a great arrangement with my employers. In addition to my monthly pay and at a discounted rate, they would provide me an instructor and an airplane to work toward my private flying license in a "square-tailed" Cessna 150. Twelve hours a day, six days a week was my work routine. My paycheck totaled about two hundred dollars a month, no paid overtime. I squeezed in the ground school classes and flight time somewhere during the long days, and my flight time began to build.

The airport's charter flight school owned a Piper Apache (four passenger, twin engine) and a Cessna 320 Skyknight (six passenger, twin engine). I was awed by both. At the time, they looked like "heavy metal" to me (a term used by aviators for large airplanes). I dreamed some day of getting checked out in one or both of them. In reality, they were far from "heavy metal," but in my world, they were the inspiration for greater opportunities.

As part of a flight lesson on mountain flying years later and after Vietnam, I would sling that same Apache airplane out of a 9,000 foot accident site in the Rocky Mountains west of Jasper, Alberta. Its pilots, disoriented by the low visibility from the smoke of a forest fire, had been scouting for the Forest Service and turned into a box canyon. With just 150hp per engine, the small twin could barely climb in the thin air at such an altitude, and when they attempted to turn 180 degrees to exit the canyon, the airplane didn't make it. It crash-landed in a giant boulder field, but the pilots miraculously climbed clear of the wreckage only battered and bruised.

Parked near Calgary's Fixed Base Operation across the taxiway on the grass was a line of Harvard airplanes. One silver airplane was parked in the line, the others were yellow, purchased surplus from the Canadian Air Force. Two-place tandem (one pilot behind the other) aircrafts that had been used as advanced trainers in WWII before pilots transitioned into larger aircrafts, including single-engine fighters. A big round radial engine, a 600hp, Pratt and Whitney, hung off the engine mounts. Known as an AT-6 Texan in the U.S., they were configured as a tailwheel airplane, its entire canopy made from separate panels of glass in a metal frame.

These same kinds of airframes had been disguised as low-flying Japanese planes, Zeros and Kates, in the original movies *From Here to Eternity* and *Tora! Tora! Tora!* by Hollywood production companies that had access to hundreds of surplus aircraft leftover from the world war. In today's computer age, the loss of such airframes is replaced in film with graphics so dazzling that viewers are unaware of the difference.

The silver one was missing a propeller, but displayed a FOR SALE sign. Each day after work, I slowly walked around it and peered into the interior. Flying something like that was beyond my imagination. Eventually the idea of actually buying it rooted in my mind.

This silver Harvard had been built in California in 1942. It was a Mark II gunnery trainer with narrower glass panels in its canopy; otherwise it looked exactly like the Mark IVs beside it. At one point while standing on the wing, I slid back the front cockpit canopy to stare in amazement at the "stick." It could have come out of a Spitfire, the legendary British fighter of the Battle of Britain. Rather than merely a straight stick, the top of its shaft had a metal circle encased in leather with the "firing button" for the guns set at the 11 o'clock position. To me, that said it all, and I started to scheme.

I couldn't even afford rent at the time, so how hard would it be to get this plan past my new wife? She had agreed to come to Canada from the U.S., lived with me in a barracks-style building, and suffered from our lack of hot water. Would she go one step further into questionable debt? She was young, but not mindless. I schemed anyway. When you love something with such intensity, logic is no longer part of the thought process. Why wouldn't I want to own a WWII training airplane? It was metal, had a 600hp engine, and the control stick came straight out of a Spitfire.

"We can buy a bathtub later," I told my astonished wife over a hamburger one night on our way home, "this is an investment!"

The possibility of owning the Harvard unfolded in my mind just as I began my flight training in the Cessna 150. It was summer now, so fortunately, the days were long.

My first instructor was at least three hundred pounds. With the little, two- place, nose-wheel airplane full of gas, and carrying both my instructor and me, I have no idea what it weighed, but we took off regardless into the warmish summer evenings from an airport elevation of four thousand feet, we climbed high enough to do stalls and spins before returning for touch-and-go-landings. There was so little room on our single bench seat that the instructor always draped his arm across the back of the seat, so everything he did or demonstrated was usually with one hand.

Unfortunately, his girlfriend, whom I never met, lived on a small farm along the way to our practice area. The instructor would always take the controls to "buzz" her house. Seeing an overloaded Cessna with a *thundering*, 100hp engine floating past seemed hardly worth the trip from the house unless you were interested in watching its slow struggle back to altitude.

Since the CAA required spin training and spin demonstrations on the final check ride, us student pilots had to practice them every time we went up solo. I would always climb the Cessna as high as I could, putting as much air as possible between me and earth before attempting a spin. Having less than twenty total hours of flight time while at the same time learning maneuvers you had never imagined attempting so far above the ground was unsettling, to say the least. It was nothing like reading a *Lessons in Flight* manual at your desk. While airborne, every time you moved the throttle or flight controls, things "happened." And despite logically understanding the purpose for a maneuver, soon it wasn't long before fear began nudging out reason, and survival emerged as the chief motivation for your actions, especially during spin entries.

Being nervous and in a hurry to get it over with, I constantly entered a spiral dive instead of an honest spin. During a spin, the airplane totally stalls, then drops a wing and enters a spin with no increase in airspeed. The airplane goes around and around, but the wings provide no lift. You just fall like a leaf from a tree.

On the other hand, during a spiral dive, the wings keep flying as the nose of the plane pitches down. You simply dive as if you had pushed the control stick fully forward. The airspeed immediately builds until just half a turn later you reach the maximum permissible airframe speed (red line). If you don't recover within seconds, a delayed attempt will cause the wings to bend or separate from the aircraft when you pull the control wheel back, not an easy task to recover from.

Instructors other than those assigned to us would periodically take us out to check on both our progress and our ability to comply with standard practices. During one such afternoon, Gina, an older woman instructor, met me at the office before my lesson to inform me she'd be taking me out for this type of "check." That day, she saved me from eventually tearing the wings off my Cessna.

Horrified at my spiral entries, she grabbed the controls as the airspeed charged toward the red line, recovered the aircraft, and then demonstrated "spin entry" in a way I would never forget. At the end of two or three breathtaking rotations, it was obvious her way was the way it should be done. The exit from the spin was similar to mine: throttle off, wheel stick forward, and then push the opposite rudder, but the results were much more satisfying, as the plane no longer shuddered from excessive speed in the pull up!

Gina demonstrated all maneuvers with authority, advocating that the pilot was in charge, not the airplane. Smooth was okay, but not to the extent that you forgot your specific intention and were late getting to it.

Pleasant but firm, she turned out to be one of the best fixed-wing instructors I ever had. She subsequently taught me, among other techniques, how to do cross-wind landings in a way that served me well my entire career. I don't know why she became my regular instructor after that early check ride, but as it turned out, I was one of the really lucky ones at that flight school. She knew exactly what to do and had lots of experience to back it up. I finished up with an actual mastery of basic flight techniques.

Two months later, I had my private pilot license, albeit Canadian, but considering the emphasis on spin training, I considered it of extra value.

Near the end of flight training, still determined to own the silver Harvard, I again pushed open the glass door of the finance company. I wasn't there to sit behind my old desk; this time I was there to secure a one-thousand-dollar loan to buy an airplane.

The previous week, I had approached the owner of the "cloud seeding" company who owned the silver Harvard Mark II. He confirmed it was still for sale. Its engine had only eight hundred hours on it along with a new "center section," but it came without a propeller. If he couldn't sell it, he intended to use it for parts for his Mark IVs.

"Why, was I interested?" he asked. I don't think I was able to give him a satisfying answer containing anything close to purpose or logic—I just wanted it! He looked puzzled, but cash is cash, and a reasonable use for the plane was not part of the deal.

He was a tough dude who had flown his Harvard into thunderstorms while spraying silver iodide hither and thither. The Harvard was strong and could take the beating from these attempts to rid the billowing clouds of hail by neutralizing the ice-producing cumulus nimbus, and thus avoided serious damage to the wheat crops below.

He typed up a bill of sale on a company letterhead sporting a yellow Harvard in one corner. I still have that bill of sale. We shook hands and agreed on the price of an even thousand dollars. HFC had approved the loan the previous week. No collateral, a cash loan. They knew me from the previous year when I had worked in their office after we first came to Calgary. The manager liked me and trusted me. Of course the interest was high, but putting a check in the hands of the man who owned the silver airplane was all I cared about. At last I owned a Harvard (AT-6 Texan). Now what?

I didn't think much about the "now what" of the matter, but I could be found on Sunday afternoons out at the Calgary Flying Club where I had moved the Harvard after qualifying for my private license and had it tied down for free. I would polish the aluminum and walk around and around while my wife—now pregnant—sat in the truck; the Morris had died. Sitting in the front cockpit and holding the circular, leather-covered stick, I daydreamed of being up in the air, making turns, and passing through clouds.

I wasn't an airplane mechanic in the least but was still determined to poke around where I could and "fix things" in obvious disrepair. One warm Sunday afternoon, while in the pilot seat up front, I leaned over and discovered beneath the seat a mounted, funnel device whose small end was inserted into a black rubber tube that ran toward the back of the plane, or so it seemed. An intercom to the back seat was my first unbelievably ignorant guess.

I sweet-talked my wife into getting into the rear seat—no easy task for someone six months pregnant. Her job was to see if she could hear me talking through the "horn" in the front seat. She had a similar funnel under her seat as well, which she unsnapped from its bracket to listen through. Not a sound. I repeated in a clear voice, "Test, 1, 2, 3." Nothing!

At that point, of course, I had no idea of the unusual noise level when the aircraft's engine was actually running. I later realized that such a racket would have blocked out any voices I had envisioned passing through my rubber tube to the backseat, but at this juncture, that fact passed right over my head.

Silver, Harvard Mk II

"Must be broken," I suggested, shouting over my shoulder to my very puzzled copilot. I heard her metal horn hit the Harvard's metal floor behind me. I knew she was frustrated. Her climb to the back seat had been accomplished with strange contortions and much effort, including climbing onto the wing. Her thoughts now of a return descent must have seemed daunting and even dangerous. Even more, nothing had been achieved beyond indulging my baffling invitation to help out in a plane that couldn't even start because it was missing the propeller.

Shrugging off this puzzle as something I could easily fix later, I hurried to help my poor wife clamber up and out of the plane and return her safely to the ground.

"Really Rob, how many other things are broken on this airplane? You only own a hammer and a screw driver."

She walked across the grass and opened the passenger door on our baby blue, '47 Chevy panel wagon, put her foot on the running board, and dropped into the seat that rocked slightly—it wasn't attached to the floor—and resumed reading her *Woman's Day* magazine. By the look on her face, she didn't intend to be disturbed again.

I resumed my favorite task, polishing the dull aluminum plane to a shiny luster one small section at a time. Beautiful! Satisfying!

Eventually, I traced the black hose to its exit under the belly of the aircraft, but I still didn't get it. Finally, gathering the courage to trade my ignorance for some answers, I went to my mechanic friend. "Relief tube," he said, breaking into laughter. I too have laughed many times since, but at that particular moment, I was filled with horror at the thought of where I had placed my mouth while trying to force my voice into the rear cockpit. Yikes!

The backseat of the Harvard also contained a "hood," a white canvas canopy that came from behind the back pilot's seat to latch onto each side of the cockpit. Shutting out the sky to simulate an environment for "blind flying," it was used to train a student pilot on instruments, regardless of the weather outside. The hood worked and was in perfect condition—no deterioration, no stains. Historic. I loved it!

Behind the canopy and before the vertical tail and rudder, a large, black antenna was attached. Shaped like a teardrop, it was aligned with the fuselage, its pointed end facing aft. An ADF antenna, it was a classic from WWII.

My friend Alfred, the head mechanic of the aviation company where I worked, looked like a good-natured doctor in his white shop coat with his name labeled in red on the breast pocket. His stories of the early days of Canadian bush-flying streamed easily from his mouth whenever more than two people were present. As he spoke, he always clenched a pipe in his teeth, frequently removing it for emphasis. One day, he approached me in the hanger. His face reflected anticipation, like he was about to present an award. He announced that since my Harvard was missing a propeller, he would borrow a "club prop" from the local aviation college so we could start the engine. The plane had come to me full of fuel, thank goodness; I didn't have two extra nickels to rub together to fill it for an engine start and run.

A "club prop" was a substitute for the regular prop (which I somehow still needed to acquire). Made from heavy laminated wood, it looked like a four-bladed prop whose blades had been sawed off to mere stubs. Used to break in engines on grounded planes, club props provided proper "load" for the running engine and increased air cooling, but you can't fly a plane with a club prop.

Holding true to his promise, the following week, the mysterious club prop, fastened to a large wooden pallet, was sitting in a corner of the hangar. For no charge, he helped me with what he must have viewed as a young man reaching out in a most impractical way to hold onto his dream of flight. He treated me like I was just a normal customer. He had other mechanics pull my Harvard into the company hangar with care and installed the club prop within a day of its arrival. A very kind man indeed.

As you can imagine, everyone around the airport—guys who just liked to hang around soaking up the atmosphere, local pilots, and even fellow employees—were all very skeptical of my Harvard purchase and gave me a hard time about it every day.

The club prop was attached after several hours of effort and many pauses for Alfred's yarns about the North. Then, he had my airplane pushed out onto the ramp in front of the hanger while he watched from just inside the hangar doors with his arms folded. I was speechless! I couldn't believe the engine was really about to start. After checking over his installation one more time, he then climbed up on the wing after I had settled into the front seat, canopy slid back and brakes firmly set. Alfred reached into the cockpit past me, he set the controls and cranked the engine while standing on the wing.

It started on the second turn-over. What a sound! No words could capture my mouth-dropping excitement and pure satisfaction at that first cough and then roar of the Pratt and Whitney engine that breathed life itself into the airplane now shaking and vibrating for all to see.

Once it warmed up, I pushed the throttle up and then back. The airflow off the club prop was significant, so Alfred jumped off the wing before I moved the throttle forward a second time. Then as I played with my prized possession, I looked around at the small crowd gathered nearby and the mechanics watching from the shadows of the expansive hangar entrance. There were a few smiles, but most of them were pained expressions of pure envy. It felt good!

Later that week I took a call at the office from a man with a heavy Texas accent.

"Y'all own that silver AT-6 with the blue cowling tied down near the flying club?" he drawled.

"Yes, sir, I do."

"I saw that high-speed propeller y'all got on it. Must really scream when ya get her up and goin'," he added with some degree of awe in his voice.

Not wanting to break his bubble of pure ignorance, since I was already walking around in one of my own, I simply replied, "Yes, sir, sure does go!"

"Y'all want to sell that screamer, I'll buy it from you."

"Not for sale just now, but thank you," I choked out, stifling my laughter.

"I'll check again next time I'm back in these neck of the woods, son." The phone clicked and then went to dial tone.

I was still able to keep my Harvard tied down on the grass at the Calgary Flying Club despite its still missing prop. Eventually, though, I decided to return to California to enroll in college and finish something I had barely started right after high school. I planned to tow the plane out to the ranch and talk Ernie into letting me leave it in his equipment shed. My next step was to remove the Harvard's wings, which meant hundreds—if not thousands—of bolts to be taken out, fuel needed to be drained, and more hassle.

Sounded like a plan, but like most plans, something was about to go awry. As I began the tedious task of removing the wing bolts, my pilot friends approached to insist that I was taking on too much work. I noticed, though, that no one was picking up a wrench to help. Instead they assured me that they'd watch over the Harvard until I got back. That seemed like a much easier solution. "Don't worry," they said, "what can go wrong?" I agreed.

However, not long after moving to California and enrolling in a local junior college, I was notified by letter that the Calgary International Airport planned to rid itself of "small planes" by raising the tie-down rates to $50 a week. Impossible! We were barely getting by as it was.

In California, several of my well-established pilot friends offered to chip in the money for a prop and the subsequent ferry flight in exchange for flight time on the aircraft and a check-out when they heard of my dilemma. I thought my Harvard was saved!

Next, I went up against the FAA for a ferry permit. Naive, alone, and ignorant of the bureaucracy's arbitrary nature, I called them—probably my first mistake in dealing with "Feds." A high squeaky voice informed me that I couldn't bring the Harvard to the U.S., even though it had been built there.

"What about the EXPERIMENTAL category?" I suggested.

"Only Boeing does that sort of thing," the voice blandly announced.

He wasn't inclined to help or even understand my objectives nor ask questions. It seemed that I had hit a wall, so I hung up. I then told my friends sadly our plan couldn't be carried out. Only later in life did I learn that you have to keep digging in the bureaucracy until you find someone that understands what you want and will listen, even if only briefly. The FAA is a huge agency. I had stopped too soon thinking one voice alone represented the whole agency. Yes, I had big plans, but I was still young and nowhere near any spigots dispensing helpful information. A painful lesson, but I couldn't wait any longer. The fifty-dollar invoices were piling up.

So That part of my flying dream was done for. I sold my Harvard/Texan T-6 over the phone to a man in Vancouver, Canada for eight hundred dollars. He didn't want to pay a thousand. After all, it didn't have a prop.

Imagine my chagrin three months later when I read an article in *Air Progress* magazine that four Arizona pilots had bought four Harvards in Canada and then ferried them to Phoenix under the EXPERIMENTAL category. Ouch, that really stung!

The first book about flying and pilots I read as a boy of fourteen was the *Big Show,* Pierre Clostermann's memoir. He had joined the RAF (British Air Force) after France fell during WWII and her Air Force vanished as a functioning opponent for the German invaders. His breathtaking tales of Spitfires and Tempests flying daring missions fueled my dreams. It never occurred to me that I would fly anything other than a fighter when I grew up.

That pressing goal now spurred our move back to Washington state after losing the Harvard. I enrolled in another local college and joined the Air Force ROTC, determined to get on the fighter pilot path. Later, I applied to the Navy Flight Program, but each time, I ran out of money. I knew nothing then about student loans or financial aid. I thought that when it came to money, you were on your own. Pumping gas and washing windows at the local Chevron station wasn't producing the financial stream I required to stay enrolled.

About that time, I picked up a single sheet, an unsophisticated mimeographed flyer printed on green paper stock while I was on my way out of a store or coffee shop. Something about flight training had caught my eye. I took it outside and walked along the sidewalk—I read it a second time. My curiosity up, I leaned against the wall outside of an old barber shop I always visited growing up and read about the Army's Warrant Officer Flight Program.

"Okay, they have airplanes, right?" I asked myself.

Take a test, pass a board interview and a physical, and you're in. How hard could it be? After basic training, you would get higher pay as you progressed through nine months of flight school achieving the rank of Warrant Officer when you earned your wings. They only required a high school diploma. This would work.

My young wife wasn't happy about moving to Texas just so I could enlist in the Army, and she let me know it through two days of tears and yelling at me. Nevertheless, I held on with calm reassurance and finally prevailed. Then, I went to the Army recruiter in town.

Just off main street, the recruiting office sat in a row of glass store fronts with heavy metal awnings. I opened the glass door and was greeted by a Staff Sergeant with hash marks on his sleeve and a colorful array of ribbons on his green uniform. He was neat, but slightly overweight with thinning brown hair. He stepped from behind a desk that was also neat and extended his arm. His toothy grin was more menacing than inviting. The room was open, and the walls were covered in recruiting posters. Two teenagers sat in metal chairs nearby thumbing through hotrod magazines.

"I want to fly airplanes for the Army," I stated in no uncertain terms.

"No problem, sir," he answered with the total confidence that that was absolutely possible. "Just go through the paperwork with me, and you'll be in the Army before you know it. It'll just take a few days to process everything," he assured me, pulling forms from his desk and turning to find a pen and a clipboard on a nearby shelf.

During the next few days, he did a background check without the aid of a computer—desktops were still a long ways off—and then called me to come down to the recruitment office. He stayed seated as I crossed the floor space to his desk. He looked up with an indifferent expression.

"Son, I'm real sorry," he stated, "but you've got a criminal record. This ends any chance of you getting in the Army." He sounded disappointed, although his manner was dismissive. Likely, he was just worried about his monthly quota.

I leaned forward, "I've never been arrested!" I objected as surprise, mixed with fear, flushed my face. My final shot at flight school was about to disintegrate on the spot.

He picked up the report, then proceeded to read off the charges, "Resisting arrest, striking the arresting officer, property damage—pretty serious charges," he replied with a hard stare suggesting disgust. How could I be so bold as to take his time up with such a rap sheet?

"Can I see that?" I asked, reaching for the heavy paper he held. I searched it slowly from top to bottom. The name was right, Robert Fulton, but the arrest date was wrong. "Look here, sir," I said, pointing to the paper, and shaking it back and forth in front him. "I wasn't big enough to strike an adult in 1947. I was only two years old!" I stabbed my finger sharply against the form, pointing at the date. Now I was getting pissed.

To me, this was deadly serious. I thrust the paper back at him, and he snatched it from me, rechecking the details. He stuck to his story for a few more minutes until it finally sank in that this was his mistake; no one was pulling a fast one on him, and he had a hard time admitting he was wrong.

I got the story from my dad later. Back in 1947, he had been stopped at night by two policemen he had known from high school. He had been drinking and started wisecracking about the two cops he knew well. It went south from there. In the end, it took five policemen and a fire hose to get him into the jail cell for the night. Once a fullback for a professional team as well as a professional boxer, he had always loved a good fight and sure enough he managed to get in a good one that night.

Several months later, with my infant son and wife in tow, I pulled a small UHaul trailer to Texas with our meager belongings after having completed basic training at Tigarland, in Ft Polk, LA. Now I stood in front of the assignment table on my first day of Army flight school and carefully explained my expectations of being selected for the fixed-wing training section, followed by assignment to a Grumman OV-1 Mohawk (twin turbine-powered airplane) out of flight school. Brother, was I ever wet behind the ears! I wasn't going to be assigned to even a Bird Dog after flight school. I was going straight into helicopters, no discussion. Next!

So there I was, a straight-wing guy who had owned a share in a small Piper Colt before joining up, but that fact wasn't going to help me a bit. I had even convinced myself that I was already halfway trained since I had a flying license. However, the Army had invented the "Warrant Officer Program" primarily to train pilots for the increasing number of Huey helicopters swarming the skies above Vietnam, and I was added to that conveyer belt right there in front of the assignment desk.

Every week in flight school brought new concepts of flight to the inept student. I mean whoever knew a thing about hovering a churning machine over one spot before they got here—until you figured it out there was no next step. Angles of approach, hovering turns, landing over obstacles, and keeping your head on a serious swivel were all part of the curriculum. As a neophyte airplane pilot, hardly a single term or theory was recognizable.

Deeper into the training, more difficult control challenges emerged, stretching your overloaded brain to adapt to numerous variables that often had to be explained a dozen times and practiced even more before it could be imagined, understood, or even accomplished. Landing on a slope was one of those.

At one of the satellite training bases surrounding Fort Wolters, the Army had pushed up a mound of dirt that extended in a straight line for a quarter of a mile. Like a giant log cut exactly in half, it lay in the center of a dusty field. Much of the perspiration that poured from beneath your flight helmet would also soak your flight suit as you desperately tried to master a machine you neither remotely understood nor appreciated. Seen from the air, the entire sloped landing practice field looked like bees swarming over a giant heap of spilled sugar, buzzing here and there, pausing, and flying away.

Landing on a slope of any kind is a difficult challenge in a helicopter, especially when you are just learning. Done successfully, it is a dance you must master since not everywhere you can land a helicopter will be perfectly flat. The ground might slant down to the left or right or even upward. Within the limits of the particular helicopter model you are flying, you must, for a successful landing, put both skids on the slope and have the collective (power lever) all the way down. Since the helicopter is now on a sloping surface, you must hold the cyclic opposite of the slope's direction in order to keep the machine from rolling down the hill.

The principles are straightforward: hover low over the slope, lower the collective, and back off the throttle until one skid—not two—rests firmly on the ground. Use the cyclic to stay level, and hold it. Now, begin to lower the collective, reducing the twist throttle as needed to maintain rpm and lower the other skid, still in the air, onto the slanting ground. Keep the spinning rotor disc level by pushing the cyclic away from the slope angle as you let the airborne skid downward until it rests on the surface of the slope.

Successfully accomplished, the landed helicopter's fuselage will be at a substantial angle with both skids on the ground, the collective will be fully down (no lifting power), and the cyclic will be pressed hard against the pilot's uphill leg so the rotor stays perpendicular to level ground.

Was there a downside" Yes, literally. If you let down the second skid too rapidly and your momentum exceeded the main rotor's ability to stop the aircraft's tipping motion, you would roll the machine down the slope into the field of red dust, and the helicopter would be in pieces. The main rotor would shatter against hard ground and fly in every direction with great energy while the rest of the machine was catapulted into the air. Your body and that of the instructor would be somewhere in the mix, perhaps still belted to their seats. The plexiglass bubble surrounding you earlier would also be gone, having exploded into large, jagged shards.

Another faulty maneuver would be turning your tail rotor into the slope rather than keeping the machine parallel with the slope as you approached or departed the exercise. This produced the same results as rehearsed above. These two potential disasters remained only microseconds away from becoming reality throughout the entire maneuver. Not every day at the slope practice area, but often enough, you would catch out of the corner of your eye a great commotion and a cloud of dust as some poor student lost it, taking the instructor with him into a cloud of flying debris and red Texas dirt.

No one stopped or hovered clear of the slope, waiting to land until things were cleaned up. If you weren't directly involved, you kept going—but now clutching the controls so hard that your knuckles turned white inside your already damp leather flight gloves.

A lot of pressure was on the instructors as they taught the "landing-on-a- slope dance." No instructor instructing in such a small helicopter was fast enough to regain control in the split second between no control and hearing the rending and tearing of plastic and metal as the aircraft suddenly rolled over and over, and the helicopter with all its spinning parts disappeared instantly as a functioning flying machine. No wonder new pilot candidates concluding their basic flight training and leaving their instructor had a tradition that every student gifted their basic instructor a bottle of their favorite beverage—and I don't mean Kool Aid!

Midair collisions became almost common, often happening several times a month. A sky filled with helicopters flown by low-experienced aviators was an accident waiting to happen every single day. In the middle of one of my training sessions on an especially warm afternoon, sitting inside the plexiglass bubble oven of a running helicopter, my instructor and I were practicing touch-and-go landings from a practice field helipad. Before departing, I slid my helmet's sun visor up one more time to wipe away the dripping perspiration that steadily filled my eyes. Then I slid the visor down and locked it.

Just as I looked up to clear the airspace we were about to depart into, my gaze fell on the exact spot at the very moment when two helicopters collided with a loud dull thud. If I didn't actually hear the thud, I felt it. No flames, just folded-up rotor blades, cabin parts, tail booms, and spinning debris rained down from a cloud of intertwined machinery that suddenly had no purpose at all except to die horribly. We made our takeoff anyway. Sitting side by side in the enclosed cabin, my instructor and I were only one among four hundred helicopters—a giant, whirling machine where not one gear could stop turning, or the consequences of a delay or a sudden diversion would unwind the whole system.

So without hesitation, we flew up and over the smoking remains of four pilots and two machines, searching the surrounding airspace with renewed vigilance, our hearts remaining heavy. We were not indifferent, only well- trained to continue with our part. Later in the war, these cataclysmic events would be repeated often in combat. In a rather gruesome way, we had just witnessed an extension of our training that would prepare us further for the experiences that lay ahead.

Night flying was a large part of the basic curriculum at Fort Wolters. The same number of buzzing machines left the earth almost simultaneously to head out for night auto rotations with an instructor or a cross country with a fellow student.

One night, we all sat idling on our individual helipads, waiting for instructions from the tower to begin our various assignments up in the dark sky. But since the wind was gusting to almost 40mph we expected a cancellation and were anticipating an idle evening back in the barracks.

"Listen up, all you trainees!" a deep, gruff voice suddenly boomed over the tower frequency. I was startled by the sharp change in tone from the normal, business-like instructions that usually came over that channel.

I imagined the scenario—a General Officer grabbing the microphone from the tower operator, just like in movies when the landing pilot being "talked down" begins to lose his nerve.

Suspecting a cancellation for the night, the General must have decided to put a stop to all such speculation by issuing a prompt command.

"We need pilots, and we need them now" he growled, "so cinch down your GD seat belts and get out there and train!"

Hardly inspirational, but to the point. The man with the microphone had one expectation at that moment—we were leaving, period. Damn the wind or anything else that might make us hesitate. I have no idea how many helicopters ran out of gas, then sat down or fell from those dark, windy skies that night over Texas, but I do know that the entire night mission was punctuated fairly often by calls of "Mayday! Mayday!"

Not all, but at least some of the calls were in Vietnamese since their pilots first had to learn English and then learn how to fly. The Vietnamese, "Maydays" often began in English, but quickly switched to their native tongue as the "pucker factor" went up. Autorotations into the blackness of unlit and unknown ground could only be terrifying. Those were very brave soldiers, determined to meet a towering challenge. If they survived the stateside training, they would go home and not just for a year like US Army pilots, but until the war was won or lost.

That same inky and windy night found my WOC partner and I on a triangular cross-country. The small Texas town in the far distance was our turning point for the second leg of the trip. The TH-55 we were flying had a top speed of 90 mph and a cruise speed of 75 mph, which the Army had red-lined at 60 mph for cruise. We didn't go anywhere fast in calm winds, but tonight with 40 mph winds at altitude, everything became more dangerous—slow ground speed (more gas burned), severe crab angles (confusing compass headings), downwind turns, and a helluva tailwind confusing us further in our navigation challenges.

Helicopters flying at night are identified by just three lights: green on the right, red on the left, and a white taillight. The bright-orange paint job that helped in the daytime was invisible in the dark. Another added difficulty.

The distant lights twinkled crystal clear with no dirty plexiglass to block our view. We were crabbed 90 degrees into the wind and had to look out through the empty space where the right door would have been. These training helicopters were flown with both doors off for ventilation as well as ease of entry. Besides, the doors on these machines were too flimsy anyway to be opened and closed a thousand times a month. Those far off lights never seemed to draw closer as we frequently checked the fuel gauge.

Suddenly, the lights of the distant town disappeared behind a helicopter that filled our vision! The stunned face of the pilot, bathed in both our green navigation light and the red glow out his own left door, filled the space where we had been tracking our progress. He looked frantic as he appeared to lean away from us, willing his machine to turn sharper to avoid the collision that seemed imminent.

Then, his face and the red navigation light vanished in an instant as he rolled away. Losing altitude, his white tail light disappeared behind us. Our machines had not touched—both were still flying. Regardless, when you see the detailed expression on another guy's face at the controls of a second helicopter, that is less than a breath away from a deadly bang and a falling tangle of wreckage as you both tumble out of the night sky together.

Advanced training, the second half of Army Flight School, was carried out in and around Ozark and Enterprise, Alabama, at Fort Rucker. Fort Rucker had been the primary training center for Army Aviators before the heavy demand of Vietnam required additional training sites, such as the one we had just left behind in Texas. In fact, a new site had just been opened for advanced training at Fort Hunter-Stewart outside of Savannah, Georgia. I volunteered to go there, I loved the beach, and the classes would be relatively small.

At last, it was Huey time! No more small stuff. We were finally flying the birds that we would operate in combat. This was the real thing and a big step up from the little orange TH-55s we had flown in basic. The Hueys weren't even painted orange. They were OD so it was easier to imagine being in the real Army when you were flying them. Basic had been demanding with plenty of bookwork, but paled in comparison to the challenges of learning the Huey and the techniques of instrument flight. Lots of scholarship was attached to the program. It wasn't all flying.

We went back to "small" after flight time in the Huey. An OH-13 (a version of the type used on the TV show *MASH*) was the instrument trainer of choice for the Army at that time. Coupled with a light blue and yellow Link Trainer simulator, one of a hundred in an aircraft hangar full of them, we mastered "blind flying."

The panel in the OH-13 was far from normal, stretching almost from side to side with all kinds of dials for flying with no outside reference. Believe me, "shooting an approach" at 40 knots gave you all kinds of time to second-guess yourself and over-control in a way that would lead to total confusion. Most of our approaches were the non-precision, ADF type unlike the GCA in which we were guided to a landing by a ground controller using radar that gave us constant corrections vertically and horizontally. The procedure could bring a slow-moving helicopter almost to a hover over the runway.

A small book could be written about that whole nine-month experience, but it did finally come to an end in a crowed ballroom with a bar where all the WOCs were decked out in brand-new dress blues (now the standard-issue Army uniform, but then worn only for special occasions). And since we had been commissioned Warrant Officers prior to graduation, we proudly sported brown and gold shoulder boards and brown and gold stripes on the sleeves of our jackets. When combined with the light blue trousers of the nineteenth century Army officer trimmed with wide gold stripes down each outside seam, we felt dashing indeed. In our young minds, we were a tangible commodity waiting to be poured into the mold of destiny.

The military ball was a very happy occasion for the six hundred graduating pilots present, along with their wives and girlfriends (mostly girlfriends, as very few were married at nineteen or twenty). I was one of the older guys in the group, twenty-two and married with both a toddler and a new baby. Socially, I was out of place.

My dad had flown in for the "wing ceremony" scheduled for the next day. That evening, he made friends with a General Officer while they were at the bar. They must have chatted for over an hour. My dad loved to swap stories and points of view about people, not politics.

When future WOCs left from basic training as buck privates carrying their rifles to the rifle range and back and started flight school, the Army upgraded them to E5s for pay purposes. My wife, having just delivered our daughter the previous month, was decked out for the ball in a new gown purchased with our extra pay and was delighted it did not hint of maturity.

No doubt all the gaiety was tinged with a certain amount of disbelief and perhaps some trepidation. This was the end, but also a beginning. Tomorrow, our silver wings would be pinned on, and we would step off the stage into the next phase: Application of skills. That new chapter would be filled with bullets and other hazards even more lethal.

The next morning, we were all assembled, again in our dress blues, for the graduation ceremony. The crowd filled every nook and cranny of the auditorium, well over a thousand friends, family, and sweethearts—a fitting conclusion to our months of effort. Getting those silver wings on our uniform was the final step of the tens of thousands of steps required to win them.

Halfway through the Commanding General's speech, he paused and searched the audience, obviously looking for someone. My dad was seated close to the stage in the vast auditorium next to my wife. The General motioned to him, calling him by name.

"Mr. Fulton, Mr. Bob Fulton, would you join me on stage?"

I couldn't believe it! My dad was mounting the stairs at the side of the stage and then reaching out to shake the General's hand. The General drew my dad next to him, and put his arm around my dad's shoulders. The room grew quiet as everyone waited the General's next words.

"Mr. Fulton and I struck up a conversation and a friendship last night," he began, grinning broadly and totally taken by the unique circumstance he was about to create.

"I want him to tell you what he told me," he continued, "about young men and motivation and what it means to work." Then with his palm up and arm extended, he introduced my Dad, "Bob."

The General stepped back from the podium and directed my dad to take his place at the lectern. Without hesitation and with no apparent nervousness, my dad poured out an extemporaneous speech on those very topics. When he stepped away from the podium fifteen minutes later, the General warmly shook his hand. I don't remember a standing ovation, but the applause was loud and sustained. I was proud of my dad. I probably didn't hear much of what was said subsequently until I stood in line to get my wings. It had been an amazing two-hour assembly.

The graduates, though, weren't quite finished. We had a meeting the next day to sort out preferences for our next official posting. It seemed that demand for helicopter pilots in Vietnam had slowed slightly as the US began a "draw down" that would last for the next four years or so, until all US military had vacated the country, but it didn't mean the war was less "hot." In fact, in the year I served there, it heated up significantly with the Cambodian invasion and the beginning of the Laos incursion.

Graduating Class AH-1G (Cobra) School—Savanah. GA

This slight hesitation in the flow of Army pilots to the war zone meant there were openings stateside that would delay an assignment to Vietnam by six months. Those who chose that option, including the few I knew, later regretted it. The six month break caused them to arrive in Vietnam rusty and not on top of their game like they had been on the last day of flight school. Some of them never came back. Maybe from playing catch up, maybe not, but having everything possible going for you when you arrived in the war zone was an offset to the downside, which was being there at all.

I was ready. I wanted to get on with it and do exactly what I had been superbly trained to do. Among other things, I wanted to prove I was worth the expense that had been lavished on me by the U.S. taxpayer.

Having stayed in the top 5% scholastically throughout my basic and advanced training, despite having struggled during the instrument flight segment, earned me one of the first chances to choose. There were five Cobra gunship slots, and I got one of them! I was elated.

It wouldn't be a Tempest fighter over occupied Europe searching for trains to blow up like I had once read about in Clostermann's memoir, but I would be flying a gunship that went faster than any other helicopter. As a result, I would be able to help out in meaningful terms as I imagined them at that time. I wasn't in the least "bloodthirsty," only filled with romantic thoughts of fighting a war from the air.

The Cobra School was also in Savannah, so we didn't have to move, and I would have almost three months of stable duty to enjoy our new little girl and play with our two year old son. We would also enjoy the extra money in our pockets before I was shipped out.

Prior to my departure for Vietnam, we would be given time to move to the West Coast (Olympia, Washington) where I had grown up and my mother and stepfather lived. I planned to move my family into a semi-attached home, one side already occupied by good friends. I hoped to surround my wife with all the support she would need for the year she would be alone. I would really miss my two children. My daughter wouldn't know me when she walked up to me in the Sea-Tac airport over a year later. My son, although shy, remembered me.

Cobra school was great duty. No harassment or curfews, and I was home every night. I was a Warrant Officer now, and even got saluted, which seemed strange. The NCOs salutes, though, were less than enthusiastic since they knew we were still bright green officers with no proven standing, whose very uniforms were brand new.

Every day, I climbed into the new Cobra with my instructor. The ship's performance was amazing. We practiced gunship tactics at the firing range, flying there very low and very fast, literally skimming the east Georgia wetlands. With winter approaching, the weather was turning cooler so the temperature was perfect. The whole exercise was just plain fun, including the "full touchdown" autorotations, which meant reducing the engine to idle and gliding steeply downward until you pulled the nose up to reduce airspeed just before sliding onto the ground with some forward speed and your engine still at idle.

My affection for the AH1-G (Cobra) grew in Vietnam. I never regretted choosing it for an assignment. I can't imagine having done my tour in another ship, either. The initial excitement of Cobra school later matured into a profound attachment for the machine.

I wasn't joining the long, oscillating line over Weatherford, Texas, anymore, but that had been my first step toward where I now found myself—flying and fighting and learning to live with fear. Being a gunship pilot didn't erase the loneliness that every solider feels in a foreign war; however, I was flying, and from the beginning, that is all I had ever wanted to do.

Chapter 3

SNAKES AND ROCKETS

A pack of Marlboros with two or three cigarettes extended was suddenly thrust in my face as I stared, unseeing, at the reddish soil below my feet. Startled, I looked up. The Colonel was offering me a smoke. I hadn't even noticed his approach. My gaze slid past his face—surprisingly smooth for his age—to focus on his unfastened helmet strap moving slightly in the faint breeze. His stubby fingers waved the red and white box.

"You wanna smoke?" he asked, his raspy voice broken by irregular breaths from what must have been a fast walk to reach me. He fixed me with a stern gaze, his eyes wary, as if trying to gauge my next move.

Without thinking, I reached for a cigarette, then stopped midway and dropped my arm as I caught sight of the smoke still curling up from the valley below.

"I don't smoke, sir," I stuttered, thinking this might be a good time to start.

My copilot and I had landed just minutes before. I had thrown the switches to kill everything, removed my "chicken plate," and climbed out of the cockpit. The rotors were still turning, causing the gunship to rock slightly fore and aft. I heard the soft "swish" of the heavy, wide blades slowing overhead, their metal clicks signaling the last rotation of the main rotor. They came to a stop, one blade drooping in a kind of salute to silence.

Where was my copilot? Was he still in the ship? I had no idea.

We were on a remote airstrip forty miles from our main base at Phuoc Vien, where we had launched earlier—had it been only that morning? Then the day had been abruptly emptied of time at that appalling moment no more than fifteen minutes ago. No late, early, or later existed for us. Time had stopped.

We had briefly stayed in the helicopter, following our usual routine of waiting for the second ship to land and cover us in a cloud of red dust. Once it settled, then we would swing open our canopy doors. But no red cloud engulfed us. Nothing. Only our helicopter—singular and alone—sat on the empty strip, while the towering jungle surrounded us like a giant wave about to knock us off our feet.

"Are we reloading here, sir?"

The voice sounded urgent, unlike mine. It seemed high-pitched and just on the verge of control. "Is there an ammo dump anywhere here, sir? I need more rockets." It wasn't a request; I was stating the obvious.

I scanned the airstrip. Although we had landed at its highest point, there were no signs of piled sandbags or a perimeter for security, only a restless group of troops at the far end. My ardent desire for more ammo drained from me like a deep sigh.

The Colonel assumed a firm stance. "We're not sending you back up," he said, speaking with authority. Then he leaned closer. "We're taking no more casualties today."

You could hear a political undertone when he said casualties.

This can't be over, I thought. Not yet! We aren't finished. We just need a plan. I could feel my heart pounding as I looked hard at the Colonel.

His firm, direct stare ended the conversation.

I looked away, glancing over my shoulder at our solitary chopper. All its rocket pods were empty. And there was the copilot still in the front seat, his head in his hands. The ship's original, olive-drab color had blackened from nearly two years of Asian sun and monsoon rains. It looked spent.

Its darkened hue had given it an aged appearance when parked near the bright, newer ships back in Phuoc Vien, but here and in this moment, it looked wise and very tough, a survivor, a veteran of a war that took the very young and very new and made them old in an hour or a day or a week.

My thoughts drifted back nearly eight months to my first night mission "in-country." Another very green pilot, a man from Texas, and I had been assigned as copilots on the "hot" crew (ready to launch just two minutes after the horn went off). Like showing up for our first day of kindergarten, we didn't know a thing.

As we walked along the rusted metal planking that formed the flight line, the Cobra gunships parked beside it in L-shaped berms were blending into the growing twilight.

The heavily sandbagged bunker serving as an operations center stood across from the shadowy line of helicopters. We stepped into the brightly lit room where the flight crews slept for the night and immediately approached an NCO for our briefing. Night operations were entirely new to both of us, and we weren't sure how it all worked.

Our Aircraft Commanders were in the back room, scarfing up the remains of a dinner brought up on soggy paper plates from the distant mess hall. It would be barely warm after delivery by an NCO who most likely paused along the way. No doubt our dinner would be ice cold before we reached it.

Our first question was, "Where should we go when the 'incoming' starts?"

They seemed to rain down almost every night. We were cautious.

"Get under this table," piped up a sergeant pointing to a large, makeshift table piled with radios of various sizes. Its bare, thick boards and closely positioned, rusty nail heads appeared stout enough to survive a direct mortar hit.

"You mean under here?" we asked, bending slightly to survey the available space. Would two prone bodies fit all the way under? Without question, it sounded like the smart thing to do, just where we would want to be during explosions.

Next, they casually pointed out the bunk room for the night. A rough set of bunkbeds were nailed to one wall. Constructed from 2 x 4s, they offered only eighteen inches of space to get up and in, or down and out. No fan, no air-conditioning. (To my knowledge only the Air Force rated air-conditioning on the big airbases around Saigon).

We were expected to sleep fully clothed as the two-minute time limit included rising from a dead sleep. Army mattresses lay thin as blankets on the underlying cross boards. Striped in navy blue and dirty white, they were otherwise bare, and they had frequently been soaked in sweat as the lingering odor testified.

Before midnight, not yet desperate enough to fall into the smelly bunks for some rest, we heard incoming mortar shells falling in the distance. As the thumps grew louder, shaking the building harder with each subsequent crash, we ran into the radio room, dived under the table as instructed, and covered our heads, waiting. Almost immediately, heavy boots jabbed painfully against our ribs and legs, as urgent, angry voices seemed to bombard us.

"Not there, you fucking idiots. Get to your ships!"

In shame (who but greenies would buy the table story) and total confusion, we lurched for the open doorway. We pushed off the soft wall of sandbags protecting the entrance, then darted around each end into the open. We were instantly blinded by flashes of light brighter than the sun and so loud we couldn't even distinguish them as sounds. In unison, we did a 180 and rushed back to the bunker as we thought, surely they're not serious?

Met with more screams and obscenities, we did immediate about-faces, again raced around the sheltering wall of bags, and threw ourselves into the nearest ditch. As we inched forward on our elbows and edged up over the ditch edge, we could see our aircraft commanders starting their ships and preparing to leave the berms at a hover. Aware of their empty front seats, the PICs (Pilot in Command) urgently motioned the ground mechanics crouching in the shadows of the berms to take our places. They were leaving without us!

Ignoring the explosions now, we leapt from the ditch and dashed to catch the helicopters moving forward from their hovers.

As they gathered speed, we sprinted beside them, slapping their sides and wings with our open hands. In desperation, we yelled, "Wait! Wait!" as we raced to overtake them.

They rapidly accelerated away, their pounding blades deadening the ungodly noise that swallowed our hearts each time another mortar shell exploded.

Each bright flash backlit the departing Cobras until they disappeared into the darkness, beginning their hunt for the source of the mortars and rockets falling on the flight line.

We had been left in the middle of the short airstrip, bent over and gasping for breath, thinking we'd rather be dead than standing there after such a performance. We probably waited an extra second or two just to see if that might happen before diving for the nearest ditch. Unfortunately, there wasn't enough water to drown us.

During Cobra Transition training back in the States, the instructors had specifically addressed "night flying" in the AH-1G (Cobra), telling us that there would be none when we got to Vietnam. Officially, the aircraft was not designed or equipped for such a task.

I flew over 900 combat hours in the Cobra "in-country," and at least 30% were at night. Regardless of the manufacturer's intentions or the Army's specifications, we innovated. No one said, "It's too dark outside to fly." We took every mission that came up and worked out ways to get results as part of the normal course of things.

Before the Cobra came into country, earlier aircrafts, like the troop-carrying "Huey," had been designated as gunships by hanging various weaponry out of their sliding doors on each side, (rocket pods, 30 mm machine guns) and poking rocket launchers through the aircrafts nose section. Many had been lost because they were 8 feet wide, started their gun runs at about 60 knots or less, and couldn't go much over 90 knots in a dive. Big target, slow target, easy target!

The AH1-Gs were called "Snakes" in 'Nam slang. When they came into country in December of 1967, they brought a very big change in gunship tactics and performance. They were as long as the H model Huey and had the same engine, but exceeded Huey performance by cruising over 120 knots and reaching up to 190 knots in a dive before pulling out. Earlier gunship models had pulled 100 knots less at the end of their dives. Heroic, but scary!

The Cobra fuselage was a mere 36 inches wide and almost 50 feet long. Under its two stubby wings, rocket pods hung with a certain menace, two pods under each wing: a fat 19-rocket pod inboard and a smaller 7-rocket pod on the outside hard point. Other units carried a different mix under their wings, but we were a First Cavalry ARA (Aerial Rocket Artillery) unit, so rockets were our stock in trade.

The PIC in the back seat flew the aircraft and fired the rockets. The front-seat copilot had small flight controls in front of the arm rests on either side of the cockpit as well as anti-torque pedals on the floor, so he could fly the aircraft when needed yet still operate the movable mini-gun sight between his legs when not flying. This flight control arrangement was unusual for a helicopter.

The fully articulated mini-gun was located in a turret under the forward nose of the helicopter. The front-seat pilot operated its gimbaled aiming device, which automatically compensated for wind and airspeed, by manually positioning its sight so the bullet rounds hit the target every time, even down and behind the diving ship.

The electric mini-gun spit out 7.62 mm shells at the prodigious rate of 6,000 rounds a minute. Outside the ship, the rotating gun made a noise like a monstrous cow wailing from the mud hole where it was stuck. That was the psychological warfare part of the weapon. It made a deep impression with its chilling rates of fire and a noise like no other—but only when it worked.

The Cobra's standard performance at sea level and in cooler conditions made it an impressive helicopter, though its fast cruise and load capabilities were reduced in the high heat of the tropics. For the Vietnam Theater, it was impressive.

These AH1Gs were among the very effective "engines of war" in the close contact between the enemy and the helicopter pilot and the "grunt" soldiers (ground troops) calling out day and night for help and support. Besides their mini-gun fury, they also carried fifty-two rockets that fell on the enemy in pairs.

More than anything, Vietnam was uniquely a "helicopter war" that will arguably never be repeated in exactly the same way. In South Vietnam, we had total air superiority. MiGs and other enemy aircraft didn't fly below the DMZ to attack us or our airbases. We never had to look up and over our shoulders for trouble. It was always waiting straight below us.

Over the course of the war, more pilots died from trying to make underpowered helicopters do things against steep odds than from being shot down by large caliber bullets.

Often, though, we were our own worst enemies when it came to aircraft losses in spite of heroic efforts and amazing feats of airmanship. In the heat of combat we attempted actions we could never reasonably accomplish. We made many poor judgments about weather and fuel and the location of the enemy. At times, the complexity of the machines we flew overwhelmed us, and they often broke under the strain at just the wrong moment. The chances of dying in your helicopter piled up once you started down the wrong path for the wrong reason, and it didn't take long for that to happen.

Regardless, ground troopers loved the helicopter for its protection, the ammo it brought them, foods like steaks and beer, and especially a better chance at a longer life from the needed gift of time. Time you would never get in the back of a truck or waiting in a LZ (landing zone), hoping a medic could stop the bleeding. Hope blossomed in the gut of every grunt when a Huey's or Cobra's pounding pair of blades sounded in the distance, coming for your rescue or bringing the firepower you needed to stop the enemy.

We were as numerous and busy all over the war zone as jeeps had been in the Second World War. Early on, the Army had mounted big guns on the slowest and smallest of the helicopters, just like a .50 cal on a jeep. It didn't really work out as a flying tank, but it did evolve into a weapon of real utility in the Cobra (AH-1G).

But the Snake had limits. It could roll into a 110-degree bank and pull up from a dive at 210 mph, but it was short on tail rotor authority and low on power, especially in the first operational model, the AH-1Gs that we flew.

The Cobra might slide 800 feet through the level of altitude where you had intended to start climbing. More and more pitch (power lever) was required whenever you attempted to arrest a diving helicopter and then climb. It was like driving a car up a steep hill. You push on the gas harder and harder until the pedal hits the floor. Then, if you don't immediately let up on the gas when you reach the crest, the engine will "rev" up and—if you try to shift—over speed the engine, or in our case, the helicopter's main rotors.

These phenomena, coupled with an occasional "hard over" when the electronic flight assist fails and rolls the aircraft on its side (fatal at low altitudes), always kept you anticipating and planning ahead in what was at the time a "high-performance" type of gunship. The ground was always closer than you thought, and even an inch off the ground, you were "in flight" and anything could happen.

The Army gave you good basic skills in flight school in the States, but then threw you as far as they could into that stormy, churning "ocean of war" to sail around amid the fray, later counting you up on the far shore—if you ever reached it.

For those who flew them every day, our aircraft were not just aluminum panels and honeycomb sandwiches with rivets everywhere and a screaming jet engine. We wore them. We often experienced the full range of emotions while flying them into battle and came to recognize aspects of ourselves we had only imagined were part of our being. Not a few of us died in them.

Each machine had its own personality and could be counted on in special ways. Each time you put on your "chicken plate," strapping that loose square of armor onto your chest underneath the seatbelt harness, you became attached in some emotional way to the bird.

The starting whine of the turbine and the slow rotation of the main rotor blades as the aircraft came to life was an awakening of sorts, a standing up to squarely face whatever lay ahead. You and the bird you had drawn for that mission were headed into harm's way, and today or tonight, anything could happen.

Mounting Up For a Mission—Cobra Backseat

Between missions, we spent time in our living quarters, located parallel to the flight line and a mere stone's throw from the L-shaped berms—constructed of sandbags and rusted PSP planks—that sheltered the parked Cobras.

Each pilot in Bravo Battery built his own quarters out of empty rocket boxes he broke down into individual planks and then reassembled into walls under the tin roof of the screened-in, wooden-floored building the Army had built for us to live in.

No ceilings, just walls and a hall were all we created. For effect, blow torches served to "stain" and bring out the grain of the wooden planks. Creature comforts were up to us.

Everyone nailed together some type of door, but no two entrances were alike. Sometimes parachutes stolen from a "parachute flare" canister were strung above as make-shift ceilings, although they soon sagged heavily with accumulated dust from the nearby flight line.

Rather than building a small room above, some pilots cut through the floorboards to dig out a cave in the sandy soil below with steps leading down to their rooms. They used the same rocket box lumber to wall up the dirt against a possible cave-in.

Those guys felt safer underground. Plus, it saved them multiple night excursions out the end door of our hooch to the trench dug as shelter from enemy incoming. A wall of sandbags and wooden boxes filled with dirt ran halfway up the sides of our buildings, but no one wanted to experience an explosive attack above ground if he could help it.

We all coveted the underground rooms, but not enough to dig one for ourselves. We just made the trips to the trench and in the process figured out how to stay partially asleep on the way there and back.

Regularly, incoming enemy 122mm rockets, 81mm mortars, and 75mm recoilless rifle rounds were lofted onto the flight line across from our quarters. This bombardment went on most nights, and often in the daytime. Ninety percent of the attacks at Phuoc Vien were directed at our aircraft. The VC hated Cobra gunships!

One memorable "incoming event" burst into the middle of a warm afternoon about halfway through my tour. I was tipping my chair back against a corner pillar in an unused, underground bunker somewhere on the compound. A number of "Willy Pete" (White Phosphorus) grenades hung from a large nail jutting out of the stout timber above my head. Dim light filtered through several ground-level openings along both sides of the bunker.

I was reading leftover Sunday comics from a stateside paper I had found in the corner of the small room. Having flown the night before, I was passing the warmer part of the day where it was cooler. Only a few other troopers were present, sitting on benches and decrepit chairs and stools. It felt like a Sunday—quiet with no radios squawking. It was midday, the sun directly overhead.

The roar of an explosion! Dust and hot air blasted through the ground-level openings, replacing soft light with a fury of debris and sound. After the briefest moment of silence, the bunker erupted into a frenzy of voices filled with alarm and confusion.

A whistling stream of bright steel shards invaded our cubicle, hidden within the cloud of sand and noise that engulfed us. In just a microsecond, they had peppered the room, tearing through flesh before finally being stopped by abrupt contact with the wooden walls and support posts.

I don't remember rocking forward on my chair or even dropping the newspaper. Suddenly, I was on my feet, looking for anyone nearby. The trooper closest to me had his hands pressed over both ears, while narrow streams of blood ran down his cheeks and throat. He was still sitting.

Opposite the corner where I had been leaning, I could just make out a cluster of men gathered around a soldier. I pushed forward to see if I could help. A nasty wound had mangled the side of his throat, spreading pools of blood across his chest just below the right shoulder. We awkwardly attempted to cradle him and get him up the stairs and out of the bunker.

Once the medics came, I went back into the bunker to look for some of my personal stuff. I kicked through a tumble of overturned chairs and stools to reach the far corner where I had been sitting. I picked up my few bits of gear and brushed off the dust. As I turned to leave, I noticed several large chunks of steel protruding from the corner post above where I had been sitting and just below the WP grenades that hung there. The properties and uses of White Phosphorus during war are too horrifying to explain.

Six inches lower, fatal for me; six inches higher, fatal for all.

On moonless nights, the Asian sky opens wide its giant throat and swallows aircraft into its darkest depths. Just above the jungle, where danger lurks, the night is blacker still. Neither light nor a glimmer of reflection can penetrate the triple canopy of such a tangled forest. Only the aircraft's altimeter and a map can save pilots from flying into solid ground.

On occasion and during certain missions at night, we would fly under parachute flares dropped from a plane that circled high above us. On especially gloomy nights, those flares resembled the lanterns struck by miners in a cave. Flying beyond that glow would immediately plunge us

into the dark cavern of the night sky.

The flares descended slowly, swinging from side to side on their parachute risers, past our circling ships, extinguishing far below, either somewhere above the trees or as they struck the earth. As their last light sputtered feebly, they were replaced by a second or third pair pitched with a flash from the unseen plane far above—falling globes of bright, smoking light.

During other nights, no descending flares assisted our vision. On those missions, we were vectored by a radar operator, often in the dark hour just before sunrise, to a single point on the ground, its location defined by the numbers a soldier had relayed from somewhere far ahead, his hand-held map clutched in a sweaty palm and illuminated by a shielded Zippo lighter. The coordinates were his best guess. His position, given in degrees of latitude and longitude, was generally within the border regions near Cambodia, where seven or more grunts most likely huddled within an area less than ten yards square.

Crouched in the sightless darkness of the jungle, they were at risk of being overrun by the far greater number of enemies around them. Hot, soaked in sweat, and worried, they waited in dense foliage, their senses attuned to the snap of a single twig. They listened with stealth for the first distant thump of our rotor blades.

Our first message to them would come as a whisper on the radio. Hopeful, but cautious, a single soldier would then whisper back, giving instructions for where our rocket fire should strike.

At those moments, no niceties or joking ever came through the headphones buried inside our flight helmets. This was immediate and all business. They had been waiting. We were charged with helping or even saving those we could neither see nor hear except for the hushed voice carried by a thin, electronic signal binding our purpose with their need.

Most likely one of the grunts would be up a tree. Whether high or low, we did not know, and it made no difference. His sole purpose was to shine a flashlight that his cupped hand directed straight up—not out—from the ground far beneath his dangling boots. Sighting that glimmer of light was the most important event of our mission. It would give us a vital visual reference, the only one connecting us with the LRPs (long range patrol) below.

At first sight, the light appeared brilliant, when in reality it was tiny; our relief at finding it seemed to magnify its rays. We acknowledged the sighting with a radio call.

"Fire twenty-five meters northwest, fifty meters southeast," came the hushed reply.

It was never loud; the enemy was near. It was never one hundred meters, it was less. Close, close as death, which was the alternative.

Four pilots, two Cobras, our sole task: hear the voice, find the light, figure out the direction, estimate the distance from the light—not by technology, but by eye and good sense. All this from thousands of feet above the straining soldier, whose singular but vital beam would trigger killing explosions raining down from the black sky and envelope him in brilliant light. His job: hang on, maintain the light. You can't plug your ears, buddy; you can't dodge flying shrapnel. Stay with the light—the single key to the gate that will bring you out.

Timing is crucial. The beat of the rotors has already announced our approach. The Cong know. We don't have the luxury of flying in circles to get this all straight and avoid a fatal error. The lead pilot decides, the plan is acknowledged, the first ship gets in position and pushes over, not at a shallow angle, but at 45 degrees—steep.

The tiny light shines above the nose of the diving ship or to the side or disappears below. We are aiming for the imaginary spot the whispered voice had asked for, and it is close to the light as the dive enters the blackest black that can be imagined. The first rocket motors ignite as they fly past our canopy, momentarily stripping us of night vision and blotting out the pinpoint of light. Then a second pair of rockets flashes by as the first pair strikes the forest. Fire and light blossom like drippings of yellow and red paint splashed against a black velvet canvas.

Sometimes, an experienced Cobra pilot, the aircraft commander in the backseat with a "green" first-week or maybe first-month "in-country" copilot in the front seat pushes over into his dark dive and flies straight into the ground. It doesn't happen every week or even every month in our unit, but it does happen more often than one would believe. The PIC flying with a combined sense of confidence, need for accuracy, and fatigue gets "target fixation."

The new pilot in the front seat, on the point of the pencil, is probably terrified, unfamiliar, overwhelmed. He sees the altimeter unwinding fast, he sees the streaks of fire going by to his left and right. It seems like they've been going downhill too long, but why would he correct a seasoned pilot in the back, or even say anything? His commander has done this many times, for months in fact, before the green guy ever got here.

So in less than a heartbeat, their ship follows the rockets through the trees and into the ground. The pilot, his mind filled with concentration and determination, never thought about the solid earth racing toward him outside the aircraft's glass canopy. The soft glow of his instrument panel with its unwinding altimeter did not alert him. His sole focus had been to put his rockets into a small, unmarked target, defined only by his imagination.

My thoughts were pulled back to the Colonel as he stood around awhile scuffing his feet in the red patches of soil, waiting to see if I was going to stay put. Wisps of white and black smoke still rose from the jungle about a mile south of the hilltop airstrip where we stood. Trails from that smoke hung beneath the low clouds, trapped and not going away anytime soon.

Earlier that day, Dennis Brault had been the PIC for the second Cobra in our two-aircraft flight. Short with black hair, he was an energetic and good-looking guy who had transferred from the Americal Division to the 1st Cavalry Division a couple of months before. He was an above-average pilot with just two weeks left in-country. Although we were not best buds, we had been together in some very tight spots during the short time we'd been acquainted.

We had flown together on one such dicey mission near the border regions of Cambodia about a month earlier. Brault had been in the back as the PIC, and I had been up front. A second Cobra had accompanied us. Our aircraft did not have GPS or anything like it. For navigation, we used a map and the given heading and distance to a target or a ground operation. The maps were huge, old French maps, taped together into a five-foot by five-foot sheet.

A smart pilot or ground soldier with time on his hands had devised a novel type of fold that reduced the entire map to twelve inches by twelve inches. As long as you unfolded it a section at a time, the fat but perfectly folded map remained manageably functional in the pilot's hand. The grunts on the ground had a radio and a map to relay their positions, but if they were on the move at night, their position was always just their best guess.

Brault and I had just flown to a position that had been estimated from a map in the dark. The science of locating an estimated ground position from 3000 feet in the air, at night and at 130 mph, was not an exact science, to say the least. We had finally located the grunts after circling for some time, followed closely by our wing ship. We unloaded our rockets at various targets in the area, but now low on fuel, we announced our departure to the units on the ground. We were out of time to linger further.

Our two Cobras turned away and headed back to our base at Phuoc Vinh on a black and what was fast becoming a stormy night. Since we only carried an hour fifteen of fuel, and our best cruise speed, depending on the weapons load, was 120 to 130 mph, our loiter time was very limited. At this point, we could afford no deviations from a straight line home.

The Cobra did not carry radar, weather or otherwise, as part of its avionics package. We generally flew at lower altitudes where all the weather was concentrated, although sometimes a daytime patrol would be clear, and we could get up high where the air was relatively cool.

Missions were not planned around weather forecasts. We had two minutes to be in the air, and we dealt with weather circumstances as they came up. On that night, sheets of lightning up ahead revealed a wall of clouds that appeared as sentinels to a giant cavern.

Despite our being very low on fuel, the storm ahead blocked our path, lying exactly between our home base at Phuoc Vinh and ourselves.

Our only other option was to land below in the black jungle and wait out the storm. All things considered, it was not a real option, since most likely it was impossible to do safely, if at all. Doing a 180 would take us nowhere. So, during a short exchange with our wing-ship, it was agreed that we'd put several miles between our ships and penetrate the squall line separately.

The Army had trained us in instrument flying techniques only to a minimum degree of competence. After that level of training, they issued what they called a Tactical Instrument Card. I believe it was pink, implying beginner, not sissy. The training was honest but minimal, as they believed we should fly VFR (Visual Flight Rules, meaning you can see the surface, even at night) not IFR (Instrument Flight Rules, meaning you must rely solely on the instruments in your panel due to obstructed visibility, but will need an electronic path to guide the aircraft to the surface).

Army aircraft had certain devices for instrument flying, basically a very good altitude gyro (artificial horizon), but no autopilot (a copilot, even if terrified, was sufficient in the Army's mind), and generally no special approaches had been set up for the helicopter side of combat operations. So the "Tac Card" was not pretend, but had been designed as a basic survival certification during short—very short—intrusions into a cloud bank and out again.

Thus armed, we entered the center of what was probably a severe thunderstorm (they all seemed severe in these tropical latitudes). The lightning was nonstop and lit up the ugly underbelly of the storm. Churning clouds and what seemed like a solid wall of water instead of rain submerged us in a phantom lake. Although Brault was doing the flying, I was trying to help by reporting—probably shouting at one point—what I felt the ship was doing.

"Diving and banking to the left," I called out, barely keeping the high pitch of fear from creeping into my declarations over the frequency that connected our headphones.

"No, we're climbing," came Brault's anxious reply.

We both had serious vertigo, and it was not just the copilot who was terrified. The ship dropped hard, as if the rotors had suddenly run out of air to stay aloft. That sensation was regularly followed by a feeling like being T-boned by a car speeding as fast as we were. The one question that crossed our mind each time a lightning bolt flashed around us was, "Can the engine keep running under water?" The entire experience lasted maybe ten or fifteen minutes, but to us, each minute seemed like forever.

Brault hung on and brought us out the other side. We burst through a curtain of hanging cloud into a clear sky. Phuoc Vinh lay spread out below, its twinkling lights, artillery flashes, and parked helicopters illuminated by the dazzle of it all. The sudden tranquility thrust upon us was a staggering contrast to the extreme violence of only moments before. Such a transition felt dreamlike.

I don't know if our wing ship had similar experiences in their slice of the storm, but we heard them call the tower to enter the traffic pattern, so they, too, were safely on this side of the furious gale. No one really knew that we were directly above the base where the roaring tempest had spit us out. We had been concentrating so hard on staying upright and were always so unsure of our position that formal radio transmissions had never occurred to us.

As it turned out, we had flown across the wrong part of the perimeter, through—or at least above—active artillery fire, but such news didn't faze us. We were still in our ship, it was running, we were alive, and nothing we could think of at that moment seemed more dangerous than our most recent experience.

And so it went in the ARA (Aerial Rocket Artillery) in the First Cavalry Division north of Saigon. With few exceptions, we were young. A year or so ago, no one here had ever flown a helicopter, and now we found ourselves in one of the most challenging environments on the planet in underpowered machines, being asked to accomplish missions that had never before been attempted, at least by us personally. Our training had happened stateside, but in-country, you watched, listened, and hung on, figuring it out as you went along.

Some pilots drank themselves unconscious almost every night. Some accepted and said yes without question or hesitation to every possible behavior option found in a war zone.

Me? I was old, twenty-two. I was married with two small children at home. All my wages went to my wife, except for $25.00. I could hardly get in trouble with that kind of funding. I couldn't even afford one of those nice, rotating fans. The fan nailed to my bunk just inches from my head had recently been recovered from the dump. It hardly turned, was noisy, and must have been manufactured when the French had occupied Vietnam, but it did move air, if only barely. My $25.00 went for toothpaste and laundry soap, and an occasional treat, as I remember. My sole attempt at poker (many guys lived off their winnings) meant squeezing the toothpaste tube tighter for four more weeks.

War in a helicopter could be terrifying and was more marginally sustainable than any of us ever knew at the time, but it could be downright exhilarating when you returned from any mission in one piece and had helped or saved anyone out there in the fight.

We did not operate in the heavens at 20,000 feet and 400 knots; our world was down in the dust at a hover and in skies filled with flying bullets at close range over triple-canopy jungle 300 feet thick and in weather—the monsoons as well as the liquid heat of the tropics.

Our airspeed was not spectacular when compared to our fixed-wing brothers, but it was plenty fast relative to the obstacles we faced, although a little bit of "afterburner" (unavailable in a helicopter) would have been greatly beneficial at certain moments.

Occasional, zero-visibility approaches to a bright light bulb on the ground during driving rain and wind was not considered extraordinary. It was one of those things no one trained you to do; it just happened and you did it so you and whoever was with you could get down to a hover in a safe zone, turn the helicopter off, and be able to walk through the hot rain to your small, wooden cave of a room ready to start again the next time the horn exploded in your ears.

Three sections of Snakes were on stand-by 24/7 in our unit. Each section was made up of two aircrafts: the "hot section" (the first in line, departing in two minutes), the second section (five minutes to takeoff), and the ten-minute section (if called, departed within ten minutes). Earlier today, the two-minute and five-minute flights had been scrambled on other missions. Our ten-minute crew was all that was left, and we were short a pilot.

Brault and I were on deck as PICs for the ten-minute crew, but Brault was missing the front-seat pilot for his ship. Ten-minute crews weren't called up often, as the two-minute and five-minute crews frequently returned before the next mission. Flight Operations, who scheduled the crews and managed the missions, knew that ten-minute crews were seldom launched on a normal day unless a big operation was in progress. Although our unit was currently short of pilots, no doubt Flight Operations had been 99% sure there was no urgency to fill Brault's front seat. They were wrong.

A young Specialist from Flight Operations found Doug Vergimini in his army khakis, bags packed, waiting for the driver who would take him to Bien Hoa for his flight home after a year in-country. He was the only pilot left in the battery, so it didn't seem to matter that he was really only half there. His mission for the day, when he had gotten up that morning, was to go home to his family.

Flight Ops found Doug leaning against a jeep, killing time, and told him to change out of his uniform and into his flight suit and flight gear to go as the front-seat pilot with Brault. They assured him that he'd be back in time for a flight to Bien Hoa; there were plenty of chopper flights to the big airbase near Saigon. Besides, this mission was simple—a couple of VCs popping off shots at a passing Chinook. It wouldn't be complicated—no waiting around on station or dawdling on the ground in some hot, sticky jungle clearing.

I remember Doug kicking the dirt once with his boot. A small dust cloud drifted up into the sky, caught by the light breeze, but he made no other comment. It wasn't the mission he minded, and he wasn't a whiner; it was the change of clothes. He was ready to fly, but home, not on one last mission.

Doug Vergimini was classic Italian. Tallish, his dark eyes were always closely focused on matters at hand, but he quietly distanced himself from most discussions unless lubricated by alcohol or anger. Although quiet, he was cheerful and magnanimous if he thought you had been in-country long enough and were truly worthy of his consideration. The doorway to his room dangled with colored beads rather than nailed-together planks like the rest of us. The beads continuously quivered, pushed lightly by the swiveling fan of warm air that quietly circulated in Doug's room. My room was next to his but not nearly as inviting. His fan never stopped, and the beads never rested. There was always a semblance of life in his room.

The pungent smell of tobacco abruptly brought my focus back to the Colonel, who had lit up a cigarette from the pack he still held. After taking a slow pull, he looked at me again—hard— and then strode off toward the waiting troops. Any chance of follow-up action on my part had been dropped to zero by the Colonel's firm stare as well as by his earlier order to stay put. As I watched him head down the airstrip, his loose helmet straps still swaying, I again thought about Doug—his strength and enduring presence during the past eight months of my tour.

I had flown my first in-country mission with him during my first week of duty. On that day, I had walked into a homemade, screened-in porch at the end of the pilot quarters, filled with open Madeira wine bottles, open cardboard boxes holding more wine bottles, and a lot of pilots whose boisterous racket could be heard in the next set of barracks as well as down the airstrip.

I had been introduced and assigned to Doug as part of the "hot section" that morning. It would be my first operational flight.

I didn't drink. In the words of Mark Twain, "I was a sinking ship with no freight to throw overboard." So I just sat there enduring the festivities, stone sober, and with no idea how all this worked.

Inside of thirty minutes, there wasn't a drop of wine left from three cases of Madeira. Doug, my PIC, was in the thick of the drinking and carousing. I had just met him as the party got going, but to him, I was just another new guy. That first introduction was a little chilly on his part. At that point, I wasn't any more useful than a sandbag in the front seat of the Cobra.

About thirty minutes later, the horn sounded; we had two minutes to leave the ground. Doug dutifully swayed out of the screen door toward the flight line, full of good humor and walking somewhat toward the ship. It was the middle of a very hot, dusty day. This was all new to me, so of course I followed—blindly would be the word—no questions asked.

We made it to the ship. He made it into the back command seat, while I clambered into the front, the copilot of our two-man crew. I struggled to get my chicken plate (armored chest protection) tucked in under my harness, while Doug cranked up the engine, ran the rotors to 100%, hovered sideways out of the berm, and then rotated the nose down for takeoff. Just after the ship got through translational lift at about 15 knots and 40 feet, the intercom crackled, "You got it, kid," and he basically passed out, or perhaps lost interest.

I was more bewildered than scared. Ignoring the possibility of a small explosion if the fumes from a quart or two of recently consumed Madeira wine encountered any kind of ignition, I took the flight controls and followed the other ship ahead of us.

The Army had taught me to fly the Cobra stateside, but that was all I knew. The mission—where, when, and how—were still a complete mystery to me.

That had been nearly eight months ago. Today was a grimmer day. It was Doug's last mission, and it was only one way.

My copilot, the battery "cut-up," was in my front seat and wisecracking steadily as was his habit. It was less annoying than normal because we weren't waiting for Brault and Vergimini, so we wouldn't have a second ship to talk to in-between comments from the copilot. Doug was still changing into his flight gear. Since no urgency had been indicated by Flight Operations, we took off, picked up a heading, and received radioed coordinates of latitude and longitude to a small landing strip in the area of the reported "pot shots." We gained altitude but could see that cloud cover was developing up ahead.

Our destination airstrip was a no-frills patch of grass and red dirt that had been cleared for fixed-wing, resupply missions. It had been there awhile, hacked out of the jungle by the French during their war in Vietnam. Located atop the highest of the low, rolling hills, it was about forty miles northwest of our main base at Phuoc Vien.

When we got close, we contacted a "grunt" observer who described an area south of the airstrip where they had heard the shots, then directed us there to put down suppressing fire—both rockets and mini-gun.

En route from our base to the assigned location, the weather changed. The cloud deck got lower. The ground elevation increased below as we flew north, and we found ourselves under a ceiling of solid clouds and less than a thousand feet over rolling, jungle countryside.

Our gun runs would have to be shallow and longer than normal to give us enough time on target. How bad could it be, a couple of guys with rifles somewhere down in the weeds and probably long gone by now?

We began our gun runs low—too low—but the cloud cover was solid at about 800 feet, so we were stuck getting our work done below a ceiling of gray carpet. Battalion SOP (Standard Operating Procedure) called for breaking off a steep dive after reaching this altitude, not starting one.

A third of the way into the first run on what we guessed was the target, the sky in front of the ship lit up with green .51mm tracers. Abruptly, this became a serious mission, very serious. We weren't doing much over 80 knots as we started the low, shallow dive. A .51mm machine gun was a lethal weapon to engage any helicopter up close. Taking on more than one was like taking on a WWII fighter. I punched off rockets in pairs, one from either side of the aircraft, and aimed directly at the source of the blossoming tracers. We wanted them to stop. We needed to turn off that green light!

That's when our mini-gun jammed.

When my brave, but wisecracking copilot held down the trigger on the rotating gun and no bullets erupted from its barrels, his lip time turned into dry heaves as heavy streaks of green fire hurtled at our diving ship. Each one seemed to be aimed directly between our eyes, but passed without sound and out of view both to the right and left.

Three more runs. We climbed and turned hard. The fire never stopped, and we had no mini-gun to suppress it.

Weapons designers didn't think about the dust and debris a hovering helicopter caused and what they did to low-mounted mini-guns with turning metal gears. They would have been stunned at how badly we needed the gun, yet how often it failed.

It was the same picture on each run. Same results, nothing slowing down in the way of tracers. They were trying hard; we were trying hard. Which side was trying the hardest was the question. Who was getting it right?

The heavy foliage prevented us from seeing our target of enemy troops and guns, but the source of the fire was obvious. There had to be a lot of VC (Viet Cong) with AK-47 rifles blazing away as well, if this had been set up right, but we couldn't see those bullets, and besides, who cared? It was impossible to consider other perils when green .51 tracers were in your face.

Pulling up from our last run and out of rockets, we looked for our wingman, who had radioed that he was close and inbound, and what was the story on the target?

Brault would have seen where our rockets were hitting, but depending on the angle, maybe not the tracers. We could see him flying into the target area. I told him we were taking heavy fire, but that is like one pilot telling another how bad the turbulence is; it's open to interpretation. One pilot's heavy turbulence is another pilot's light to moderate. Brault had had a lot more time in a Snake than I had.

No one was firing at the moment; the VC knew how all this worked. They were waiting for the second ship.

Brault pulled his Cobra's nose up, slowing the bird to roll over into the run. The helicopter seemed to hang against the gray overcast like a wind chime moving slightly. We could see its belly as the nose rolled to the left. For an instant, we saw the nose drop as the Snake began its shallow run toward the target.

We were out of rockets but still flying, heading back to re-arm. We kept our eye on our wing ship to see if the setup was going to work out okay. It was heavy work, but we had done four runs and would return for more once we loaded more rockets into our empty pods. There was no thought of failure or loss. Get the job done was how we all thought, then go home.

At least half a dozen heavy explosions erupted along the fuselage of Brault and Vergimini's ship. In an instant, their cockpit was obliterated by flashing red explosions and white smoke. The VC had found their range, and Brault had flown into the confluence of the .51s. The enemy's geometric solution had come together as a dark sum.

The fuselage of Brault's aircraft, with Doug in the front, rolled over on the side towards us, on fire from the shells' impacts. At that moment, my eyes stopped following the plunging ship. Although I was aware of its impact, I focused on the spinning, main rotor blades—still intact and flying as a single silver disc, throwing off reflections of light, not wobbling or rolling end-over-end, but continuing as if still rotating over a flying helicopter.

The aircraft's rotor mast must have been cleanly severed by a single fragment without causing the smallest change or disturbance to the rotor system. Like a well-thrown frisbee, the rotor disc continued to soar, and then began a slow descent.

Finally, a good distance from the wreckage, it settled behind jungle foliage. It seemed to have flown for minutes, but that couldn't be right. It was as if the helicopter had been striving to stay aloft. The spinning disk was headed in the direction of home, but nothing else was going with it.

"God damn it!"

My next encounter had been a red and white box thrust suddenly in my face as the Colonel rasped, "You wanna smoke?"

I was on the ground, and I was stunned. Grounded by the Colonel, I had been arrested mid-effort in making a plan to re-arm and impetuously return for a counterblow at the scene of the shoot down. I didn't exactly know what to do now, nor did I even know where to look. No rockets, no second attempt. Only loss.

The second ship of our pair was gone. It wasn't elsewhere; it was gone. All that existed now was an indistinguishable mound of burning metal and a lump of melted engine smoking in the nearby jungle. The two good men it had carried were gone with it. What was next?

That flight back to base would exceed the loneliness of any flight I would take during my time as a pilot—then or since. In war, it is the most desolate flight imaginable—one aircraft, two people, no wing ship. At base, we wouldn't be following our usual pattern for landing—one behind the other. There would be no post-mission gathering of our two crews over drinks, joking and talking about near misses and the simple fact that we were back.

Today's loss would be the first two-pilot loss in a string of another ten losses over the next few months. Why had this grisly procession started today?

No heavenly scale that we could see fully compensates for the weight and measure of such unjust events. Vergamini's tour of duty had ended, but fate had pulled him back into his completed year to extract a final flight. He had already been ordered home. He was dressed for it. He was on his way.

Brault was still in his year. Only two weeks to go, but still climbing the 365-day mountain to when he could leave in an airliner, cross the Pacific, and at last see home. Now only pain and suffering would be delivered there. Neither man would be present.

These missions are burned into my mind and my heart. They are just a few of the many I have lived through. Thousands of other veterans also carry experiences that live on in their hearts and minds, but we will never know about them. As the saying goes, "You can leave the war, but the war never leaves you."

Chapter 4

THE FORTUNE COOKIE

Fate is like a fortune cookie. No one at the table knows what the message will read, but you are at a Chinese restaurant and the cookies come with the meal. By breaking it open, you dare to invite the demon of consequence to participate in your life. The small slip of paper declares your fate. Is it served cold ("You will get a new job")? Or hot ("Beware a chance meeting")?

Each time you walk to an aircraft and prepare it for flight, you are picking up at least one metaphorical fortune cookie, perhaps more. The message or messages are written by an unknown hand whose presence is evident in the message, but hidden from you. Their tidings have been transcribed from a pen dipped in a well of complex contents: climate, human elements, and a perplexing machine that defies gravity and wars with the elements to meet its purpose. Any of those variables may crack the cookie and spill out the message fate has written there. It may well be an outcome or a dilemma you don't understand. It may also come with the force of total surprise as it reveals itself.

In everyday life, but most certainly during war, many more variables may be added to the ingredients of fate. These missives are still hidden within the remaining cookies you carry aloft in your hypothetical bag. Some might return with you unbroken, but once opened, the message inside may plunge you into a critical circumstance or a puzzling challenge that you must solve correctly, or die trying.

Tail-rotor loss is an example of fate served hot. Helicopters need tail rotors. Without them, the fuselage rotates in the opposite direction of the main rotor blades, the passengers are unhappy, and the ride becomes ferocious, pointless, and even life-threatening. A few helicopter designs have opposing main rotor blades that cancel the powerful torque of a flying or hovering helicopter, but whenever you see a helicopter with a spinning blade on its tail, know that it is a key component of successful flight.

One of my earliest experiences with a tail-rotor predicament occurred in Vietnam. We had landed as a team of two Cobras to arm and refuel near the Cambodian border at a remote jungle airstrip just a couple of thousand feet long. Our flight of two was part of a good-size operation that day. Late morning, the stiff breeze had already begun to dry out the steamy air as the sun climbed toward its zenith in a deep blue sky.

When we arrived, helicopters were lined up and down one side of the landing strip that was defined by partially buried and rusted PSP underlying the packed gravel and scraggly clumps of grass along its length. Every refueling pad was already filled with an idling helicopter. Others were parked on the strip, waiting their turn to hover onto the fueling pads. Our team of two helicopters split up to find openings in the line.

The wind socks at either end of the short runway stood out in opposite directions. Since we were parked at the base of a low, rocky hill, the fickle wind was ricocheting in undetectable directions.

The first models of the AH1-G (Cobra) had tail rotors without enough bite (pitch) in the blade to maintain tail rotor authority and keep the helicopter from turning uncontrollably if the heavy or the rotor wash of another helicopter blew from behind.

The wind continued to swirl any which way with considerable intensity, gusting fiercely at times. With so many running helicopters coming and going and a wind with no definable direction, concern over losing control of the helicopter was nerve racking. Losing control in such a crowded gaggle of machines would be catastrophic.

We had finished fueling. Our rocket pods were fully loaded. The mini-gun ammunition had been replenished, stored in boxes beneath the aluminum floor of our cockpits. Its flat metal links filled with thousands of bullets were fed via chutes to the underslung weapon in the nose turret. We were heavy laden with explosives and combustibles and ready to depart.

I gradually rolled on the throttle to the left. The main rotors gathered themselves, the slow rhythmic sound of the idling blades changing to an urgent throbbing. I pulled up on the collective, and we left the ground cautiously, inching toward the open runway.

A one-foot hover seemed safest since the machine promptly began twitching from side to side, indicating the onset of the tail-rotor losing its authority in the conflicted airflow around its spinning blades. I was pulling most of the available engine power just to hover, which meant the tail rotor blades were close to maximum pitch. I slowly slid the helicopter sideways away from the fueling pad into the clear space at the center of the runway.

As I hovered away from the line of refueling aircraft, the Cobra that had been parked next to us in line came to a hover. Someone or something had cracked open a fortune cookie. The rotor wash of his heavily loaded Snake spread out as a great gust of wind, catching our machine squarely in its rear quarter. Our helicopter, placed abruptly on what seemed like an icy road, began a gradual revolution to the right. Full left pedal (maximum tail rotor blade pitch) would not stop the tendency, so the machine continued toward an uncontrolled spiral.

I began lowering the collective to slide the aircraft onto the runway in a sideward touchdown. Otherwise, waiting would increase our rotation as we lost total authority for the tail-rotor. If we began to turn with any greater velocity, it would become impossible to put the helicopter on the ground without rolling it over on its side, spinning blades and all.

The increasing velocity to the right of the heavily loaded Snake's nose startled the young Captain (aircraft commander by rank) in the front seat. Some of the young officers thought it was "cool" to sit in the front and direct the mission while having the guy in the back do all the work.

The Captain grabbed the Cobra's front seat flight controls and yelled, "I've got it! I've got it!"

I felt his rough inputs and released the stick. I took my feet off the pedals that controlled the tail rotor pitch. They began marching harshly full right, then full left as they were rapidly pumped by the Captain struggling to reclaim control. A second cookie was opened.

There was no point at all in wrestling for control of the aircraft at this critical juncture. Communicating, even briefly, while the aircraft was still manageable would have saved us, but rash action came first. Panic is never the correct response. It gives fate the upper hand even before you start.

We staggered to a high hover. He must have pulled the collective lever against the stops, introducing even more torque. The helicopter made a complete turn to the right. We had not lost the tail rotor itself; however, the sudden application of full power to the main rotors amid the rotor downwash from the helicopter behind us overwhelmed our spinning tail rotor. It became useless as an anti-torque device. We were now at the mercy of uncontrolled torque, which had turned violent in the extreme.

Suddenly, I felt like I was astride a berserk pachyderm. The Cobra's normal flight comportment had been shredded. It whirled and bucked like the mad elephant I imagined. I was just along for the ride!

Looking into the front cockpit, I got a glimpse of the struggling Captain. One of his hands gripped the short collective on the left, in front of the armrest, while his right hand radically moved the stick in front of the other armrest. This unusual design for an AH1-G made room for the movable gun site that sat between the front pilot's legs.

His position, viewed from behind, reminded me of someone leaning back in an armchair with a beer in one hand and a sandwich in the other, his gaze frozen on a TV screen where a

50 yard pass had just been thrown. The helicopter went around again, even faster. In a state of unbelievable calm, I reached to lock my shoulder harness. This was not going to end well. It was getting hard to think or even reason, given the pace at which the situation was deteriorating.

We were winding up like a top spinning faster and faster. A blur of green mixed with other spinning rotor blades swept past the canopy. Each rotation caused us to spin faster and the rotor rpm to decay further. If the Captain didn't do something soon, we would fall from the sky like a brick. His helmet was bobbing from side to side, blocking a clear view of the front cockpit. Was there a brain in there that was going to act? That was the question. What could I do? How do I decide what is next? We were rapidly reaching the point where nothing we did would matter. The size of the fireball would be the measure of our failure to act sooner.

Not wanting to touch the gyrating joy stick in front of me to press the mic button, I leaned back and yelled, "Split the needles! Split the needles!" The centrifugal force from the whirling machine made it impossible to get my foot anywhere near the floor switch that activated the intercom.

Splitting the needles (disconnecting the engine drive from the main rotor blades through a clutch arrangement) was our only option for removing the unrestrained torque that threatened us. The helicopter would stop spinning and just before we touched down—if he pulled the collective with all he was worth—the main blades would take a great bite out of the air, slowing our descent. Then, if he timed it right the helicopter would have just begun to turn again as the skids touched the ground. The crisis would be over.

Whether it was my screamed demands or a message from his own brain, the Captain's left hand snapped the throttle to the right. The aircraft immediately stopped spinning. We were still high, very high for a vertical landing, but the green blur outside of the canopy suddenly came into focus.

We fell fast from at least thirty feet—our trajectory straight down. There soon would be a loud explosion or just maybe the young Captain would get it "kind of right" and return us in one piece. We were going to land where we were going to land. There was no time to pick a spot and move over it.

Seconds later, we crunched into the ground hard and slid backwards into a ditch, the nose of the Cobra pointed upward. The Captain re-engaged the main rotor. Holding his cyclic control as far forward as possible to hold our position, he shouted orders almost hysterically, "Get out! Get out! Check the damage!"

I was glad I couldn't see his face. His eyes were likely disconcerting, void of any reason. I unlatched the canopy, stood up, and straddled the cockpit rail, carefully searching out the first step with my foot. I was not really sure how stable the helicopter was, given its high nose angle—would it slide backward even farther? We were much closer to the ground, and I wasn't exactly sure why. I let myself down into the thick grass.

We had semi-crashed into a depression within a sloped ditch. The tail rotor blades were spinning normally but just inches from where the bottom of the ditch began to rise. Both skids were bent upward into the bottom of the short wings. The surrounding tall grass lay flattened from the strong downward thrust of air from the main rotor. What a sight!

The helicopter was still running, but looked humiliated in its ridiculous position, almost like a drunken man who had fallen into a hole and was staring up in embarrassment.

I climbed up the side of the machine and stuck my head into the cabin to shout my report over the sound of the running helicopter. The Captain's face was still locked straight ahead, as if searching the space before him for a solution to our dilemma. I would soon discover that his agitated thoughts were not founded in reason, but at that moment based more on hysteria.

Unbeknownst to me, he was reaching deep into our mythical bag of fortune cookies. Without realizing it, he intended to crack one open and hand me its message to read.

He ordered me back into the helicopter. That seemed strange to me, as I was outside and in one piece. Why re-enter what just minutes before had felt like a coffin about to be dropped into a grave?

I reluctantly clambered into a cockpit that now had an upward slanting floor and fell back into the pilot seat. I assumed I was here to assist in the machine's shutdown. Without saying a word or asking my opinion, the Captain took us into the air and rolled the nose over for takeoff, which we did.

Any witnesses on the ground must have been astounded by this action. You couldn't have made this scenario up, but it really happened. I fumbled to secure my seat belt and chicken plate, and then I plugged in my mic cord.

"Where are we headed?" I spit out in total surprise.

"Back to base," he said in a high voice I didn't recognize.

"Sir, we have warning lights and a couple of bells going off back here. I doubt we can make it that far," I warned.

We were joined by our wing ship. They flew close to inspect the damage.

"Damn! Your ship's pretty screwed up! How're you gonna land with the skids gone?"

There was no answer from the front seat. The Captain still held the flight controls in a death grip. Giving control back to me would have made more sense under the circumstances, as the back seat controls had a ratio of four to one in terms of authority over the front ones, thus reducing the attention needed to control the ship, but no orders or requests were forthcoming. He was determined to run this emergency on his own.

Getting the Snake back into the air and hoping we could fly a fairly long distance to our base at Phuoc Vinh had been the wrong choice. The fateful timing of the helicopter picking up behind us at just the wrong moment had deposited us on a path of poor choices that were increasing the possibility that the plight the Captain had created would soon concoct a dismal disaster.

I was losing it myself, staring at the warning lights and gauges. Finally, the intercom came to life.

"What warning lights are on?" he asked.

I looked at the panel of lights that were blinking yellow with the occasional red glimmer.

"All of them!" I said with alarm.

Just then, the voice from the wing ship came across the radio with the same question.

"What all is showing on your panel?" The radio crackled in my ear like a voice from outer space.

"Everything," I declared.

Wow, we were gonna blow up any minute! Take a deep breath, man. Get it together. With some difficulty, I tried to stay calm. Up front, the Captain had yet to tell me what he planned to do next.

I suddenly realized that I had been leaning forward and squashing the test button with my gloved finger, producing the alarming display of warning lights. Now who was panicking?

No reply came from the other Cobra, flying close by. I could see the pilots' reactions to my declaration of "all of them," their mouths open in astonishment. They both stared at our mangled machine as they slid their helicopter farther away from ours. They either believed me, which was really scary, or they thought further inquiry would result in a situation overload for us. We flew on.

Adding to my concern was my total lack of trust in the intentions and decisions of the inexperienced Captain in charge of our ship. No verbal connection had transpired, which would at least open a communication link that could lead to a mutual decision or purpose, a plan of sorts.

Recently, an order had come down from the Colonel that all commissioned officers flying with Warrant Officers would automatically become the Aircraft Commander regardless of experience by virtue of their superior rank. I considered briefly the chance of the Colonel's perspective being changed by the current situation? Doubtful.

Our wing ship's Aircraft Commander was an experienced pilot and leader. He was a first lieutenant, and his calm and measured assessment of the emergency created by the young Captain who outranked him was a breath of cool air rushing into the overheated sphere in our cockpit.

The young Captain was still frozen with indecision. The lieutenant flying our wing-ship took control by alerting a nearby Green Beret outpost that we were coming their way with a stricken ship. We didn't hear that conversation, but were given a new compass heading by the Lieutenant's steady voice coming through the radio. He also relayed the plan of how we would land once we reached the outpost.

Twenty minutes later, we briefly circled the small outpost where they had built up a "cradle" of sandbags inside their perimeter. We were going to land the Cobra in that cradle and hope it held and didn't collapse under us. There were no Army manuals for its construction. This was an emergency set-up all around and had been completed in the short timespan since the first radio call.

Our badly shaken Captain wobbled down from our low altitude to attempt a shallow approach to where the sandbags had been placed. Nothing crackled over the intercom. He was still in his own world.

The closer we got to the sandbags, the more the ship staggered. The Cobra's unique flight controls made landing difficult enough under normal conditions. This poor pilot had been gripping the controls for more than twenty-five minutes. Relaxing his grip at this point was probably beyond his ability.

Finally, the intercom came to life! "You take it!" came the voice from the front seat.

I was more than happy to take control. More than half of my fears had been erased by the pile of dusty, red sandbags in front of us. For one thing, the tail boom or some other such part was not going to suddenly come off and send us cartwheeling though the air to disintegrate in the jungle below. At this point, we had more than a fighting chance of living, no matter what happened. Hope is a powerful force. It was now magnified in the narrow confines of our ship and brought freedom from our recent dark fears.

Our wing ship circled low above us. The crew was watching intently, no doubt, to see if our aircraft was going to settle into the sandbag cradle and stay or just roll over into the red dirt and turn into a pile of useless parts.

The compound had been emptied of personnel. Likely someone there had seen a helicopter come apart and knew the air would be filled with flying shrapnel and ammunition and had warned the others. Not that they didn't believe they had done a good job with the sandbags, but one never knew, in a war zone, what might come next.

I hovered the Cobra over the sandbag cradle despite the cloud of red dust that billowed up. The cloud was created by rotor blades almost as wide as the cabin itself. I cautiously centered the fuselage with its curled-up skids over the cradle and lowered the collective. Then I very gingerly descended, and letting the weight of the helicopter gradually transfer itself onto the gritty pile of bags, feeling for any slippage or unsteadiness. Hopefully this would work the first time, since the other option was to hover outside of the compound and then roll the machine onto its side while running. No one wanted to see that happen.

When I finally rolled off the throttle, the Cobra had settled snuggly onto the mound, only tilting slightly to the left as the blades coasted to a stop. Even the rocking motion of the shutdown had not dislodged the machine from its resting place. We got out. The outpost grunts had been good engineers. It worked.

Once we were shut down and the blades had stopped turning, our wing ship left in the direction of our base. Later, the Colonel's Huey showed up to take us back "home." The Colonel wasn't on it, thankfully! The Captain didn't speak to me, then or on the way back.

I assume the helicopter was recovered from the compound by a large, twin-rotor Chinook, whose pilots would have peered out their side window to see it twisting around and around at the end of a 200-foot cable on its way back to Phuoc Vinh.

When the other Cobra picked up behind us at the critical moment, he broke open a fortune cookie. Fate moved before the thirty seconds we needed to depart came around and set off a twenty minute drama that had dire consequences folded into the initial choices being made. A good wing ship commander stepped into the unraveling situation and directed fate away from our destruction. A precise plan evaporated the short message on the slip of paper that popped out of the cookie at the airstrip.

If we had stayed in the tall grass of the sloping ditch, as humiliating as it was, the bird would have been returned to service by a safer route than the one we took. When there is a weak link in a chain, it snaps quickly under strain. The results hastily tumble into a trajectory that sweeps fear, confusion, and most likely danger along with it, producing unintended consequences. In our situation, the break in the link may have been forestalled by taking a brief minute to consider the options, but who knows where the weak links are in a tether until they snap? In war, you must suspect it and do what you can to strengthen it before the chain snaps. Often, you don't anticipate it. Its sudden and then the wheels come off.

The bird was out of action for a month—one of our newer ships—I remember the number on the tail, "206." It never failed to come back, nor did it kill anyone after that day, but it almost always came back early from a mission with something wrong with it. That had been a hell of a fall. Number 206 was never the same.

In war, you learn, when possible, not to react without purpose. Waiting an extra second to be sure can change your path significantly. This decision-making process saved me during numerous civilian flight experiences in situations as extreme as helicopter logging, flying small, commuter planes during bad weather in and out of small airports with uncommon approaches, and towing practice torpedoes along the surface of the ocean at zero elevations.

One such situation found me grinding my way north through a significant Pacific storm headed toward the US Navy's shallow water, torpedo testing range. I skimmed the wave tops of the crashing surf as it pounded the sands and log-jammed beaches along the occasionally steep cliffs of the northwest Washington coastline.

I was flying a Soloy Hiller12E on floats. The Soloy company had replaced the standard piston engine of this model Hiller with a turbine engine that burned jet fuel. Dragging along those two pale yellow, rubber carcasses—one on each side—through the spray-filled air further restrained the helicopter's already slow progress.

While immersed in such an environment, it occurred to me that most callings in aviation pitted man and machine against some combination of the elements. Who rules in these contests, nature or you? It is your innate task as a pilot to avoid being overwhelmed or disabled by nature's unforgiving bias. It is a match where only the tools and knowledge you have acquired by hours in the air can find a way through. Winning is vital when survival is the goal.

I was turned out in a bulky, bright orange float suit common to crews in danger of being washed overboard or who intended to abandon ship. It was a combination loose-fitting wet suit and life jacket. My white flight helmet topped off my resemblance to the Pillsbury dough boy.

Upon reaching the US Navy's torpedo test range near La Push, I would spend two weeks performing aerial tasks involving the calibrating of the range and recovery of torpedoes. Not included in the contract and unbeknownst to me at the time would be an unarmed aerial assault against the Russians!

It had been a ferry trip whose course had not been direct. I had left the small town airport where the helicopter service was based near the Puget Sound, holding a course northwest toward the Pacific coast. The weather had precluded a straight line over the Olympic Range, so I intersected the coastline through a somewhat twisted route, dodging low clouds and fog generated by the incoming storm. I would now simply have to fly along the shoreline until I reached the naval base.

It was going to be a long flight. I had topped off my single fuel tank and filled fuel jugs before departure. I checked over the machine. The helicopter, with floats attached, wallowed from side to side. It was like walking on a waterbed as you moved around checking the rotor head, etc. during your preflight. One of them even looked smaller than the other one, but what did I know? I hadn't flown this type of set-up before.

The small, two-helicopter outfit I worked for usually spent long days with both machines flying, slinging bundles of cedar bolts that dangled from the end of various lengths of cable secured to the helicopter's main hook. A second hook at the bottom of the cable was controlled electrically by the pilot to release the load of cedar bolts without dropping the cable itself.

The bolts (short, three-foot chunks of cedar) were cut from ancient downed cedar trees half buried in the moss and undergrowth of the Northwest rain forests. Moisture doesn't rot cedar like it does other wood. Each bundle of bolts was worth about $300. Once delivered, the bolts were then trucked to a mill and hand split into roof shakes. The money was good, and we filled truck after truck. Each had clawed its way over old, potholed logging roads to get as near as possible to the source of wood, rain or shine. And in a rain forest, the rule was gray overcast with rain almost every day.

On occasion, other charter or contract opportunities would come up. As the new pilot, I was assigned when the time came to show up at La Push. Choices were often limited by others, including the boss. The significant demands of learning yet another flying technique on my own was not picked by me, but assigned based on the higher financial return produced by a more experienced pilot hauling cedar.

The Navy contract had been signed the previous year. In addition to recovering practice torpedoes, I would be supporting the Navy's test range by dragging a small torpedo back and forth out in the ocean on a cable attached to the helicopter. The Navy Range technicians would carefully calibrate the range for the moment when actual torpedoes without warheads would be launched. With a correctly calibrated range, they could track with precision the underwater maneuvers of the torpedo as it attacked a US Navy cruiser's attempted evasion.

Bundled up in my "float/dry suit," I would drag a practice torpedo on various headings assigned by the shore team. Again, no GPS, meaning you relied on a compass heading or heading indicator adjusted for wind and variation that you computed by the seat of your pants, charts, and your best guess.

Hiller 12E Soloy—Picking Up Torpedoes

Of course, the ocean's surface is never flat or still. Undulating water of an active sea rises and falls continuously. The nose of the single-engine Hiller was always tipped steeply toward the dark water as it rose and fell.

Pulling a large metal cylinder twenty feet under water, no matter how light, was a tremendous drag on forward flight. So these flights were very slow, maybe fifteen knots, and they lasted a good part of the day with a fuel stop every hour and a half. As the sea surged higher on some days, it was a constant challenge to keep it from striking the bottom of the aircraft. Only one hard slap of seawater would erase controlled flight.

Later in the operation after the range had been calibrated, the shore crew launched dummy torpedoes much smaller than the full-blown version, to run through the course. When the run was complete, the dummy torpedoes were programmed to come to the surface and float vertically, nose up. My job was to locate the bobbing shiny metal nose of the drone torpedo somewhere across the vast ocean range, using radioed guidance from the technicians on shore.

On these recovery missions, I flew a triangular rope cage that dangled from the end of a one hundred foot cable attached to the belly hook of the helicopter. The "floor," or bottom of the net enclosure, would be pulled up by a tag-line to a vertical position alongside the net itself. This arrangement exposed an opening on one-side of the cage so that the whole device could be lowered over the torpedo. Once the nose of the torpedo touched the inside limit of the triangular net, I electrically released the tag-line, which in turn released the "floor" of the rope cage, causing it to swing level and enclose the drone. I would then lift the torpedo clear of the water and return it to shore. This procedure as described seems straightforward and easily accomplished.

Not really! To fully appreciate the task, imagine drinking a fifth of any kind of liquor before you start in order to appreciate the challenges involved in looking down through an open doorway (the door itself remains onshore), past the flapping, rubber float into the rolling waves.

The rotor wash and steady sea breeze buffets the swinging net far below. There is no solid peripheral reference, which is mandatory for a steady hover. With no fixed references, the effort of hovering over moving water is like trying to balance on a basketball on a moving conveyer belt. You are attempting the impossible. Between the waves going up, down, and sideways and the constantly changing floor angle of the helicopter, you struggle. The torpedo floats nearby, with its silver head bobbing in and out of the sea in a taunting game of hide and seek. All of this must somehow come together at one time to capture the torpedo.

In addition, you are in a Hiller helicopter, whose flight controls seem to have a one-minute delayed reaction after your manual input. You are reduced to feeling like a well-developed drunk stabbing at a moving fish. This is painful at the very least, and at best, frustrating beyond imagination.

Again, no one sat beside you for the first few hours of this unique operation, nor was there a manual on recovering torpedo drones at sea. You knew how to fly a helicopter, so you were expected to figure out the rest without risking the machine, or secondarily, your neck!

Training cost money, but losing a helicopter cost much more. Unlike the airline industry, helicopter companies generally offered no specialized training before you left on an assignment. No doubt just keeping a very complicated and expensive aircraft in the air was straining most owner's pocketbooks as well as their imaginations. Additional costs that could bring beneficial future returns were seldom considered.

Most tasks were very close to the ground with few options if things went bad. It boiled down to two vital rules in a helicopter, no matter what you were doing: One—keep the rotor rpm in the green. Two—maintain control of the machine. After that, there were literally hundreds of techniques for completing a certain kind of job with a rotor-wing machine. No one wanted to share secrets. If they told you what they knew, you might end up knowing more than they did. Ah, human reason at work.

During the final days of the contract, I was finally free of a dangling cable under the helicopter. The time had arrived when the purpose of all this preparation was at hand, and a real torpedo (minus the warhead) was about to be launched onto the range. A US Navy Cruiser had shown up in the night and was anchored offshore. I assumed my contract tasks were complete as a larger helicopter had flown in for a single day to recover the much bigger torpedo after it surfaced, nose bobbing up and down, depleted of fuel. The authentic torpedo would perform unbelievable maneuvers underwater in its attempt to close with the Navy ship.

Just before the launch of the torpedo, the horizon filled with dozens and dozens of ships. They appeared suddenly as if they had risen straight out of the ocean at exactly the same moment. They were Russian trawlers.

If the torpedo turned into a "runaway," it would be in international waters and legally salvageable by anyone out there. The Russians hoped for a runaway. They were set up to capture it immediately, if that happened.

Although I was flying the least formidable of helicopters, floats and all, I was approached and ordered to fly out to the Navy Cruiser, land on its rolling aft deck, and pick up an officer. We would then fly at least fifteen miles offshore and challenge the Russians' fishing fleet.

We circled, dove at, and flew close to virtually every ship. The Navy officer with me was looking for certain types of antennas and deck configurations. Although disguised as fishing vessels, apparently there were "wolves" among the flock capable of recovering an errant torpedo. What were we going to do about it? I had no idea.

I am sure the Russians understood the game that was being played and were thoroughly unimpressed by my seventy knots of airspeed and two yellow rubber accomplices charging at their ships. They ignored us. No one turned and pointed up at us from the closely watched decks of the trawlers. After more than an hour of "play," we returned for fuel and made another pass before I flew the Navy officer back to shore. He ducked under the turning blades and walked over to naval operations, entering by the side door. The international incident was concluded peacefully. Nuclear war had been averted! Fortune cookies served cold?

The demanding tasks of the contract paled in comparison to the trial of the inbound trip to La Push at the beginning of the contract.

As I flew along the coast on my way to the Navy test site to start the contract, I chose to fly about fifty yards offshore beyond the breaking surf rather than snake along the shoreline where swirling eddies of foam and surf concealed most patches of exposed sand. My altitude was just two hundred feet. Poor visibility and heavy rain kept me close to the wave tops.

The fuel gauge showed I was getting low on fuel, but I was only a 15-minute flight from my destination. Even if I could find a place to land on the stormy shore, it would be difficult in the driving rain to clamber over the "waterbed" attached to my helicopter while attempting to refuel from the jugs strapped to the side racks.

The fuel tank on this machine was a rectangle about twelve inches deep with the fuel pickup located at the rear of the tank. Flying with floats kept the nose even lower than normal. A fortune cookie waiting to open? In this configuration, the fuel gauge was giving questionable readings at best. As I mentioned earlier, helicopter pilots figured out this stuff on their own. There were no lined charts—time versus fuel—or blinking gauges to compute fuel burned and time left before reaching empty. Bare bones was the theme in this helicopter cockpit.

Basic configurations left the pilot with more interpretive choices and judgment considerations which led to more small slips of white paper popping from the cookie.

One accessory the helicopter did carry on the panel was a re-ignition device, attached to the igniter on the turbine engine. If the turbine fire died, the igniter—charged with electricity—automatically clicked away. If the fuel flow had been interrupted with a small amount of water or air, the continuous igniter spark would re-light the fuel again after the interruption. Because of this instrument, one less cookie was carried aloft.

Pressing forward in the wind and just beyond the crashing waves hitting the beach, the engine's high whine ceased suddenly. The aircraft began to drop from the sky. Normal procedure was to immediately lower the collective to save rotor rpm, but I was only two hundred feet in the air. Slamming down the collective would immediately put me into the wild sea. I turned toward shore, lowering the collective with trepidation. I was going to land in the churning waves of the heavy storm surf directly ahead.

At least I would have the shore in front of me. Less than thirty seconds of continued flight would have put me behind a jagged rock formation towering out of the sea, and I would have been unable to turn toward shore. Fate smiled briefly. Such rock formations dotted this part of the coast infrequently, but dramatically where the waves dashed against them..

In my headset, I could hear the constant "clicking" of the re-ignition system, but during this particular moment of peril, it didn't register. I was more focused on the sad realization that I had run out of gas. That even with floats the giant waves would not be kind to the aircraft or to me. We were about to drop into a furious, watery hell.

As I leveled the aircraft for the final step of the very brief autorotation, perhaps ten feet above the water and just before being swallowed by the wind-torn surf, the engine surged to life. Leveling the aircraft must have suddenly washed any remaining fuel across the fuel pick-up point at the rear of the tank. The auto re-ignition system had restored power just at the right moment, as designed.

Even if your equipment is basic, attention to the important components that support continuous flight, once airborne, should never be overlooked by an owner, and in this case, it wasn't. Score one for the company! Good fortune emerging from a cookie on its tiny slip is always a win.

With the helicopter level just feet away from the rolling surf, I attempted to freeze its level attitude and move at a high hover toward shore. I immediately spotted a small circle of brown sand, defined by the foam and sea water swirling around its edges. It was free of driftwood fragments and formed a slight mound on the beach. I hovered over it, and just as I started down, the engine quit again. The floats broke my fall. The helicopter rocked quietly back and forth in the moaning wind as the rotors, after a prolonged freewheeling rotation, coasted to a stop above my head. Man-made noises had fled with only the sounds of crashing waves and piercing wind remaining.

More profoundly thankful than ecstatic—that would come later—I unlatched the cabin door and stepped over the wobbly float and its false assurance that any landing in the water would be safe. I unlashed the three fuel jugs from the side racks and assembled them near the filler neck of the gas tank. Using a large rag, I attempted to shield the fuel tank opening from the rain as I emptied all three jugs into the tank. Then, I tightly screwed on the tops and re-lashed the jugs to the racks.

Next, I found a wrench. I had seen how mechanics, after working on the engine, removed the ignitor from the combustion chamber and then cleared it of air by switching on the fuel pump in the cockpit until a steady flow of fuel passed from the hose into a scavenged container.

So I climbed up and knelt on the soft rubber float near the back of the engine and loosened the ignitor/fuel line. No fuel came out. Placing the end of the hose into the container I had scrounged from the cockpit, and as best I could, stumbled along the top of the float to the front of the aircraft, then carefully opened the flimsy cabin door, gripping it against the gusting wind. I switched on both the battery and fuel pump, then struggled the five feet back to the rear of the engine to glare at the hose, watching for fuel flow.

Shortly, a steady stream of fuel drained into the container. I tasted it to be sure. I quickly emptied the container onto the sand and lurched along the float back to the cabin to shut off the battery. Then I dried the end of the hose and reattached it to the combustion chamber, cinching it tightly with the wrench.

Despite the bulky suit that made it so awkward to get around, I did not resent it. At such moments, if the incident had ended differently, it would have provided my only chance of survival, but only after getting clear of the spinning rotor blades beating the surrounding water into geysers of saltwater.

The engine started normally. I knew exactly how much fuel and thus how much time I had left in the air, as well as how far away the base was located. I lifted off, tucked the nose over, and again merged with the storm, clawing up the coast against the force of the wind.

This same 12E had a sad ending just two years later. Another new employee/pilot, married with children like myself, left La Push when the contract was over to ferry the aircraft across the remote Olympic Peninsula. He never showed up. After an exhaustive search, neither the pilot nor helicopter was ever found. The fortune cookies that carry the messages of fate on any flight are never to be taken lightly or ignored; your very life may rest among them.

The conversion from a piston engine in the original airframe to a turbine engine by the Soloy Company had made the 12E more reliable and improved its performance. The company followed that same calculation into other rotor wing airframes.

As an aviation engineering company, Soloy first took horizontally opposed piston engines out of Cessna airplanes like the models 180, 206, and 207, replacing them at the time with the Allison 250, 420hp jet turbine engine commonly found in the Bell 206 helicopter. This re-engineering of the power plant to a jet turbine engine reduced the weight significantly, and although the overhaul cost was much higher, the turbine engine lasted much longer. Its takeoff performance became literally amazing with the addition of a huge, three-bladed propeller and an extra 120hp under the cowling.

They also accomplished this same enterprise with three helicopter models, including the Eurocopter AStar D model. The Eurocopter, factory-installed Lycoming 101 turbine engine was replaced by Soloy with an Allison engine also, but it was the larger 250M model of over 700hp. The Lycoming engine had been very problematic, and both owners and operators were looking for reliability.

I had joined Soloy as a demonstrator/sales person for the Bell 47 helicopter that Soloy had converted to a turbine. Before coming to Soloy, I had purchased and operated one for a large mining corporation, so I knew the machine's performance parameters well.

Subsequently, I was asked by Soloy to be the test pilot for the AStar conversion. With no formal training as a test pilot, I followed the instructions of the resident engineer in the back seat of the helicopter who ran all the electronic equipment, but that did not prevent many terrifying moments of attempting to carry out the maneuvers asked of me. Such instances never seemed to rattle the engineer. In fact, I didn't know some of the maneuvers were even possible. Live and learn, the key word being *live*!

Once the AStar conversion had an up-and-running engine installation, the company, even before FAA certification, was anxious to market it widely.

One very gray overcast day, Mr. Soloy himself decided to fly the prototype. It had been painted a bright yellow and white in the livery colors of PHI, the biggest helicopter company on the Gulf of Mexico, their targeted buyer for hundreds, if not dozens, of the type.

Mr. Soloy's son owned a helicopter company in Alaska and just before the promotional flight for the new AStar conversion, had one of his helicopters flown down from Alaska, a Hughes 500D. The plan was to make an aerial video of the newly converted AStar.

A Tyler Mount for securing a movie camera was fixed to the floor of the 500D and partially protruded into the slipstream where the right rear cabin door had been removed. This was the same model flown in *Magnum P.I.* If you are a Tom Selleck fan, you'll know the type. The mount had a swivel seat, and the camera was fastened to it outside the helicopter with the operator sitting half in and half out of the aircraft. This arrangement gave the camera lens an unobstructed view of the subject being filmed.

All the wires and cables were draped over the back of the right front seat where the director/technician would hold the TV monitor on his lap. After a successful installation, the small cabin of the 500D was stuffed full of people and equipment.

Mr. Soloy, the film crew, and I discussed the general outline for gathering aerial footage of the AStar flying at treetop level across a fir tree plantation that ran parallel to an old taxiway along the eastern edge of the airport. It was a wide swath of concrete and was not currently operational.

I took on a light load of fuel. The filming area and plantation were only one hundred yards behind the factory hangar. The office area at the back of the hangar had a large picture window where factory staff and others were already lined up for a good view of the proceedings. I took the 500D up to three hundred feet, passing over the six to eight foot fir trees, lined up like soldiers on parade. I came to a high hover and waited for the AStar to appear. Minutes later, I heard Mr. Soloy on the company frequency, announcing his departure.

The yellow and white aircraft with PHI painted on its fuselage came hovering around the corner of the hangar and then began its first run below us, crossing just fifty feet over the small pines at a moderate speed. The business of focus, position, and how the AStar should proceed next filled the airwaves between the two helicopters. I kept a constant altitude, maneuvering here and there at a fast hover, as the aircraft below crisscrossed the plantation.

Ordered to the center of the filming area, I flew directly there and put the helicopter into a sliding right flare as I came into the wind.

Pulling the collective up to set the engine at high power arrested our sideward movement and stabilized the 500D in a hover. When I pushed the left pedal, the tail rotor blades bit solidly into the damp air for only a fraction of a second, but as we came to a stabilized hover, the left pedal went clear to the stops. I stared at it. "That wasn't right," I said to myself.

I had no time to ponder my surprise. The helicopter had begun a rapid right turn toward the cameraman positioned outside of the machine, strapped to the Tyler mount. He was about to experience the ride of a lifetime. We learned later that a nut located in the helicopter tail boom had come off a critical bolt that fastened the control rod, which manipulated tail rotor pitch to the pedals in the cockpit. The bolt must have dropped clear of the control rod just as we came to a hover. The small white slip from the broken cookie read, "*Inattention to detail, possible consequences dire.*"

In the rotor wing world, if something went wrong, it went wrong immediately and usually violently. All the parts were a complex team of moving and turning components that shared one purpose—make this thing fly! With few exceptions, all parts were required to be present for duty. There was rarely time to consult a flight manual as you fell towards earth. You were in a swirling, gyrating machine. Instinct was your best bet under the circumstances, as your senses were being trashed by either noise, wild movement, or raw gut-wrenching fear.

Myself, I go icy in a bad situation. I think it was the way the Army trained us. Fear or suppressed panic does surface in me, but usually about two days later, when I can hardly stand up at the thought of the emergency I have just lived through.

As we spun faster, I tuned out the screams of my two companions. I left the power in. We came straight down from three hundred feet. We were not in free fall, since I still had power to the main blades, but down was the only way out. It felt like we turned twenty times in those three hundred feet, but it was probably more like four or five. I had no idea where I was going to hit. The high probability was that we would land in the pines that blanketed the ground beneath us.

As the blur of the earth came closer and got darker, I "split the needles," taking the torque that was spinning us completely out of the flight equation. The helicopter straightened, and I pulled up on the collective lever. We landed rather lightly on the slanting embankment along the only road in the plantation. Fate can also be kind. As it landed, the helicopter rocked up on one skid, but came back down on both skids, meeting solid ground at the same time. We were down! The five narrow rotor blades coasted to a stop as I opened the cabin door and jumped to the ground.

The camera operator was unhurt, but pale as a ghost. He looked at me with a frantic stare that seemed to beg the question, "What just happened?" He had ridden the spinning "bull" from inside the tightening circle of centrifugal force. I helped release him from his three-point harness and held onto his arms as he wiggled limply from behind the camera onto terra firma. Unable to stand, he collapsed in a heap, struggling for breath, but for all practical purposes, he was okay.

The director/technician appeared from around the front of the helicopter, great relief smeared across his face and grinning from ear to ear.

"I'll be sending you a Christmas Card for the rest of my life!" he blurted out as he gave me a hug.

Then it started raining. There was no sign of the AStar. It was gone. I had thought that by the time the rotors stopped, an emergency vehicle or at least a pickup truck would have arrived to check on everyone. Nothing came. No one wanted to get back in the machine, so we slid next to or just under the helicopter and began getting soaked like the nearby trees dripping water from every branch and needle. We waited.

Perhaps fifteen minutes later, a white, Cadillac sedan pulled up. The son got out, his face clouded with disgust. He slammed the driver's door hard and marched around the front of the car. Putting his hands on his hips, he stared down at us like we were three bums huddled around a campfire. He didn't give anyone a hand as we struggled to our feet and walked up the slick grass to the road. Watching from the picture window, he had seen us spin down from a very high hover and land. It made him mad! He was convinced I had been "cowboying it" with his machine. A real show-off, he thought.

It took him a while to calm down. When the 500D hadn't lifted off again to return to the ramp in front of the hangar, he finally figured out that maybe something had gone wrong. He had then begrudgingly taken his parents' car and come down the concrete taxiway onto the narrow, asphalt road where the helicopter sat on the shoulder, its fuselage tipping slightly downhill.

The three of us helped each other into the car. The son didn't as much as open a door or close one. He stomped back to the driver's door, threw it open, and then slammed it shut after falling heavily into the driver's seat. At least he had waited for us to get in. Hey, I thought, it wasn't me nor a mechanic working for me who failed to secure the nut to such a vital bolt. You're really lucky it didn't come off between here and Alaska!

Two days later, he called me up at home. His mother had made him.

With little enthusiasm and barely any shame, he forced out his words, "Thanks for getting my ship down in one piece. Sorry about the mix up. My mother said I should call you.

"Yeah," I replied, "no sweat." He hung up. Would have been nice to get a job offer, but no dice. "Spoiled brat," I muttered to myself.

Fortunately, I never lost the weight of the tail rotor gear box and the blades during my experiences with tail rotor loss. When the gear box leaves, it is like someone jumping off the opposite end of a teeter totter when you are in midair. The weight loss so far back on the machine causes the pilot to run out of aft cyclic (stick) control, so he is unable to bring the nose of the aircraft level. This is especially the case with many of the Bell models, like the Huey, that have such long tail booms. Usually, the aircraft will rotate two or three times, the nose will tuck, and then the helicopter will be immediately uncontrollable.

There are rare exceptions. If for some reason the aircraft is loaded heavily towards the back, it may enable the pilot to "streamline" the helicopter by reaching an airspeed where the aerodynamic forces on the airframe will keep it from turning. If that condition can be achieved, then the pilot can slide the helicopter onto a hard surface like landing an airplane and through proper technique bring it to a stop without further mishap.

My closest call to losing a tail rotor gear box and subsequently crashing began to develop one night outside a bar in Alaska. I had just been offered a job from a very drunk chief pilot sitting in a slouch on the wooden planks of the sidewalk while leaning against the storefront of the bar. He looked up at me, his blurry eyes failing to focus clearly. "We'll fly you out to the island tomorrow," he mumbled.

My friend Clint worked for the company I was hoping to get a job with. He and I had searched for an hour for the chief pilot. It was getting darker, but in those latitudes at that time of the year, total darkness only came for a few hours in the middle of the night. The front windows and open door of the ruckus bar allowed the dirt road and wooden sidewalk in front of it to be painted periodically with splashes of noise and pulsing light as we stood looking down at the sodden human form at our feet.

His outfit had sent me a roundtrip airline ticket from Pennsylvania to Alaska to interview for this job. This was the interview, blurry eyes and all. In other words, they needed a body, one who could fly—they would take my word for it, no resume required. The chief pilot, slurring his words, explained once more that the plan was to meet in the lobby of the hotel in the morning. "Be ready to go," he whispered before he went silent altogether. According to Clint, who had the scuttlebutt on this specific job, I would be flying a surplus Huey. The pilot I was replacing would be coming out on the same aircraft I flew in on.

Later, alone in my tiny hotel room, I counted the fortune cookies I had picked up in the course of the day. All of them were partially opened, but I couldn't see the messages. However, they were in there. What did they say? Would fate be served hot or cold? I tossed and turned under the stiff sheets and prickly, woolen blanket that made up the bedding in this wild west hotel where I stayed the night.

How and when these fortune cookies would pop open was a puzzle I didn't have the powers to unwind, but in reality, they confronted me in this order:

1. When I had arrived in the afternoon, I had seen Clint for the first time in a year or two. He was at the controls of a Bell 214B with a group of mechanics, working to clear a problem with the rotor system of the helicopter. He invited me to go for a test flight while they worked on the mechanical issue. With the exception of Clint himself, the comments, proposals for a solution, and the logic of the three or four mechanics on board made me feel like I was in a clown car.

2. They obviously lacked the training, experience, and tools to resolve the issue they were discussing at length.

3. Standing quietly among the same group after we landed from the test flight, I heard the story of how previously non-serviceable parts had been returned from the main office in California with no overhaul performed, just the tag changed from red to green and returned for service. As a result, there had been a fatal crash.

4. The "blotto" condition of the chief pilot was not unusual for someone working out of a remote location in Alaska; however, it was hardly reassuring given the previous two points.

All through the night, I tossed and turned, struggling to minimize these indicators as unimportant. I really needed steady work, and helicopter logging paid well. I was never very good at saying no, and they had paid for a thousand dollar airline ticket. Finally, I fell asleep.

Early the next morning, I met the red-eyed, chief pilot and the other pilots and mechanics traveling out to the remote company camp. Various duffel bags and piles of articles cluttered the small lobby. I walked up to the chief pilot, waited for him to finish his sip of steaming coffee, and told him directly that I wouldn't be taking the job. His cup of coffee froze in midair as he stared me full in the face. He sputtered a few words, his face turned red, and he slammed his cup onto the counter. He looked again at my face, saw the resolve there, grabbed at his bags, and stomped out of the lobby.

Silently, the rest of the group milled around, picking up their gear and leaving right behind him. They all bundled into a large van waiting outside the doorway. I was alone in the lobby except for a scattered number of locals leftover from the night before, loafing in the various stained and overstuffed chairs at the edges of the room.

I felt guilty, but not guilty enough to say yes to the job. I caught a taxi later in the morning that took me to a ferry that transported the passengers across to the island airport to catch our flight. As the ferry left the dock, so did my feelings of guilt. For me, I had done the right thing.

A month or two later, I heard from my friend Clint. The pilot I was to replace that morning in Alaska had taken up the Huey I was to be assigned and lost the tail rotor gearbox while picking up a load of logs. He crashed into the trees. He didn't deserve to die instead of me. Unpredictable fate had dictated a message—it came on a small slip of white paper and it read; "*One will die, and one will live.*" The message was easily interchangeable as to who, but this time, it was not for me. I felt bad.

Chapter 5

TAILDRAGGERS, YOU'VE GOT TO LOVE 'EM

Like an acrobat beginning his cartwheel with just one hand on the floor, the right wing tip of my muscular airplane—a bright yellow Thrush Commander—had struck the far bank of a deep ditch paralleling the road where I had wanted to land. The left wing rose high above me. A glance out the right side window presented a vertical view of the earth below. My cockpit reached the highest point of the arc. The airplane completed its cartwheel as the left wing tip then touched the ground with me in the middle, the head of the acrobat so to speak.

With the throttle at idle, I stood on the brake, but neither wheel was anywhere close to the rutted, mud-choked road they had left just seconds before. I held on to the stick, but none of these actions slowed our downward velocity. The ground filled the windscreen in a sudden telescopic close-up.

The ground crew and myself were in the depths of a pine forest, flying a fertilizer contract for a large, southern paper and lumber company. I skimmed the Loblolly pines, dispensing urea pellets (nitrogen fertilizer) from the Thrush's hopper and returning again and again for another load. The remote grass strip that we used earlier had quickly turned into a quagmire of deep ruts, becoming unusable, so we had moved the trucks next to a narrow logging road to begin takeoffs and landings from there.

A round, 600 hp, radial engine hung from the extended nose of this large, crop-spraying aircraft. It was solid, noisy, and as heavy as a bag of anvils.

The cockpit was large for just a single-seat aircraft. My first flight felt like I had been swallowed by a giant bird and sat in its stomach. The throw of the "stick" seemed to touch every corner of the spacious enclosure. Wearing the right shoulder strap of the three-point seat belt, I could barely reach the right quadrant of stick movement, so I flew with just the left strap secured. Since the throttle was easily reached with my left hand, the seatbelt adjustment freed my right arm to push the stick to its limits.

Having previously flown a spray plane with less than half the horsepower, my graduating to the Thrush was a big step. I had helped the owner of the family-owned spraying service to secure the fertilizer contract from the corporation that owned the forest. I believe he wanted me to reap some benefit as well, even if it meant checking me out in the larger aircraft, the pride of his two-plane fleet.

The narrow logging road was a landing challenge even on a good day, but then difficult and uncommon situations often developed in the spray business. The goal is to minimize "empty" flight time (when the aircraft is not loaded with product), so accepting all kinds of short airstrips or even, in this instance, an unimproved road, kept the "empty turns" as short as possible.

I set up to land for my fourth trip into the muddy, narrow lane. Deep drainage ditches paralleled the road on either side, where numerous smaller canals connected in regular intervals at ninety-degree angles. I also noted a light crosswind from the left.

Besides those variables, the smaller canals separated the closely planted plantations of pine trees fifteen to twenty feet high. Thus, wind gusts struck the logging road as they blew down the smaller canals but stopped momentarily when blocked by the trees, quickly resuming at the next opening of an intersecting canal. Tricky!

Shortly after my touchdown, as the aircraft rolled through the thick mud at a good speed, it began moving to the right. A more experienced Thrush pilot probably would have stood much harder on the left brake. I learned that it took only a few seconds before the wheel dropped over the edge of the deep canal. The right wing tip then crashed into the far bank, arresting the plane's forward motion and sending it into its cartwheel.

I was now hanging by only the left shoulder strap, I realized at once that the plane's wings had pivoted ninety degrees. They were now lined up with the deep canal at the side of the road, and the Thrush's tail was positioned almost straight up in the air. The big engine was going downward to be submerged instantly and pound into the muddy bottom of the drainage ditch.

As the ground on the far side of the canal's edge rushed into my vision and I prepared with teeth-grinding tension to accept the slam of earth against my windscreen, everything came to a sudden and silent stop. The windscreen had stopped just short of the dirt.

I could see each blade of grass clearly, as if the lens of a camera had suddenly rotated to full close-up. They stood erect, very green and moving slightly, less than a foot in front of the windshield.

Steam from the submerged engine curled upward in the light wind, and blew past the outside of the canopy. The sizzling sound of hot metal in water announced the end of the aircraft's movement.

The large cockpit that protruded from the yellow airframe had not been sheared off—with me in it—by the rising ground. The canal was just deep enough for this second-best situation to work out okay. The first, of course, would have been to remain on the road.

Being such a stout bird, its repairs did not reach the threshold of an accident, but rather an incident in the FAA's books. My injuries were confined to emotions, including pride of course. Mostly, I felt I had let the owner/family down and, at the time, saw everything as a total disaster and all my fault.

Other than remorse and other churning emotions, though, my only other injury was on my torso. A perfectly diagonal outline of the left shoulder harness strap led from my left shoulder to my waist in deep black, blue, and purple bruises.

Five years earlier, I had moved with my family—a wife and four small children, one a baby in arms—to North Carolina. I accepted a job offer from a west coast forestry company that owned millions of acres of pine trees in the Carolinas and needed a helicopter pilot stationed there.

I flew their Bell 206B JetRanger, a five-passenger (pilot plus four) helicopter five days a week, logging flight time of at least six to seven hours a day, which totaled a thousand hours a year. I carried timber managers surveying the forest holdings and harvest activity, and in season fought forest fires on company land. I burned logged-over parcels of ground scattered with mounds of logging debris, using a blow torch controlled from the cockpit and slung at the end of a twenty-five foot cable dangling below the helicopter.

It was a good flying job, but with a growing family at home, one thousand dollars a month was a budget challenge, despite a monthly car payment of $75 and a mortgage of $105.

Needing extra income, I had learned of a part-time position with a local spray company. Those pine tree forests were surrounded by hundreds of square miles of soy beans, corn, and tobacco. Eastern Carolina is as flat as a board, so crops other than tobacco were laid out in very large fields. That meant crop-dusting companies.

It was a pleasant, windless morning in early spring when I showed up to interview with the owner of a small, two-plane spray service.

I parked my truck near a one-room wooden building sitting just off the edge of a well-maintained grass strip. The grass around the building was tall and untrimmed as if it had been thrust up from beneath the ground. Freshly whitewashed, it stood out brightly in the morning sun. It looked empty. Two small boys played nearby, probably the owner's sons. A strip of tall pine trees ran the full length of the runway behind the building.

Resting on the grass across from the building sat what—in my limited experience—was a very large airplane.

White with red striping, it had a single, overlarge cockpit like an upside-down bucket perched rising above the fuselage. Large struts fastened at the top of each wing connected to attachments on the fuselage, making the entire aircraft appear as though it had been buckled together from a kit.

Striding toward me across the grass, a tall, slender man approached with his hand outstretched. He wore jeans and a camel-colored shirt without a wrinkle. His handshake was firm, his expression sincere and open. His eyes, however, betrayed a certain caution as he surveyed my person. He was decidedly friendlier than the first North Carolina spray pilot I had met.

I had driven on that first day through the entrance to an old training airfield that served as the local airport. I needed directions. Soy beans grew in the spaces between concrete runways laid out in a large triangle. The entire area was more than a mile square. A tractor slowly droned along beyond the main runway, in the center of the crops, a dusty cloud rising behind it.

The only building on the ram—a small, white office with a flat black roof—stood where the entrance road ended in a small parking lot. After parking the car, I walked past the building onto a deserted ramp where numerous small airplanes were parked hoping to ask directions of the first person I came across. Up ahead, I saw a man working on a large, yellow spray plane. His back was to me and a large greasy rag was stuffed in the back pocket of his overalls, one end touching the back of his knee. He didn't turn to face me when I approached.

"Excuse me, sir, I wonder if you could help me and, by the way, nice airplane!"

Large in girth with an oily baseball cap, he laid down his wrench and slowly turned to face me, the stub of a cigar stuck in the corner of his moth.

"You're a Yankee, right?" he spat out with contempt, his piercing look bored into me.

Taken aback by the simmering disdain contorting his face, I took a short step backward.

"Kind of," I stammered. "I was born in Canada, but moved here from the Seattle area," I meekly added.

I believe the Canada part was lost on him. He removed the cigar, "Not my habit to speak to Yankees," he growled before turning back to this airplane as he chomped down on the cigar. Ignoring me, he briefly arched his back, picked up the wrench near a small pile of parts on the wing, and resumed his former task.

This rebuff was not at all typical of the people I later met in Carolina, but that first encounter had left me with no doubt that the "Old South" lived on in the hearts of some.

Now, two years later, I stood in front of another native of the State, trying to be seriously considered for a position flying his spray plane. The interview began with, "Have you ever flown a taildragger?"

Not specifying the exact types I had flown, I looked him in the eye and declared, "Yes, sir, I have!" The plane I was thinking of at the time was a small one (the only one I had flown with a tailwheel), a really small one compared to what sat in front of me on the grassy strip. I had purchased it a year before for $4,000, a perfect Cessna 120.

My little, two-tone brown Cessna had a bench seat for two with a small space behind the seat for luggage. Total horsepower, 85. It was a high-wing airplane with a tailwheel under the rudder at the very rear of the fuselage. The plane we were currently discussing had only one seat, but a 235 hp engine and a low-wing just for starters. I swallowed hard.

From my short but direct answer, the owner made a significant assumption, that I could actually fly the airplane we were standing beside. Clearly, southern men take you at your word. No further explanation was required. Perhaps it was beyond his imagination that I would stand in front of what to me was a "giant" plane and boldly state that indeed I was experienced in flying tailwheel planes with no reference to the size of the aircraft, nor what I had actually done with them when I flew them.

Tailwheels on airplanes, even something as large as a DC-3, pitch the nose of the aircraft toward the sky because the tail is barely held off the ground by a relatively small tire. When you taxi one of these, you have to strain to see over the nose, often resorting to "S turns" to avoid running into anything or anyone directly in front of you. This also means that when rolling down the runway for takeoff, you must get enough speed to raise the tail and level the aircraft, while at the same time keeping it straight and centered on the runway with the remaining two wheels. And oh, yes, see where you are going!

All of this rushed through my mind as I attempted to maintain eye contact with the owner. A gaze that spoke confidence and comprehension was my goal. Was the small plane harder or easier to control on the ground? Would the lessons of one transfer to the other? If I ran off the runway, what would I say in my defense? I needed the income, but he needed his airplane in one piece.

Unlike taildraggers, nose wheel planes are level already. To drive one, you just steer with brakes at the top of the rudder pedals or use a small steering device at the side of the cockpit. Since you are moving a wheel virtually below where you sit, there is no long lever (the length of the fuselage) to move side to side, threatening to pitch you off the runway if you fail to pay attention.

The spray plane in front of me, a Piper Pawnee, had wings and a fuselage covered in fabric and dope (makes the fabric stiff). Metal surrounded the engine and hopper. Like all tail wheeled airplanes, the wheel under its tail was small, so the long nose pitched up. The two wheels under its wings looked stout. This was the one I now had to fly and land in order to prove I could do the job. Only one seat—you were on your own.

It had a very long—and I mean a *very long*—nose, as measured from the cockpit/windscreen to the nose cone of the propeller, containing not only the hopper with its liquid or solid load, but also the gas tank and, of course, the engine. At the moment, it seemed to be about 20 feet long, but in reality it was 6-8 feet. My little Cessna, the only tailwheel plane I had actually flown, also had a nose, but one just 2 feet long.

I tried hard to act nonchalant as I climbed up on the wing, over the cockpit rail, and then dropped into the bucket seat. I avoided looking forward in the direction of the propeller. I did not want the owner to glimpse even a glimmer of the amazement registered across my face. The realization of what I was about to attempt in broad daylight crept through me like I had just been wrapped in a functioning electric blanket.

The owner climbed up on the wing after I was seated and helped me with the shoulder harness and seat belt. Leaning into the cockpit with his arm resting on the cockpit rail, he showed me the controls, throttle, etc. He then went through a dry run of the engine starting sequence. He slapped the side of the cockpit twice, then jumped off the wing and strode over near the building, where he turned, folded his arms, and watched. I looked up and above the instrument panel toward the propeller. Wow!

The 235hp Lycoming engine whirred, coughed, and came to life almost immediately. The propeller, way up there in front, blurred. Everything was waiting for me.

The nose seemed to stretch to the sky, and I could see small, puffy clouds through the arc of the whirring propeller. I thought to myself, if I can fly this, I'm sure to get the job. After all, I didn't have to "spray" anything or take off loaded; I just had to look like I knew what I was doing and make a decent landing within the confines of the grass strip. The moment I pushed the throttle forward, though, I wasn't really sure it could be done.

I turned the nose of the Pawnee so it pointed to the other end of the strip and began to taxi. My heart was pounding! As I swung the aircraft around at the end of the grass strip, the small windsock hung limply nearby. I did a check of the magnetos and controls before takeoff and took a really deep breath.

Minutes later, advancing the throttle firmly to full open, I stepped on the pedals to compensate for torque, raised the tail off the grass, and before I could worry about my next move, the white Pawnee was airborne and climbing. I was much calmer as I busied myself for the landing. The aircraft was responsive and with no load, it begged to soar much higher.

Keeping the flight short and focused, I flew a wide pattern, lined up with the grass, and landed just past the threshold of the airstrip. I taxied to a stop about where the airplane had been parked, killed the engine, and climbed out of the cockpit onto the wing. The grin on my face was so wide I doubt I could have moved my lips to speak just then.

I jumped off the wing and walked confidently to where the owner was standing, extending my arm. He took my hand and shook it firmly. No doubt he was relieved that his gamble had paid off. I could tell by his face that I had passed the test and would get the job.

Spraying crops was useful, but also fun in the Pawnee. Loaded, it could takeoff from small, scattered airstrips in less than a thousand feet. Often we landed into the wind, as close to the loading truck as we could get so we lost no time taxiing. The mixing guy then loaded the hopper, and we would turn the aircraft around to take off downwind and not waste time circling.

The owner often flew his yellow Thrush, a much larger plane, off the same strip, working on another nearby job. The days were long when the weather was good and the wind calm, but I was making the extra money I had hoped for with each load.

The large fields of corn and soybeans often meant running out of product after just one or two passes. Turning the Pawnee and coming into the field at about three feet, making sure each swath overlapped the previous run, was challenging at first. We would aim for the very tightest turns to get back in the field quickly. Like any high production activity, we couldn't afford to waste time. When the spray gate was open, the company made money; when it was closed, we didn't.

Turning the spray plane tightly meant flying on the edge of a stall throughout the turn. When the plane was heavy with a load, it was tricky, but after a while you could feel the plane "talking to you" in the seat of your pants and through the controls. You flew on that edge all the way around. Turning and swooping and diving was a special kind of flying, and it never got old.

The smaller the fields, the quicker the spray runs and the greater the number of obstacles—and I mean wires and tall trees. Tobacco fields in eastern North Carolina came in all sizes and shapes. Twenty-five acres surrounded by 100-foot Loblolly pines was not uncommon.

On the Pawnee, the handle to turn the spray off and on was right next to the throttle. Diving straight down into tiny fields with the throttle off the entire way, then switching to the spray handle as you level out, back to the throttle to keep going, then turning off the spray handle before pushing the throttle to its limits so you could climb almost straight up to clear the trees was always a thrill, or to be honest, at times downright terrifying! It was a dance—complicated like the tango, but with the cadence of a waltz, one, two, three, one, two, three.

Just two or three passes would do a small field, but what passes! If you mistook the spray handle for the throttle when pushing forward to climb, you would be dead instantly. You had to pay attention, never daring to look at either handle or take your eyes off the field where things were happening very quickly.

Since I was spraying part-time, my availability got around. I was approached one Saturday by a man who owned a spray plane but worked a regular job. He needed a pilot on weekends for individual spray jobs he picked up. He owned a Cessna AG

Wagon (Cessna 188). It had 65hp more than the Pawnee, but like the Pawnee, there were metal struts bracing the wing. The Cessna was an all-metal aircraft, newer and quicker going into the field, but the extra speed had to be managed for even product application.

I received the same kind of aircraft checkout I had in the Pawnee, but of course, by this time, I had a much better handle on the job and what was expected from the aircraft.

The owner of the airplane would pick me up in the evenings before the weekend or early Saturday morning and drive me around to each job. There was no map to lay out the job sites. I would just mentally remember landmarks and house or barn characteristics or certain road intersections. There were usually no more than five locations.

Since I wasn't native-born and, therefore, lacked the inherited knowledge of the location of each farm in the county, I screwed up. I sprayed the right crop with the right product, but sprayed the wrong field. It was owned by a farmer who hadn't ordered his crop sprayed. That added a sour note to the relationship with the aircraft owner. He took the cost of the product out of my pay, which was fair, but I didn't mess up again. A five-gallon can of chemical was more than my monthly car payment!

I continued flying the Pawnee, as it was steady work, but enjoyed my stint in the Cessna as well. I picked up a compliment while flying the Cessna, one of those you tend to remember over time, not that you ever got many when you were just doing your job. I heard it from a group of farmers who standing around their trucks near the field where I had been spraying, their weather-beaten hats pushed back on their heads or pulled down over their eyes.

After I had landed and shut down the aircraft, I walked toward my truck and passed the group with a wave. One of them fell in behind me. "Ah… hey, buddy," he said.

I turned to face him, noting his baseball cap sporting a chemical company's logo. I smiled, expecting to exchange pleasantries.

"We were just talking," he said, nodding toward the group behind us. Then he pointed toward the parked Cessna.

"We all knew you could spray," he continued, "but seems like you almost dance with that airplane."

I stuttered a thank you, no doubt with some embarrassment. I was surprised. These hard-working men were not known to offer such comments, which made their mutual observation pretty darn special.

When flying helicopters, I had learned early that smooth and deliberate was the key, while being "rough on the controls" was a sure-fire way to get in trouble and fast! Considering the farmer's remarks, I gave myself credit for having translated that same rhythm and motion into my fixed-wing flying, and that felt very good at that particular moment. By the way, I am a pretty good dancer, or so I've been told.

While we are talking "tailwheels" I would like to return to my Cessna 120, the little guy I mentioned earlier. We, my small children and I

(and I emphasize *small)*, were loaded in the 120 for a local excursion. Officially a two-seater airplane, we filled it up and made it a five-seater airplane!

Someone else had had the same idea, as behind the 120's bench seat was an unattached, hand-riveted, aluminum, concave seat. A large seat belt connected to each side of the fuselage met in the middle of the plane. Connecting the two metal pieces at the end of each strap created a large, heavy buckle that probably would have kept three hundred pounds from budging!

I put the two older children, seven and nine at the time, behind the bench seat on that contraption, belting them in with the one heavy belt. The two youngest, three and five, sat side-by-side on the bench seat next to me, belted in with the single, adult seat belt.

They were so short that only the kid seated next to a door could barely see out. Of course, of the two seated behind the bench seat, only my son, the oldest, could see anything. His younger sister—my oldest daughter—sat uncomplainingly next to him, her only view the back of my seat.

Cessna 120—Five Passenger Airplane If Your Small Enough!

The Cessna 120 was the first model designed and built by the Cessna factory in 1947 to sell to all those returning WWII pilots. The hope was that those aviation veterans would buy a private airplane for recreation and sport.

The seating was side-by-side rather than in tandem like the pre-WWII Piper Cub. It was all metal, except for wings that were covered in fabric and had no flaps. The later 140 model was identical to the 120, except the wings had been upgraded to metal and wing flaps added.

The 120 we owned was a fine example of the type. Freshly painted in beige with brown stripes, it was a perky little plane that was really fun to fly. It had a rather old radio, and I remember saving for some time for a new Narco VHF to put in the panel that was already bare bones when it came to avionics (communication and navigation radios).

The interior had been freshly recovered in vinyl and fabric, and the panel was painted in a matching copper brown. Being only twenty-eight at the time, I could easily slide in and out of the cockpit, but it would no doubt present a challenge for an older, heavier man. It was a very small airplane.

Our 120 was tied down under a wooden structure, open on all sides. The wood holding up the shake roof was well-weathered but sturdy, and I was happy the cloth wings were shielded from the Carolina sun. The plane was secured with rope that extended from a heavy cement anchor in the ground to the steel rings attached to the strut under each wing.

Struts were a staple of the high-wing Cessna design and are still found on their modern models, such as the four-passenger 172 and six-passenger 206. The tie-downs on any airplane are stout because extreme winds can actually lift the aircraft off the ground.

Such a wind came through our town one night. The gale was so strong that a three-bladed helicopter, whose blades were not tied down while parked in front of the FBO building, had a blade snapped off at the root. Now that takes a real breeze!

That night, I lay in bed listening to the sudden rise in the wind, wondering if I had tied down the airplane securely enough, but never dreaming the wind would exceed 60 mph!

As the wind hammered against our roof for what seemed like hours, screaming through the magnificent pecan trees in our backyard, fear began to grip me. I dreaded the morning and the probable sight of a ruined plane crumbled against the pine trees lining the airport or upside down in the soybean fields within the triangular space of the vintage, WW II runways.

The ropes held! However, what had been perfectly round, steel tie-down rings several days before were now oblong, with each side now firmly pressed against the rope passing through them. They had been seriously tugged! The plane must have been inches or maybe even a foot off the ground through the entire event. In its element—alone—without the propeller turning or anyone onboard.

On the subject of weather and the 120, there was another incident when my two youngest daughters were onboard, seated beside me and, at the time, sound asleep.

We had been on a cross-country flight and were coming back to a small airfield near home. Despite its size, it had paved runways, an operating tower, and available fuel. As is often the case in the humid South, the sky was very hazy that afternoon, the squall line of a moving thunderstorm hidden in the soggy air.

My first call to the tower had been to report my position and get the wind and active runway information. They returned my call promptly. A small, general aviation airport, it had minimal traffic, except on Saturday mornings.

The air traffic controller reported the wind as down the runway at 8 knots. A piece of cake. The forward visibility was just legal at about 3 miles. I don't know if they had radar in such a sleepy location, but they didn't call out the approaching squall line. They probably couldn't see it either.

Having been spoiled by a helicopter's abilities to land almost anywhere, I was most likely guilty of a poor pre-flight weather check. I was used to getting back to base by just dealing with weather as it came. The helicopter flying had been all VFR technically, so instead of "shooting" an approach, I only had to follow roads during low visibility or even hover from tree to tree while crossing a swamp in extremes of rain or fog.

On the other hand, with flying fixed-wing VFR only, especially in the beloved 120, the prospect of landing in a tobacco field at 40 mph when the weather was getting close to non-flyable was not an option. Getting down at the nearest grass strip or airfield safely was always preferable.

That particular afternoon, I lined up for a longish final approach. Although I couldn't see the airport in the haze, I was confident that the landmarks below would lead me to the end of the runway. The tower called. The wind was now 10 knots down the runway. Almost immediately they called again. The wind was up to 15 knots. I had the runway in sight, but because of the increasing headwind, the airplane's progress across the ground slowed, delaying the 120 from reaching the end of the runway quickly. The girls heads were drooped almost touching their chests. They were sound asleep.

The aircraft was starting to rock its wings. It could have been worse. The next call from the tower announced a pick-up in the wind to almost 30 knots. I acknowledged, but continued to press toward a landing. It was getting scary. The girls slept peacefully beside me, and I tried to inhale their serenity.

I didn't have a plan B! Landing was my only plan, and it was just outside the window and only a minute away. I could see exactly where I hoped to plant my wheels. The last call from the tower announced gusts to 50. The tower operator's voice had replaced its previous matter-of-fact tone with a barely controlled concern.

Of course, this was going to be a two-wheel landing, not three. The airplane needed to be driven onto the pavement instead of the usual procedure of stalling it in a three point landing with the nose in the air. Business as usual would have brought immediate disaster! I needed to make the 120 stick as soon as the wheels struck payment. Our goal now was just survival—us and the plane—if that was even possible in such wind velocity. The little plane lurched and rocked fiercely. Still, the girls slept.

I was attempting to land an airplane that had a lift-off speed of 40 mph. The wind was now higher than that number and rising. Thank god the wind was down the runway! The first time the wheels struck pavement, we bounced back into the air. I pushed forward hard on the control wheel, knowing this was a one-time shot. The sky above us was filled with an unseen giant of great force. We could not return there.

It was a very long runway, but that didn't really matter as I was almost hovering over it. When the two wheels contacted pavement the second time, even at the risk of striking the runway with the propeller, I pushed forward hard on the control wheel to glue the little airplane to the earth, despite the savage wind outside.

It wasn't that we really even rolled to a stop. The airplane rather froze in the same configuration it had during touchdown—tail up, level, main wheels on the runway—but I wasn't going to leave the ground no matter what. I had a lot of throttle still in, so we just sat there. I couldn't possibly consider a turn either way. It reminded me of the dude in a TV ad for mega speakers who sat on a stuffed chair two feet from the speaker with his hair blowing straight back. At that moment, we could have been that dude.

I wasn't sure what to do next except hold my position right where I was. The howling wind would not allow the tail to quit flying and settle to the ground. It didn't matter that I had no idea what to say to the tower; I was too afraid to take my hand off the throttle to pick up the microphone.

After what seemed like half an hour, but was in reality only minutes, I saw movement from my left in the direction of the ramp. Men, about five or six I guessed, hurried toward us though I wasn't sure why. They circled to the back of the plane. I couldn't possibly take my hand off the throttle or control wheel to open the door and ask their intentions.

I had never experienced men running toward a plane while the propeller whirred and I was on the runway still landing, sort of. In reality, the 120 was still flying, despite the two wheels firmly planted on terra firma. My right hand kept the throttle partially open. To my relief, the men began piling onto the airplane's tail section, fanning my fervent hope that everything would be okay.

Suddenly, the Cessna's nose went up and the tail went down. Two men dangled from the struts under each wing. Their added weight made the 120 too heavy to fly, so all three wheels were now pinned to the ground. With the men holding on, the plane was safe to turn and taxi to a tie-down on the ramp in front of the tower.

The men, who only minutes before had been hanging out in a comfortable lobby probably telling flying stories, ignored the high winds and the blast of the propeller to keep to their chosen mission of not allowing the plane to tip or leave the ground. They had risen to an immediate need for aid, dared to take it on, and then afterward thought nothing of it. They were all valiant!

The winds were still so high that no exchange of words was possible as they unwrapped themselves from the tail of the plane. The guys on the struts dropped to the ground and secured the plane with stout ropes and knots, then secured the tail. The 120 was now fastened to the ground.

Without comment, the men nonchalantly and in a rough line that still leaned into the strong wind, paraded back through the double glass doors they had charged forth from just a short time before.

They resumed, no doubt, their discussions and stories, having now been favored through their efforts with an additional tale. I looked down at my two young daughters: one was barely waking, while the other was looking around and rubbing her eyes. With the sudden dying of the engine noise, they both must've have thought we were home. Oblivion, as in this case, had its useful purposes.

In the spring another family excursion would hatch in my head, prompted by a chance discovery during a work-related, low-level reconnaissance. I crop dusted in planes part-time, but my full time job five days a week was flying a helicopter almost everywhere in Eastern North Carolina. I soon knew the terrain in the area and its features intimately and seldom referred to an aviation chart.

One particular morning, I flew right over a small grass airstrip bordered on two sides by tall pines. The location was within walking distance of a nice beach of brownish sand along the south bank of the Neuse River, where its brackish water flowed into Pamlico Sound and on into the Atlantic Ocean. I had had no idea it was there, but it looked like a possible candidate for a family field trip in the Cessna 120.

The grass strip was perpendicular to the beach, and a small motel sat between them, its sign MOTEL—large letters balanced on the roof— announcing its sole purpose. I could not tell from the air if it was occupied, but there were no cars nearby. The area was remote compared to the surrounding population.

The building was approached by a dirt logging road, which paralleled the river and stopped at the motel's entrance. A single-story structure, it crossed the north end of the airstrip like a "T," its main doors located dead center with rooms extending on either side of the entrance.

The only intrusions into this rustic getaway from the hustle and bustle of modern life were the modestly high power lines strung on well braced weathered, gray poles. Forming the "H" construction design from several decades earlier, they ran just behind the motel and parallel to the river, seeming connected more to the building than to the tranquil scene beyond, where the ground sloped gradually toward the beach spreading north and east along the broad river.

I envisioned a picnic with the kids on some pleasant Saturday morning. Traveling there by car never occurred to me, nor did I consider calling the motel for permission to land a plane. With crop dusting, a grass strip was a place to land an airplane. It seemed obvious.

That morning wasn't far in the future. In spring, when the days were warm and the weather pleasant and predictable, we packed a cooler with fun food, gathered towels and a blanket, and headed for the airport. The kids were in bathing suits with t-shirts, already enjoying the warm air and light breeze blowing in the car's windows. Half an hour later, I packed—stuffed actually—the cooler, the towels, and the blanket behind the bench seat of the 120, partially burying my son and oldest daughter. I couldn't risk anything being held by the two youngest up front because of the dual control wheels.

We lifted off the long concrete runway near the Pamlico River and made a turn to the southeast, heading for our beach getaway about fifty miles away. Map and compass were the tools of the day. No GPS existed then. We chugged along at 2,000 feet just under 100 mph, the air smooth. The children were in high spirits! Funny how they poked and fought and chattered in the station wagon, but not in the airplane.

The little 85hp engine made plenty of noise without any increased racket from unlatching the window for cooling air. With it closed today, the temperature was just right.

Arriving at the strip, I set up for an approach over the trees at the opposite end from the building and wires. The 120 had no flaps for a slower approach, but I had often practiced "slipping" the aircraft and frequently used it as a landing option. You had to be mindful of a possible stall during a slip, especially close to the ground however, done properly it works very well and it was the best approach for this airstrip having to cross the tall pines rising across its end.

After clearing the pines, I took the 120 out of its sideslip and dropped swiftly the last twenty feet to land softly in the tallish grass. I taxied to the far end near the motel and then parked the aircraft.

Walking around to the side door, I lifted the little girls from the front seat and then folded the bench seat down, separating the two oldest children from all the beach stuff until all had been lifted out.

The emptied airplane sat with its nose in the air, a sort of perky stance, having met the challenge of transferring all of us to this remote place. Its beige airframe seemed to reflect its satisfaction in the late morning sun.

The beach was not far away, so I picked up the cooler, handed the towels to the kids now running around, happily released from the plane, and then led the hike to the beach. No one from the motel greeted us, so my former assumption that it was unoccupied was probably right, although the caretaker might have been absent in the off season or working elsewhere. It looked cared for, not abandoned.

When we reached the beach, we spread out the blanket in a good spot near the water and began enjoying ourselves. The children loved the water and were dripping wet in minutes.

Several hours later, our picnic lunch devoured completely, we picked up the cooler and blanket and headed back to the plane. The kids were wrapped in towels, still drying off as they walked along the path. The early afternoon was pleasantly warm, not hot and humid.

Even as we approached the Cessna, I took no special note of the tall grass covering the airstrip. I did a quick walk around, checked the oil before loading, and then buckled everyone into their seats.

The two oldest were again in the back, but now partially buried by damp towels. The two youngest were content up front. No one ever argued about seat arrangements in the airplane; regardless of age, they seemed to understand there was purpose to where they sat. And they were never fearful. This trip had been special, but in their young lives, it was just another car ride.

The 85hp Continental engine shuddered to life, we began our taxi to the far end of the strip, which by most standards was rather short. I was sure I couldn't lift off in time to clear the tall pines at that end. With the calm wind, I elected a takeoff over the motel and wires, since beyond them was the wide river with no obstacles at all.

After a pre-takeoff check of the magnetos, the controls, and the engine instruments, I swung the tail of the airplane as close to the tree line behind me as I could. Unused runway behind the plane was not going to help a departure, so why give it away for no reason?

I fully advanced the throttle while pushing hard on the brakes. The engine sounded nice and smooth. I lowered the pressure of my feet on the toe brakes and was mildly surprised that we weren't accelerating with the usual initial surge, even though we were on grass, not concrete.

We were halfway down the strip before the tail started to rise slightly. That was not good! I looked at the airspeed indicator. The needle registered nothing; it only showed the occasional feeble bounce. Then everything happened quickly. The strip was small and short. Really short! I realized it about the time the motel began to fill the windscreen.

With a sickening feeling, I instantly realized that the long grass was tugging at the Cessna, slowing its acceleration. Vital insight, but too late! My only choice was to fly or go straight into the motel. There was neither time or space to stop. As I pulled back hard on the control wheel, the little plane struggled along the ground a bit longer, and then lifted into the air.

The building no longer loomed in the windscreen, but its image was immediately replaced by the large, heavy wires of the power line just beyond.

Maybe my flying routine of hanging on the edge of a stall during crop dusting turns had been a factor. I couldn't say for sure, but we were so slow clearing the last wire that I could no longer hold the climb. I pushed the wheel full forward, wondering if the tail would bring the last wire with it.

This was a "fly as you go" proposition. Not only was I not scanning the flight instruments, but I also didn't give a damn.

Getting over the wires was all that mattered. As they say, *"Everything was open but the tool box, and the only thing on the airspeed indicator was the manufacturer's name!"* I pointed the nose down towards the broad expanse of river and prayed for the best.

With the nose down, we finally began to accelerate. It had been too long without any recognizable airspeed, so I welcomed the rising noise of air pushing against the fuselage. We weren't very high when we cleared the power line, but because the ground sloped some distance to the river, we had enough room to dive.

I held the nose down as long as I dared, but like spraying soybeans, I was only a few feet above the water when I pulled the wheel back and soared across the river's calm surface in the direction of home.

My hearing came back into focus as I began to climbing with real airspeed, and I actually started breathing again. That's when I heard my youngest two squealing like they were halfway through a ride at the fair. They thought, I suppose, that I had been showing them a fun time with all the climbing and diving we had just been through.

The two oldest in back, however, were quiet. They never said a word, but I wondered what the takeoff must have felt like when you were stuck in the shadows behind a seat draped in damp towels.

It is curious that on certain occasions in aviation a miracle occurs. Not for everyone, and not just for those who seem to deserve it, and certainly not each time. Since airspace is shared with angels, you tend to think of them first, but gremlins and other questionable creatures have also been blamed or credited for either hindering or helping the struggling aviator trying to save his bird. It wasn't by chance that the old song "Coming in on a Wing and a Prayer" was one of the most popular Army Air Force tunes during WWII.

After landing safely, you look back and wonder while engineers or more experienced pilots declare that it could never have happened. "Are you sure you got your facts straight?" they'd ask or boldly declare, "The plane couldn't possibly have stayed in the air!"

I humbly believe, my foolishness and ignorance as a 120 pilot aside, that without doubt, a "gentle giant of the sky," inspired by God or angels, tenderly lifted our small plane—because of its precious cargo—up and over the high wires and gave us back our airspeed.

Taildraggers! You've got to love 'em!

Chapter 6

NORTH TO ALASKA

Hawaii was 5,000 miles away from my starting point in Toronto, Canada, and it is south of Nome, Alaska. I wasn't headed for Hawaii, but that was one way of gauging the distance to Nome, near the Bering Straits. It would be a stretch for any helicopter, let alone one that cruised at 70 knots, but that is where I had agreed to ferry the Bell 47 G3B-2 helicopter.

You would recognize it. Although it was a more powerful model, its profile came right out of the TV hit show *M*A*S*H*. Big plastic bubble and open tail-boom, but unlike the *M*A*S*H* model, it had two saddlebag fuel tanks, one on each side behind the top of the clear plastic cabin and centered on the main rotor mast.

It had been a close call. I had almost missed the opportunity. The random swinging of an entrance door, mere seconds, gave me the chance I had been looking for with some desperation. A real job that paid!

Having quit my job at the paper company and crashed the Thrush (as seen in chapter 5), I was hunting for steady employment in the region. With four small children to raise, I could have used a steady paycheck.

At the time of that random encounter, I had been poking around the ramp of a small local airport, hoping to get wind of a job opening. The airport was north of my home where the spray company I had flown for previously was based. Walking toward the FBO (Fixed Base Operation) building to escape the midday sun and grab a Coke, I studied the large corporate jet sitting on the ramp.

Just as I opened one of the double glass doors into the FBO, the opposing door swung open, and a pilot with shoulder boards on his shirt flashed a cheerful smile and said in passing, "Do you know any helicopter pilots around here? We're looking for one."

"Yeah, I'm one," I replied, turning to follow him, more of an automatic response than anything else.

He paused, then turned back, looking me over more carefully. He seemed surprised to find a helicopter pilot standing right in front of him. His company's search, although urgent, had apparently been random. His casual query while passing through the double doors had suddenly produced results.

"We have a four to five month exploration job up north of Nome, Alaska, cranking up soon. It needs a pilot. Would you be interested?" he asked with some urgency—and hopefulness—in his voice.

As I stood on the hot ramp of a Southern airfield, the concept of Alaska was a little hard to grasp, but who cared? "I'm available and would love to work for you guys!" I burst out, lowering my voice to avoid sounding over- anxious, which in fact I was.

"I'm down here from Westchester, New York," he explained. "I fly for TexasGulf. They own the big phosphate mine down by the river. Do you know where that is?"

He touched my arm, looking a little unsure of exactly who he was addressing. In the world of fixed-wing pilots, a certain suspicion persists that rotary-wing pilots possess a complex and peculiar personality. After all, who would freely accept the peril of flying one of those machines? He was friendly, but cautious. He took a step closer.

"Here's the deal as I understand it," he said, pointing his index finger into his other hand for emphasis. He struggled a bit with the concept of helicopter pilot requirements, gladly skipping the technical details he may have been expected to address.

"The pay is $4000 a month," he continued, "and the job starts in Toronto." He searched my face to see if the money offer had struck home or was too low. I fought back a strong desire to shriek with joy. Satisfied with my reaction, he squinted a little before addressing the next item on the list. Bracing himself for what he likely expected would be a deal-breaker, he added in a somewhat lowered voice, "You will have to ferry the aircraft to Nome."

He rubbed the back of his neck and looked a little bashful, wondering if he had said too much all at once. He hadn't even invited me to discuss the matter over a Coke. Had that been a mistake?

Not at all. Holy Cow! In the past five years, I hadn't seen more than $1500 a month and at times even less. I was going to be rich! I was so focused on the salary that I didn't hear the Toronto part at first.

Pilot to pilot talk is supposed to be cool, especially if you don't know each other. I got a hold of myself. Warmly and with real curiosity, I asked, "When would I start?"

He swayed, one foot to the other, clearly gearing up to say something difficult. He put both hands in his pockets.

"We need you in a week," he said all in one breath, and then gave me a pleading look before adding, "Would that be a problem?"

I assured him it wouldn't.

No resume, very little discussion of experience, yet for all intents and purposes, I was hired on the spot. Kind of. He wasn't the Chief Pilot. He pulled a pen and a small notebook out of his shirt pocket and wrote a name and contact number before tearing it out and handing it to me.

"Look," he said, pointing to the name he had printed, "Mark here is a great guy. Call him today. He'll give you the details."

We shook hands. He walked away toward the big jet, joined by another pilot who had just exited the FBO's double doors. No passengers appeared, so I stood there watching as they departed, pinching myself, wondering if I had heard everything right. I took the small scrap of paper from my pocket and looked at it hard. Yeah, it was real.

It was fairly late in the afternoon, so I called Mark the next morning. He knew who I was. Then without hesitation, and probably worried that I had changed my mind, he poured out the plan. They would send me a plane ticket to fly out of Raleigh to Toronto on the following Friday. I would be gone for four months. A company helicopter waited in Toronto, a Bell 47, he wasn't sure of the model. The job started with the ferry flight.

Mark was the Chief Pilot of their flight department yet seemed hesitant when helicopter questions were asked. The company had two other helicopters, he explained, but the pilots ran their own shows. He didn't want to discourage me at all, so he spoke bravely about a machine he knew nothing about, including how it managed to stay airborne.

He continued. This job would be a seasonal position and would end when I got back home. My pay would start right away, and they would send me a check and company credit card for expenses and gas. The employment package would come through FedEx. He gave me the contact numbers for Toronto and explained about the hangar where the aircraft was kept at the International Airport.

I asked questions. He listened without interruption. I think he was just happy someone was willing to fly the damn egg beater! He treated me like a big fish on a line he was very gingerly reeling in. He did not want to lose the only candidate they had managed to find.

"How is the maintenance going to be handled?" I asked.

"We have a great helicopter mechanic working for the company; I'll send him to you for all of the inspections." Then, he timidly added, "We can send him with you if you want?"

I hesitated. I had known some great mechanics who were personable and always helpful, but I had also known some real introverts and had been stuck with them in remote locations for many unpleasant weeks on end. It hadn't worked out that well. I decided the ferry flight would be best accomplished alone.

"I prefer solo," I replied, "but only if I can do the daily checks and greasing." This older helicopter was like keeping a hay baler running, lots of grease! Avoiding a bad matchup of personalities on a very long flight worried me more than a possible breakdown along the way.

Mark countered, "However you want to work it. We'll send a box of standard parts with you."

I had flown this type of helicopter during Army instrument training, but I had never been responsible for its daily maintenance. I quickly did a mental inventory. I'd need a very good grease gun, perhaps two, and lots of cans of good grease. Also, numerous rags and rolls of paper towels to wipe the airframe clean from all the grease flung by the centrifugal forces of a flying helicopter.

The grease guns would have to be loaded by hand, a trick in itself. No drop-in, pre-packaged tubes were available then. The machine required greasing every morning, and after flying through rain, I would have to land and grease it again.

I would make sure all of the greasing issues were addressed with the maintenance guys when I stepped off the plane in Toronto. Right now, I didn't want to confuse Mark with those kinds of details.

My more pressing issue was that I had four young children and a puppy at home, but no wife. I had custody of the children, but their mother was in California. I couldn't take them with me. Caring for them while I was gone filled my thoughts on the drive home. I had a job, but, oh yeah, I had a lot of responsibilities on the home front, and only one of them was providing a paycheck. I had to make this work out for everyone's sake. The story of how that all happened would rate its own chapter, but that is a tale for another day.

Loose ends finally wrapped up, I stood a week later on a sunny ramp at Toronto's International Airport, inspecting the helicopter I was about to fly 5,000 miles to Nome. It looked brand new, although it had been parked there for a while. I would need supplies for getting to Nome, like all the 5 gallon (19 liters, if you speak Canadian) fuel jugs I could bungee to the baskets (trays, you might say) secured externally on each side of the airframe.

I spent the first day rounding up gear, buying maps, making up a survival kit, and packing the helicopter. The copilot's controls were removed to open up more space in the cabin. As far as I know, this was the only helicopter model Bell ever made that placed the pilot on the left side, probably because the only seat was a bench seat for three adults. Dual controls would have limited it to a "two-seater" only.

When I left home, I knew I would be gone for at least four months, so I packed lots of books. I carried in an old Army duffel bag, along with a small overnight bag plus a sleeping bag. I would be staying in motels along the way, mostly in small towns and even villages. No planned camping, therefore no tent. If stuck in weather or during a breakdown somewhere in wilderness, I could shelter in the large, bulbous cabin.

There was no baggage compartment; everything except the fuel went in the cabin with me. The spacious bubble contained only a central pedestal for the radios and instruments, so all the space on the passenger's side was available. Besides my personal gear, which included a large, goose down parka, that space was soon crammed with plastic bottles of engine oil, yellow cans of grease, helicopter parts, a small tool box, grease guns, a survival kit, and rags and paper towels wherever they would fit. I couldn't see out the right side of the aircraft. However, I was cautious. Not wanting to scratch the plexiglass plastic cabin, I had packed accordingly. I hated looking through scratched windscreens.

Using heavy bungee cords, I strapped five gallon "jerry cans" (three per side) on the external wire racks just behind the cabin doors. With such a long flight and such a slow helicopter, planning fuel stops would be critical. I carried all the extra fuel I could manage, refilling all tanks and jugs at each stop.

Cities in Canada do not "bleed" into the next city or town. When you leave their outskirts, you are in the wilderness of the Great White North, so you must carefully navigate to your next fuel stop, as there are no options in between. The Precambrian igneous rock of the great Canadian Shield covers Ontario and is dotted with thousands of lakes, each one nestled among its own unique, rocky shoreline. Rolling hills covered with forest cap the province. The highest peaks are just over 2,000 feet. My first fuel stop would be at a lake where a floatplane base was indicated on the chart.

I navigated with a paper map and compass, except when I could hook up with a remote road to nowhere that wended its way in my general direction. When I crossed into western Manitoba, the hardwood forests behind me were gradually replaced by the vast, rolling prairies. Not a tree in sight except as windbreaks surrounding farmhouses and barns that were widely scattered like islands across an enormous archipelago of grass. As I traversed the Canadian prairies, I planned to follow the transcontinental Canadian Highway whenever it led directly to my next fuel stop. GPS navigation was still years in the future.

The immediate challenge of my first fuel stop presented itself as I circled over the lake. How was I going to land close enough to the fuel tanks, situated near the water for fueling the float planes, without bringing havoc to the scene below when I landed?

Fixed-wing aircrafts' ground operations do not mix well with helicopters. Airplanes taxi on water or land with relatively little commotion other than the prop's air blasting back over the wings and fuselage. A helicopter, on the other hand, brings a tornado with it wherever it flies, even at one foot off the ground.

Its rotor wash increases as a cushion of air builds along the ground beneath the hovering helicopter, often generating initial rushes of air over 100mph. Scraps of plywood or tin, empty boxes and cans, and especially patches of dirt among sparsely seeded grass become airborne and are flung in all directions. An airplane's wings will rock violently if parked in the vicinity of a hovering helicopter. Float planes tied to a dock would fare even worse. All of this spelled expensive damage if ignored.

I decided to make an initial landing well away from the buildings, as well as the docks where float planes were lined up like so many boats, nose to tail. I hoped that from there I could find the manager of the operation suggest a plan he would accept.

In the States, most operational managers would suggest that you leave and fuel elsewhere, but in the North Country, fuel stops could be far apart. Every pilot and operator was well aware of that critical operational reality. Airplanes and helicopters flying in the far reaches of the barren wilderness operated together to service oil rigs, various hunting lodges, villages, and exploration efforts. Out of necessity, they resolved conflicts amicably. No one wanted to run out of gas in the middle of nowhere and maybe lose a machine as well as a pilot.

It was only midday, but thick fog was beginning to roll in from the edges of the broad lake. I shut down the helicopter and waited for the rotor to stop before walking over to the small operational shack. A bearded man of advanced years sat behind a desk. He had seen me land and knew what I was about to ask. He pushed back his stained cap and spoke first.

"Which direction you comin' from?" he asked in a flat voice.

"Toronto, headed west," I answered. "Hoping for some fuel, but it looks a little complicated out there. How should we handle this?"

He had difficulty rising from his chair. With a slight stoop and shuffle, he stepped outside, motioning for me to join him. He nodded toward a small dirt road just behind one of the large fuel tanks.

"Can you get in there?" he asked, pointing his gnarly finger at the spot.

"Yeah," I replied, "if I hook around to the north and land into the breeze coming from the lake. That'll put me downwind from your aircraft and keep my rotor wash under control and behind the tank."

He nodded; we had a plan.

I hadn't needed to break into the extra fuel in my "jerry cans" on this first leg. That was good. The range for this most recent helicopter model had been increased, ensuring that while cruising at about 80mph, I could stay in the air three and a half hours and still have a fuel reserve. That gave me a no wind range of about 300 miles. Although my speed was slow, this aircraft's range equaled the distance a faster helicopter could cover before landing for fuel.

This advanced model of the Bell 47 had been manufactured in the very early 70s, and thanks to its 280hp engine and turbo charger, plus longer rotor blades, it had great altitude performance (ceiling 20,000 feet) a long with a longer range. I would eventually find myself on the higher slopes of what was then Mt. McKinley, now known as Denali. Those three improvements, which dramatically increased this versatile helicopter's utility, would make such a feat possible.

However, this was Canada, not western Pennsylvania. The landmass was vast, to say nothing of the Alaska interior. The jerry cans carried an extra two hours of flight fuel. I would need all of it. I was flying east to west, meaning I would fly almost daily against the prevailing winds. Seldom would I have a tailwind. Knowing this deepened my appreciation for the improved range of this model.

Ten minutes later, I slid the helicopter skids onto the dirt road and came to a stop. The wings on the docked float planes barely rocked. This strategy kept the rotor wash to a minimum and certainly made the manager, watching me from his porch, happy and—no doubt—relieved.

Dragging the long black hose over to the helicopter and rewinding it afterwards took extra time, but I topped off my tanks, paid the gentleman, thanked him, and departed before the fog caught me on the ground. I climbed to 2,000 feet and glanced at the map. My next stop would be a small town where I would stay the night in an ancient motel. Getting a ride from the unattended, small fields near each village or small town was uncertain, so often I walked.

My plan was to reach the north shore of Lake Superior and skirt its upper reaches before connecting with the sweeping Canadian prairie that extended to the edge of the Rocky Mountains. The prairies covered most of the immense center of Canada with a gently rolling plain stretching far into its northern regions.

The next day as I approached Lake Superior about mid-morning, light fog was already building. A local pilot would know the region and its weather very well, but there were no books of local knowledge for the strange territory I would soon attempt to cover. I would have to rely on experience alone, which in my present proximity to such a large body of water could be dead wrong.

As I neared the lake, the fog thickened. I dropped to a low altitude and attempted to follow the highway to a lakeside town. Wires started appearing with discomforting regularity. The fog got worse, but I had a long way to go and couldn't stop yet. The day was too young. The now commonly sighted wires increased the probability of a nasty wire strike, so I retraced my earlier flight path until the fog began to thin and lift as the highway crested the surrounding hills.

I tightened down the collective and throttle, using their individual control frictions, and then flew with my knees clamped around the joy stick so I could study the map. A railroad track just ahead led to the same lakeside town I had been trying to reach. I guessed that railroad lines wouldn't have fewer overhead wires since the tracks ran through uninhabited wilderness. The map indicated no towns located between my current position and the place the tracks crossed the highway.

At that intersection, I turned westward again, following the tracks down toward the lake. It felt safer. I flew for some time with no wire sightings, although the fog began to thicken—I flew lower. Soon my rotors were just clearing the trees on either side of the tracks, and the fuselage was below the tree tops. I was down to about 100 feet, but still had fairly good forward speed. The visibility seemed to be about half a mile.

Suddenly, out of the gray mist jumped the sagging wires of a large power line. I immediately pulled hard on the stick, dumped the collective, and kicked pedal. I rotated the helicopter to the right, but couldn't see through all the cargo piled up on that side of the cabin. As the ground rushed into my one o'clock position, I pulled hard on the collective to level the machine. Jerry cans still attached, cabin cargo still intact, I landed on the railroad cross ties. As the aircraft settled on its landing skids, my large orange parka slid off the boxes and bags to the center console. I didn't lift a hand to stop it. I just sat there taking deep breaths as the helicopter kept running. If I had been a smoker, I would have lit up. My hand shook slightly, so I probably couldn't have put a smoke between my lips anyway.

The goal was to get the helicopter to Alaska in one piece, and I had only just started. I was scared; my judgment was suspect. It had been a very close call finding my way to the lake, but now I was only twenty miles away. What to do?

The helicopter was on the tracks facing back toward where I had just come. In spite of the vibrations of the running helicopter, I suddenly felt an additional unfamiliar rumble. Looking up and peering ahead through the mist, I caught the headlight of a barreling train with attached boxcars less than a mile away.

I quickly grabbed the collective and pulled up. Within seconds, it seemed, the orange blur of the charging locomotive and its attached cargo passed beneath me. I couldn't go any higher, as the fog was solid above me. Entering it at a low altitude would immediately put me into a different pickle jar, perhaps as nasty as the one passing below me. I held a high hover and waited for the train to pass. I couldn't believe what had just happened! Thankfully, I had landed facing the oncoming train, not the other way.

Sometime later, I would look back that event with dark humor, imagining my narrowly avoiding a major wire strike only to land on a track and be immediately run over by a speeding train. A very good day had morphed into a very bad day in the span of three minutes.

Without another moment of doubt or hesitation, I moved the helicopter forward through a translational lift and then headed back to the highway where I had started. There had been a small motel near where the tracks had crossed the highway. I landed in the yard behind the motel and checked in for the rest of the day. The next day offered blue skies, but I stayed right where I was.

I needed to gather my wits and reset my urgency meter. I had a long way to go, but I clearly needed to be more thoughtful, less compelled to rush madly across the continent to my destination. The geologist could wait. As simple as it sounds now, back then I needed to recognize that getting there would be much preferable to never getting there, even if it meant I would show up late. Calculated risks in the helicopter world came with the territory, but taking unnecessary risks, as my dad had always said, was a fool's game that usually ended just one way.

Now above the Canadian prairies, I saw green, rolling hills stretching to the horizon, a view I endured for the next several days. Often, cars and trucks along the Canadian highway would pass me below as I struggled into a headwind. This is where I began reading my first book of the trip. I had learned to fly well with just my knees clamped around the stick, and the other controls held by tightened control friction. With power set at a consistent setting and altitude smoothly maintained, the game went like this; cross check, read, check airspace ahead, read, cross check, and so on.

I usually flew at a leisurely 800 feet—above the ground, below other air traffic and, most importantly, clear of wires. Flying competently with my knee and joystick arrangement was often useful. I couldn't land each time I needed to unfold and consult the map that I often referred to when calculating my progress towards the next fuel stop.

Thank goodness for my books! Three-hour legs at least three times a day with ground speeds of only 40-50 mph could be mind-numbing, since scenery never changed at those latitudes.

Although I grew up in the States, I had been born at the Gray Nun Hospital in Regina, Saskatchewan, located in the middle of the Canadian prairies. I was determined to plan my route westward through Regina, learning where the hospital was and then flying over it. And I did! To this day, that moment when I looked down at the square, dark grey building isolated amid towering, glass skyscrapers remains a fixed picture in my mind.

On the day I was born, my mother had walked with her sister the two miles to the hospital because she didn't want me delivered in a taxi cab. Near the end of January, the temperature outside was 40 below. The possibility of giving birth in a snowbank hadn't occurred to her.

Much later, I had learned to fly in a straight-tail Cessna 150 on these same prairies, just after I was married and before Vietnam. Once, when finding myself lost on the solo cross-country for my private license, I had zoomed low over solitary towns whose names were painted on the weathered grain silos along the railroad tracks. It always worked. I would know exactly where I was as I climbed away. Although not lost on this flight, for old times' sake, I buzzed a few silos along the way for good measure.

On the fifth day, I finally reached Calgary. I landed on the ranch west of town where I had worked in the summers during high school and visited with my good friend and former employer and his family. Then turning north past Red Deer and parallel to the foothills of the Canadian Rockies looming majestically in the distance, I began to see more trees.

The North American Boreal forest began to present itself solidly north of Edmonton. Fittingly named for the Greek goddess of the North wind, this mostly coniferous timber stretched far north into the Arctic regions. I frequently saw moose and other animals below, moving through its woodlands as I passed above. Further west in the mountains, the timber would be taller.

Entering the Peace River country south of Grande Prairie, I planned to continue northwest to Fort Saint John and the beginning of the Alaskan highway. That 130-mile leg would take me out of Alberta and into British Columbia. However,

I encountered headwinds that pushed against the aircraft as if compressing a giant spring. I tried different altitudes within reason, but I was almost going backwards. I would never make it at 10 mph, even with extra fuel.

I turned around, landed in Grande Prairie, and headed into town in a borrowed "airport car," an aging Dodge sedan. The streets were muddy from recent rain and the buildings weather-worn from wind and extreme temperatures. The hotel situated about a third of the way down the main street, had recently been painted a robin's egg blue with white trim. It stood out like an Easter egg in a basket full of brown ones.

The lobby smelled of stale beer, its walls covered in outrageous patterns of wallpaper, partially torn in places. Various people gave me blank stares, lost in alcoholic dazes. Others seemed curious at first, but quickly lost interest, walking past me toward the bar at the far end of the room.

I proceeded to check into what would become one of the most damaged hotels of my journey. The door frame of my room had been recently shattered, the splits and fragments of wood still fresh. It had been re-secured with large nails not quite pounded in. The door hung at an odd angle and opened with a tortured moan, a fitting welcome to the putrid green walls with numerous holes punched out by fists and boots.

The room itself had seen heavy usage. The remaining furniture was meager, but included a freshly made bed where a large woman—passed out in an inebriated stupor—sprawled with her nylons rolled down around her ankles and paper money poking out of her bodice. Wrong room! At my request, the desk clerk came up with another man and removed her. Tragically, I had now entered the hard drinking zone of the Great White North.

The Alaska Highway was still mostly gravel in those days, and no doubt things have changed greatly since then and for the good, but back then, I had the feeling that I was walking through the Old West until I remembered that I had arrived in a helicopter.

Each day, I pushed farther north and west, dealing with the weather as it came. The odd Canadian Transportation (Canadian FAA) weather office was seldom open when I stopped at night, if one existed at all. Without the utility of a weather app, a cell phone, or opportunities for a regular weather briefing, I realized that my slow speed would render most weather reports useless for my needs.

Bell 47-G3 B2—Refueling Stop—Headed for Nome

My flight paths were unpredictable and dictated by fuel stops. Filing a normal flight plan was inconvenient and unnecessarily time consuming. To make sure someone knew my plan for the day, I called the corporate flight office in Westchester, New York, before I left each morning and then checked back with them at the end each day. It was often hit and miss trying to catch someone at the other end who would write it down, but I would have been derelict to have made no effort at all. I was now flying over endless tracts of unspoiled wilderness, taking shortcuts through the mountainous terrain where I could, rather than staying with the Alaskan Highway, trying to make time by flying as directly as possible. Thinking back, I have no idea how the company would have initiated a search from New York or even pinpointed my location within a hundred miles of the projected route.

Corporate was likely aware of that disconnect, but they needed me north of Nome, and operations like theirs tended to regard any helicopter pilot as having less than a full deck anyway. To them, such pilots seemed a bit extreme or at the very least, irrelevant to their focus from the cockpits of speeding jets at 35,000 feet.

Now crossing the mountains whose peaks had hidden the sun earlier that day and whose terrain was more menacing, I often found myself landing on a gravel bar somewhere beside or in the midst of a roaring northern stream to refuel out of my fuel jugs. Tricky for two reasons.

One, I thought it unwise to shut down in such remote locations. If for any reason I couldn't restart that big engine or if I ran the battery down while trying, my goose would be cooked. I wasn't equipped to walk a hundred miles through the bush and over mountain passes to find a phone and call home.

Second, standing on the side racks while tipping up the jerry cans to pour fuel into the saddle tanks was a feat of balance, to say the least. I had to maneuver both myself and the jugs to avoid the spinning main rotor while the jugs were fully emptied. Any mishap could precipitate a small catastrophe, especially if I was injured in any way. And believe me, that eighteen inches of clearance seems much narrower once you are up there near the spinning blades.

Ninety degrees from the rotor and fastened just below it on the mast was a long, steel rod with weights on each end. It was attached to the mast in such a way that, like a teeter-totter, it could move up and down. It helped stabilize the helicopter mechanically, but it offered another dangerous variable for refueling with plastic jugs while the helicopter was running.

I carried out that refueling process numerous times, including on the tundra of Alaska, where you couldn't walk a mile in three hours. Thankfully, I never had a collision with a jug or any of my body parts.

After covering the 1300 from Fort St John, across the Yukon, and past the Alaskan/Canadian border, I arrived in Delta Junction, Alaska, southeast of Fairbanks. From there, I turned almost due west, flying north of Denali (Mt. McKinley) and south of Fairbanks. The impressive slopes of the mountain seemed to pierce the sky itself. At 20,000 feet, the highest mountain in North America added another unforgettable image to the dozens already accumulating in my brain as I flew toward Nome.

It was an event to finally reach Alaska. Nome was almost the same latitude as Delta Junction, which meant I would cross Alaska's wide interior to the Seward peninsula bordering the shores of the Bering Sea where it began, just one hundred miles east of Nome itself.

This wasn't the first time I had flown the North Country. I hadn't been in Alaska before, but I had operated out of Inuvik, NWT, for over a year. My first job out of the Army (see the "Thirty Seconds over Tokyo" chapter) had been in the Canadian Islands six hundred miles above the Arctic Circle. I wouldn't quite reach the Circle on this expedition, but since it was summer, that fact wasn't even relevant.

I was navigating to Unalakleet on Norton Sound, a large bay on Alaska's west coast, bordering the east side of the Bering Sea. There was an Eskimo village there with an airport where I intended to refuel before making the last leg to Nome where I would again refuel for the remaining eighty miles to the camp, my final destination.

This last leg—a long stretch—would end my journey. I had been flying from dawn to dark every day with the exception of the "wire incident" way back on Lake Superior and a "weather day" at Fort Saint John. Fourteen days straight. I wanted to reach Nome sooner rather than later.

Unalakleet was on the water where the shoreline went due north before turning ninety degrees westward to become the south shoreline of the Seward Peninsula. Shaped like a square you would find in a toolbox, each side was about a hundred miles long. Direct to Nome from Unalakleet would require a straight flight over one hundred and twenty miles of open water. Definitely anxious to reach my final destination on this particular day, I could sure use a shortcut!

Rechecking the map, I noticed a small peninsula jutting out into the sea about halfway up the shoreline before it turned from north to west. Flying to its tip, about fifteen miles, would allow me to "cut the corner," thus shaving close to two hours and probably another fuel stop from the 90-degree follow-the-shoreline route.

Skirting this peninsula for the first third of the shortcut would help me bypass much of the water before I actually had to get my feet wet. But I still would be crossing at least thirty miles of open ocean. Now that's a crazy notion in a single-engine helicopter. Hardly a reasonable "calculated risk." However, at that moment, I was feeling a little inflated from having crossed North America, and I really wanted to sleep in Nome that night. Make sense? Probably not, but I set up to do just that.

At the time, I had no idea that the frigid water temperature would allow me only a ten-minute window before severe hypothermia set in and I sank to the bottom of the ocean. There wasn't a life raft or life jacket onboard, and no floats were attached to the aircraft's skids. The chances of ditching the helicopter and exiting it successfully were zero. Plus, I would be bucking a slight headwind. I needed a break to rethink this option.

I followed the peninsula to its tip, landing at the edge of a high cliff that dropped vertically into the water. The sea, dark blue and very cold-looking, surrounded me on three sides. It felt like an island, since I could no longer see the original north-south shoreline where I had made the left turn.

Leaving the helicopter running, I got out to stretch and study the situation one more time. Was it too much of a reach? If I flew back to take the shoreline route, I would definitely need another fuel stop, having now flown at least a 30-mile round trip out of my way, making my land fall about 60 miles east of Nome.

I walked away from the running helicopter and stared hard at the horizon. Was this doable or just foolish?

I could feel the cold breeze on my face. The edge of my jacket fluttered against my leg. I stared hard across the proposed course one more time. Yes, bad things could happen, but that had been the case all along my two-week route.

I devised a way to ignore the danger and cross in a more reassuring frame of mind I would fly with my knees while I read Dan Rather's book that I was already halfway through and not look back to check my progress until had I reached the far shore. Okay, I had a plan.

Back in the helicopter, I checked everything twice, making sure all was secure, including the door latches and fuel jugs. I ran the rotor up to 100% and did a mag check twice. The engine sounded good. You had to love the sound of the turbocharger spooling up behind the cabin wall. I miss that sound to this day. Although mechanical, it spoke to a combination of strength and determination.

I picked the helicopter up to a hover, rolled the nose over, and was immediately 800 feet over gently cresting waves, looking down on the spray at the base of the cliff where the water struck with some force.

Anyone who has piloted a piston-powered, single-engine aircraft over water some distance from land will understand the term "automatic rough." All of a sudden you are convinced the engine has a different sound. You think *trouble*, when in fact, most likely nothing has changed. When I started to hear that sound, I forced myself deeper into the content of my book.

Turning page after page, I read on. Okay, I must be halfway across at least. I broke my own rule and looked back. It felt like I was fleeing with Lot and had turned into a pillar of salt! It appeared that I had barely left land. The cliffs I had launched from still seemed to tower above me. I swallowed hard, forced myself back into the semi-interesting text, and continued.

Turning around and flying back was just too hard to do. I had committed to a plan, and surging fear seemed like a poor reason to change it. I could overcome that, reducing it to a kind of throbbing nervousness, and still succeed. It was the longest thirty miles of the trip, maybe the longest thirty miles of my life.

My mind still holds vividly the vision between the rudder pedals as the blue sea and white-laced surf turned to solid land the moment I crossed onto the Seward Peninsula. A huge sigh followed that sighting, announcing deep relief, at least to myself. I turned west along the shoreline toward Nome. I would have enough fuel.

Flying low over the brown, sandy beaches approaching Nome, I felt like I was entering the terrain of an alien planet. Strange forms, partially buried, protruded from the wet sand. Like skeletons of strange creatures, painted in reddish shades from rust, they hunched over, towers of metal etched with channels that suggested ribs and the parts of a creature's torso. Vein-like rods were all that remained of a few of the exotic bodies. Drums wrapped in cables looked like giant eyeballs whose capillaries had been exposed. Metal machinery frozen by eighty years of salt water. These unusual monuments haunted the landscape, debris from the great gold rush of 1899.

That stampede for easy riches was unique in that the gold had been discovered in the beaches themselves. Get off the boat, find a space on the sand, start looking. Until 1909, Nome had been buried in a mass of humanity looking to get rich fast. Today, it was just a small town with evidence of past glory scattered around its faded edges.

The owner of the largest saloon in Nome, its car rental business, and most of its other enterprises had, in the previous month, returned from a five-year prison sentence for manslaughter. He had shot and killed a man for making unwelcome advances towards his wife in the bar he owned.

Nome was a town just barely out of the Wild West. Nevada-like in its remoteness and history, it was not hard to find lookalikes from a Gary Cooper western walking the boardwalks and muddy streets.

The Iditarod, the annual dog sled race originating in Anchorage, ended here on the main street when the ground was frozen hard and covered in snow. The celebrating crowds at the end of that race would likely make an average cowboy's Saturday night in town pale in comparison.

The finish line archway had been chopped and carved from rough logs, stained, and then varnished. When I saw it, it sat at an angle beside the main street, covered in summer dust and splattered mud, pushed aside to await winter, but still present as a promise of good times to come.

I slept in Nome that night as I'd hoped. The main airport was paved and accepted a steady stream of bush planes and even the occasional airliner during daylight hours. Hoping for an early start in the morning, I fueled up right after landing.

An ancient gold dredge still labored 24/7 at the end of the main runway surrounded by a freshwater lake of modest dimensions. Its long, conveyor-belt tower angled high into the air with a ponderous back and forth motion that reminded me of long-necked dinosaurs in old films, standing in lakes as they munched on nearby tree tops. The masses had not taken all the gold when they finally left. Lots of it had been left behind; it just required more money and patience to find.

Climbing up from the Nome airport and heading almost due north, I could easily identify the small range of mountain-like peaks that crossed east to west just beyond the town. They were solid rock and rugged, but a mere shadow of the mighty ranges in the lower part of the state.

A dirt road ran up through the middle of those small peaks, seeming to split the range deeply in two on its journey through a narrow pass. Adits occasionally penetrated the walls of rock on either side of the pass, hand dug by miners under horrific conditions, no doubt while seeking the source of the gold found on the beaches below.

Just beyond this jumbled pile of granite, the dirt road descended, the ground spreading out into a broad green plain, devoid of trees. It was dotted with sagging and blackened buildings, collapsing from years of heavy snow and surrounded by decaying piles of boards and rusting metal. These abandoned mining camps had been built close to or beside small streams running roughly east to west along the remainder of my route.

This far north, building materials came in the hard way, so no one was going to take it out again. Material of any kind—and certainly shelter, intact or not—was left standing rather than burned because of its rarity and potential usefulness.

Rolling hills and the occasional sharp point of worn granite gradually appeared in the distance. The ground generally also started sloping upward. The map confirmed that I was close to the campsite, which lay on the far side of a rather broad, but sharply ridged hill. Butterflies fluttered in my stomach, I was almost there. What conditions would I find? What were geologists like?

As I rounded the final ridge of a large hill, a circle of six or seven tents appeared just ahead with people waving wildly as they ran in from the grassy fields of mixed tundra and rock. They must have heard me coming. This was it. After 5,000 miles, I was finally here. Perhaps unremarkable to others, to me it was spectacular! No dust arose as I landed away from the tents. The ground was packed hard with granite chips.

The geologists surrounded the helicopter from several directions, some bent over with their hands on their knees, recovering their breath. None of us knew each other and avoided eye contact through the plastic bubble. It was an awkward five minutes until the cool down was over, the blades drooping and banging as they slowly came to a stop. I pushed open the small pilot door, avoiding the metal racks holding my trusted fuel jugs, and stepped onto the ground where I would walk for the next four months.

The five geologists immediately crowded around me, asking questions and verbally reassuring themselves, hardly believing I had arrived. Some questions were tactfully put, about why I was late, but that was between them and the company.

From the story they told, I must have been hired around the time they had expected me. That confirmed my initial impression that Mark had, in fact, been very desperate at the time he hired me. It also struck me that for whatever reason, Mark's permanent helicopter pilots had refused the assignment—at least the part of ferrying the aircraft.

There was no cook on staff, just scientists. None could cook, as I would soon learn. These were outdoor types: thin, in good shape, and mostly vegetarians. I had had my last cheeseburger for a while.

As the geologists gathered around, their distinctive features already indicated that they would be a very interesting group to be isolated with in the wilds of Alaska. A husband and wife team—he a very bright, but silent type; she a more outgoing collaborator—were the first to welcome me. They were flanked by two others—a tall fellow whose shock of dark red hair and ever present sunglasses set him apart from the mild-mannered, slightly "geeky" fellow behind him, wearing thick glasses and sporting a Beatles haircut. Most of them looked to have been out of their advanced educations only a few years—hard to tell.

The last person to arrive at the scene turned out to be the manager of the group, a rather cocky man whose Hungarian name had been Americanized to George. Very short and with a receding hairline, he was older than the rest of us and wore a tan shirt with epaulets that would become a sort of uniform for him in the coming months. I would soon learn that he was very dogmatic and rarely hesitated to share his rather extreme views.

Over the summer, however, I would find him to be a good sort and perhaps the most intriguing member of the group. More about George in a later chapter.

Geologists, George and Me, North of Nome

Their initial anxiety had arisen not so much from the delay in beginning their search for a tin mine as from the three-mile walk to a nearby hot springs. Attempting to cross tundra was somewhat like trying to hike across a field of basketballs on springs.

So, first things first. Since it was only noon, everyone packed lunches, and I ferried them to the nearby hot springs. Of course, they had first helped me unload the helicopter and store the oil, grease, etc. in the corner of the single umbrella tent I would occupy. As the last one to show up, I got the tent without a door, which stayed that way for the duration of the summer. Did I mention that George was cheap? No, make that "seized right up" when it came to expedition funds.

I ferried them two at a time until we were all there, and then I shut down the helicopter. It was a great way to start a four-month relationship. The hot springs were very remote, reached in the winter only by snowmobile. The warm waters were housed in a roughly constructed building that had been erected by natives who then enjoyed them year round. Imagine sitting in there when it was 30 below with four feet of snow piled outside.

A wide, very cold creek ran partially through and under one wall of the building and out the other. It was used to dilute and cool the hot springs, which otherwise would be absolutely scalding. The hot spring was boarded off to create a pool as deep as a private hot tub. Water temperature was adjusted by lifting or lowering a gate in the board wall that defined the soaking area. Ingenious!

Thus began an adventure that included unforeseen events such as a harrowing evacuation of the whole camp to Nome during a late June blizzard that destroyed the camp with its high winds.

Among other discoveries that summer, we encountered the aggressive, but smaller, Barren Ground Grizzly in his habitat. With no trees whatsoever on the Seward Peninsula, there was no way to escape the bear's rage. One hundred miles was just too far to run! Somewhat naively, we poured a giant circle of mothballs around the entire camp, having been assured by locals that it was guaranteed to keep out bears.

The company armed each of us with Black Hawk (long barrel) .44 magnums as a self-defense weapon, psychological boost, or both. This was during the era of Clint Eastwood's *Dirty Harry* movies. If he could rollover an 18-wheeler with one shot, then we could stop a bear, right? Wrong!

When we overnighted with a famous Alaskan guide later that summer, he wouldn't stop laughing at our explanation for the heavy side arms. He flopped backward onto a camp chair still chuckling. Then shaking his head, he assured us, "They're noisemakers only, boys. Or if you want, you could turn them on yourselves as a last resort!" Humiliating and humbling. I don't think my companions even liked guns. They were just too afraid not to carry them.

Our camp north of Nome was the beginning of a summer odyssey that took us back across Alaska to its eastern border prospecting for tin. We missed the hot springs from our first camp, as we could never reproduce that condition a second time during our exploration swath across the Alaskan interior. Often our chances for bathing existed solely in a glacial stream of unimagined temperature. The water always gurgled by at a swift pace and wasn't frozen, but just barely. It was a matter of jumping in and losing your breath to get wet then struggling out over slippery stones to the shore where you had to stand on the bank to lather up—soap doesn't happily lather at those temperatures, by the way. The second plunge into the icy creek or small pond was the rinse cycle. If you were lucky, you could half walk back out, but often a crawl was all you could manage in your semi-frozen condition. A third immersion was out of the question!

I tried to bathe and shave every day, but on occasion rationalized a postponement for up to two days. I had to shave since my facial hair refused to produce a beard as thick and well-trimmed as others at the camp. I would never be able to sport a pilot's perfect mustache; it just wasn't in the genes. The comforting thing about shaving daily was that the water was always hot in the bucket near the campfire.

We camped within range of an airstrip of some kind, whether riverbed gravel or an area hacked from the brush atop of a hill, so we could receive our fuel in fifty-five-gallon barrels (about five hundred pounds each), as well as our supplies. The barrels were always painted in the two Shell colors, yellow with a wide, red stripe. Often, I would hook a barrel under the helicopter on a cable or in a net and sling it to camp. These large, heavy barrels were grappled with, rocked to an upright position, and stood up in a row near the machine, or else stored on their sides. Once they were upright, I would screw a hand pump into the open bung and then pump away until both tanks and sometimes all the fuel jugs were full. At the end of the summer, I am pretty sure I could have gone home and lifted one side of a car off the ground.

There were many more shared and solo experiences that summer—some funny, some serious, some downright terrifying—but this story is not about that summer. Instead, it's about the journey of a lifetime that took me across North America from one end to the other in a low flying, slow-moving fish bowl that allowed me a view that few will ever see—at least the way I saw it that first summer, going north to Alaska.

Chapter 7

END OF THE EARTH: LOST RIVER

The following summer, I returned to the Seward Peninsula and the city of Nome, having been hired full-time by the same mining company I had worked for the year before when I had ferried a helicopter 5,000 miles from Toronto.

At the conclusion of that previous season, the summer skies had become tinged with a creeping darkness after midnight, and the light no longer shone 24 hours a day. The leaves on the low bushes turned yellow, signaling the end of the exploration season. I ferried the helicopter to the town of Galena in the center of the state. We were able to rent hanger space there for the winter.

This season, the company had elected to relocate its exploration efforts northwest of Nome, along the coast just short of the Bering Straits.

Having stopped in Nome after flying the helicopter from Galena, I met with the crew. George (remember the Hungarian manager?) sent me to the camp ahead of everyone else to check things out and park the helicopter. From there, I would be picked up for the return trip back to Nome by a fixed-wing aircraft after it unloaded supplies at the camp.

I left the shoreline on my way to the new camp and turned north into the entrance to a coastal river valley. Our camp was located at the head of the basin formed by the valley. As I flew low across the rising ground just beyond the canyon's entrance, I discovered the bones of what I guessed was an old Fairchild airplane. The twisted tubing outlined a high-wing plane with struts, a good size cabin, and fixed gear. This patch of ground had been a very long way from civilization when the plane had made its last contact with earth. I landed the helicopter, but left it idling as I struggled across thirty yards of spongy tundra to inspect the wreckage up close.

From where I stood, Nome was seventy miles away. In this era, I could leave there on an airliner and arrive in Seattle or Hawaii about five hours later. If the pilot of this crash had survived and walked the beach to Nome, he still would have been nowhere. What had brought him this far in a fabric-covered airplane during Alaska's early aviation days? Had there been others with him?

His aircraft would have flown here before the Second World War, perhaps in the early thirties, so it may have lain here undisturbed for the better part of fifty years. The remains of a handmade wooden propeller lay near the single engine, its varnish long gone, its broken edges smoothed by wind, ice, and rain to a grayish white.

A stainless steel plate, hand-riveted to prevent erosion, was still solidly attached to the leading edge of one of the prop's splintered blades. The other blade had been broken off close to the center of the propeller, below where a second plate would have been attached. Its fractured remains had cracked hard against the rising ground at the moment of impact. That sound of cracking wood would have flushed hope from the pilot a mere second before the entire aircraft followed the propeller into the tundra.

The hub of the propeller where it attached to the engine was neither distorted nor cracked. All six holes looked as if the steel bolts securing it to the drive shaft had been carefully removed. They must have rusted and perhaps been dislodged by a curious animal, causing the remainder of the broken prop to fall to the ground long after the crash.

These three maimed companions now sharing the tundra grass had once been joined for one purpose—flight. Separated by violence, they had lain in this cold remote wilderness where the abrasive elements had gradually worn them away; in a few lifetimes, they would disappear.

The shattered prop told me that the engine had been running when the aircraft hit the ground, a desperate crash. Here the narrow valley was closed in by steep hills, devoid of vegetation, black and gray even in daylight. The hills curved around to form a large "U," creating a box canyon with only the sea at the southern end where the plane had entered, perhaps in bad weather.

The valley floor climbed gradually inland. The aircraft had impacted halfway between the shore and the first inkling of a riverbed. The river itself ended almost a mile from the shore and then disappeared. The sinister dimensions of this bear trap were two or three miles deep and perhaps a mile across, set at all hours of the day and unapproachable at night by flyers.

A long, straight scar of river gravel extended down the center of the valley floor almost 4,000 feet. One-way in, one-way out. When the mine was first opened years before, a Lockheed Hercules aircraft most likely had flown in to offload its heavy cargos of tools, mining equipment, and building supplies.

Early in the project, a dozer had somehow made its way here from Nome by either a land route or a sea barge to push out the landing strip, making the valley a destination and launching point for airplanes. This was Lost River, and I had come here for the summer to fly the two aircrafts assigned to the project.

I had landed the helicopter at the first aircraft wreckage in the valley—the Fairchild. As I flew over the abandoned camp, I spotted a second wreck, a large twin-engine, aluminum Lockheed with its tail high in the air. It had been pulled to the side and sat in a low wash a third of the way up the gravel airstrip.

I would later crawl in and out of it to probe its secrets. I could see there was a lot more to this wreck than the one I had first encountered. This one looked like a converted corporate aircraft by its paint and window layout. It must have been dragged to the side of the runway after its crash. I flew the helicopter low over it and then headed up to the camp site.

What remained of the mining camp was a string of old shacks painted yellow, faded and peeling under the gray overcast and surrounded by acres of gravel. The buildings were in perfect rows, what was left from the early mining effort that had created this airstrip. The whole scene resembled a picture of a remote POW camp minus the fence.

Our crew of four geologists and six diamond (core drill) drillers were not here yet. I had come to reconnoiter the terrain and location and park the helicopter. The diminutive Hungarian, still head geologist of the project, was back in Nome managing the stores, supplies, equipment, and diamond drill all bound for here, a place as remote-looking as a moonscape and as surreal as a whiff of smoke.

Adding to this improbable atmosphere, the black, gravelly beach below the entrance held numerous human skulls. Whether ancient Eskimos or bodies thrown up by the sea, who knew? Since only geologists, not anthropologists, were arriving, no answer was forthcoming.

One of the skulls, later brought in from the beach by one of the jolliest drillers during our first week, would sit on top of a time-worn piano left behind by the previous miners. Occupying the corner of the shack we used for a kitchen and mess hall, no one ever played it and not because it was out of tune.

The skull gazed at us with its blank stare at every meal, the a daily reminder of the oppressive and lonely atmosphere of our present workplace. Its presence became part of our camp routine and was never moved from its place of honor, although our native cook was known to have occasionally draped it with a towel when he was alone in the kitchen after meals.

Lost River, sitting at sea level with rounded hills and treeless terrain, wasn't a problem for helicopter operations, but it was a risky place for airplanes. The scattered wrecks along the narrow, three-mile valley was sufficient evidence of that.

In order to haul fuel for the drill and make good time to Nome for supplies and crew changes, I was about to become an Alaskan bush pilot of sorts, flying a leased green and yellow Cessna 185 (tail-wheel type) with an external slip tank for the drill's diesel fuel. I had owned a Cessna 120 (two-place, 85hp, tail wheel) in North Carolina and had also flown a Pawnee, a Thrush, and a

SkyTruck while spraying tobacco and soybeans on the coastal plain there (see chapter five). North Carolina, however, was not Alaska, except for the flying-low part.

The Bell 47 would be our back-up aircraft. We remained friends, that particular helicopter and I, but a new relationship was about to develop with a different airframe that was faster and the wings stayed put when airborne. However, my flight options would change. Hover power was gone, and air speed became king.

The only similarity between the Bell and the Cessna 185 was the flap handle (like a collective lever), located between the front seats of the Cessna. In a helicopter, the collective provides liftoff whereas the flap handle in the hands of a fixed wing pilot initiated the action that put the airplane in the air. It resembled the emergency brake lever in a VW Bug, and it worked much the same, except that it was attached to the airplane's flaps, not its brakes. Once applying power to start the takeoff roll down the runway, you then grasped it firmly, pulling up slowly until the airplane left the ground.

You were now flying, if just barely, held up by the ground cushion below the wings and the extra lift from the flaps. Six inches was as good as ten feet, as long as you were clear of obstacles. The wheels had done their part, and now you were in the air, no longer slowed by the wheels' friction against the surface. If you continued maintaining the flap lever's exact position, the plane would accelerate quickly. Then as soon as you had sufficient fly away airspeed, you'd lower the flap handle, and you were out of there!

That particular trick, shared by a good Alaskan bush pilot, was the best tip I had been given during the airplane checkout, and I used it plenty.

The Bering Straits lay a short flight to our west. They seemed to be the source of all of the bad weather for the continent stretching thousands of miles to the south, but Nome pilots flew in it first. On the only cloudless day in four months, with unlimited blue sky, two geologists and I happened to be working exploration tasks with the helicopter. We went up to 8,000 feet to see if we could glimpse the Russian coastline across the strait. And there it was on the distant horizon, a reddish line where the bright blue sky met the dark green sea. Breathtaking!

At first, the head geologist tried being the head cook, wanting to save the budget for his drilling project. That plan looked good on paper, but never worked out in reality. Setting aside the tasteless and tortured food he spread before us, we chose to spare his feelings by convincing him to find a cook so he'd have more time to look at rocks.

I inquired in Nome for a seasonal cook. We hired a short, slightly built Eskimo man, always happy and energetic, and very well-organized. Our meals and their regularity improved dramatically. He had a dog, a small black and white terrier-type, also very energetic. It was his constant companion.

The new cook explained cheerfully that he had been in many snowmobile wrecks, dozens. As a result, his right leg was as stiff as a 2 x 4 from the hip down, but he managed very well and never drank a drop of liquor all the time he was there. His white paper cook's hat was always on and sat at a jaunty angle. His white cook's uniform was always clean, top and bottom, and he was never grumpy. He taught me to never leave a pan soaking in the sink. Get it done and start fresh each morning! A lesson easily applied to other matters in life, I have found.

Located virtually on the Bering Strait itself was an Air Force early-warning radar station. A local native, it was discovered later, had turned off the single fuel valve to the back-up generators, which shut down their whole enterprise. That brought the FBI to the region to investigate fears of espionage. The subsequent spurt of investigative activity somehow involved me in a flight to a small hunting village near the radar site, where the rugged coast had vertical cliffs dropping straight down to the sea.

The map indicated a nearby airstrip as well, but since the topography had been tightly drawn, it was sure to prove interesting when it finally appeared, and it was! About three hundred feet of dirt sloped up a hillside, followed by a 100-foot flat section along the hilltop that then descended 200 feet off of the proverbial cliff toward the circling seagulls and foaming waves below.

I showed up with two FBI agents on board the airplane. They had luggage—and quite a bit of it. The airstrip, as already described, lay perpendicular to the sea, but as was common along this coast, there was only one way in and one obvious way out—off and over the side, so to speak.

The uphill slope of the runway, more like a small scar, I'm sure was not 45 degrees, but it looked like it on the way in. With full flaps and a three-point touch down, it felt more like a fly landing on a wall. The remaining forward momentum brought the plane to the flat hilltop area where we rolled to a stop, but just barely.

After what seemed like a very short ceremony of shutting down the airplane and unloading the passengers with their bags, they seemed unusually quiet. I walked to the edge of the way out and looked down into the green sea. Back at the aircraft, I cranked the engine, put a heavy setting of flap down, and, from exactly where I sat on the airstrip, ran the engine up to takeoff power against the brakes. As soon as I released the brakes, the aircraft lurched over the edge onto the shorter-than-short downslope. Before I had time to take my first deep breath, I was over the edge, nose down, diving past the seagulls toward the water below to get airspeed. Flying speed came quickly with what seemed like a vertical fall, and I swooped the Cessna out over the ocean with a feeling of true flight, engine or not. You wouldn't want to do them in every flight, but falling/diving takeoffs had profound appeal as a rush!

Nome was still a wild west town: dirt streets, wooden sidewalks, and monuments to the gold rush in the form of abandoned mining equipment around town and in the brown sand beach that bordered the town. The large, gold dredge still operated where it floated in the channel it had created over many years between the airport and the ocean, a major landmark for incoming aircraft of any size and shape. A square box on a large flat deck, it floated noisily when working the huge conveyor that protruded from its front end at about thirty degrees.

The company had leased a reasonably large apartment in Nome for incoming crews and for me to stay overnight when in town, as well as to provide a shipping address. That apartment is where I was often required to play "psychiatric nurse." Alcohol had been a problem in my family, so I never took it up, unlike most people who lived near or above the Arctic Circle.

Also, I believe I may have been one of the few local pilots who had yet to discover weed, which was more convenient than booze and easily carried. A bag of weed didn't break open or spill, and it was cheap and available because it was legal to grow it in Alaska. I base this on the stuffed baggie commonly passed around after any dinner event. Yes, at the time "Naïve" was my middle name!

I mention the alcohol part only because I did my fair share of drying out drillers coming in from the lower 48 and nursing some fairly severe cases of the DTs before I could pack anyone into the small cabin of the plane and fly them the seventy miles to Lost River. All of this was done alone, part of the job when you work remotely. And there was no first aid manual for treating a condition that was down-right scary for the sober guy in the room.

The other part of my psychiatric nursing effort was trying to reason with our head geologist, George. Since he was very small, he preferred to mount the coffee table to make his point, pacing back and forth across it during every conversation, his full, sandy beard a sharp contrast with his shiny, domed noggin. Apparently, this elevated position made him feel more than equal to those he addressed. He was a very smart geologist, despite his extreme theories on population control and the causes of war, delivered in a thick Hungarian accent and punctuated with dramatic gestures. His temper, though rarely expressed in its full glory, was not just hot; it was white hot. His eyes glaring from beneath shaggy brows warned possible death to anyone who continued to challenge him.

I preferred clashes with George to take place at the apartment in Nome where the coffee table somewhat contained him. But the tables in the mess hall at Lost River elevated him into a neck-craning diatribe that went on endlessly.

The trip to Nome in the Cessna was not every day, but frequent, especially when the drill was running and drinking fuel at a good rate. The slip tank on the Cessna 185 worked well for that purpose.

Regardless of low visibility in the valley during takeoff, once a plane reached the shoreline just beyond the entrance to Lost River, its pilot could turn southeast toward Nome and follow the white surf crashing along the beach—a singular white line marking the way to Nome itself.

If visibility was poor, even very poor, the pilot could hang in the air above the boiling waves with a lot of flap down until eventually he could glimpse the gold dredge at Nome, turn 90 degrees, and then fly a heading and time to the runway at the main airport. The plane would already be slow enough and low enough to make a good landing upon sighting the runway, no last-minute adjustment required. You were already in landing configuration. It worked every time, and we all did it. It was Alaska after all, not downtown Chicago.

Leaving Lost River for Nome, the shore made a large hook back to the north, almost touching the beach at the entrance to our river valley. Most of the area within the hook's arc (perhaps fifty square miles) was dotted abundantly with small bodies of water, forming a giant tidal basin. As the hook straightened, the shore turned southeast toward Nome.

Where the hook base attached to the mainland, a set of low hills thrust upward at its edge. Their altitude was only 100 to 300 feet, but for any plane following the shoreline with 30 degrees of flap down, anything over 50 feet was too high.

Three weeks into the season, it was time for two of the drill crew to escape to the south and a well-deserved break. They had fidgeted for two days in the bunkhouse, waiting for improved weather conditions. As is normal in that latitude, it remained too foul for flying. On the third day, after checking the weather for the twentieth time since breakfast, I at last could see the ocean at the opposite end of the valley from where I stood near the plane. What was I waiting for? It was a possibility, and cashing in on possibilities, no matter how thin, was how things got done around there. I gave in. I would make an attempt.

I put both passengers with all their gear in the back two seats and then piled their duffel bags and sleeping bags in front of them all the way up to the ceiling so they could only look out the side windows. I hated back seat drivers on days like this. You can only answer the question, "Are we going to make it?" so many times without wanting to scream, "Hell, yes!" about an outcome that was still a mystery in your own mind. As we exited Lost River across the black beach, I had enough visibility to take the shorter route across the tidal basin, saving time and fuel. I would cut the southeast shoreline about where the basin ended and then follow the beach to Nome.

Over the lakes ten minutes later, the fog began shortening my forward view dramatically. There was nothing to hit, so maybe with fifty feet of altitude and twenty degrees of flap, I could count on dissecting the beach before reaching the hills.

The low visibility, however, began forcing the plane farther east toward the high ground, when I really wanted southeast toward the beach and the breakers. However, I had a good sense of how long I could stay on an easterly heading before running into the low hills. In my mental hourglass, though, the sand was already getting low in the upper chamber.

I strained for views to the south and turned toward southerly headings anytime I could. Much faster than I liked though, despite resisting, I would again be on an easterly course. It became an ongoing struggle for southern mileage. The hills were bad news. In this weather, I would never clear them. A low turn at this altitude and visibility would be a killer. If I lost sight of the ground for even a second during the turning arc, we would immediately be buried in the brown sand. This was a 30-degree, off-the-nose trip to Nome; turning back was not an option.

We came over the beach just as the ground began to rise. A black shoulder of a large rock flashed by as we turned to follow the long white line of continuous surf. The rising hills could still be a mile or so to our east. I strongly sensed their presence through the gray wall of fog out our left window. My passengers, however, remained totally ignorant of our predicament, and that worked for me.

Almost at full flap, we droned along, looking for a landmark. I yearned for the ancient dredge to appear ghost-like out of the fog to our left and release the tightening in my gut. Missing it would mean an eventual beach landing, which could end badly.

Just when it seemed that we had missed it, the dredge appeared abruptly. Not marked in any special way, its graying planks were barely discernible, but on a day like this, even the briefest glimpse sent the same message as a flashing beacon or a brightly burning bonfire: "Home safe." Hallelujah!

I turned and took up a heading for the final approach. As we flew low over the grassy tundra, I watched for the end of the runway and soon glimpsed the outline of its concrete edges. The runway numbers jumped into view as they passed low under the main wheels. The landing was a piece of cake! However, shortly afterwards, the inevitable inquiry came from the backseat, "Are we in Nome?"

Toward the end of the season, we moved into an upstairs, very "posh" apartment in town. With everything new and modern, it could have been the best of downtown Anchorage. That counted for a lot in a town like Nome that had barely improved its worn-out look from the turn-of-the-century gold rush. Opening the door to that new suite helped me stay mentally grounded, a sort of micro-vacation from the remote location and damp cabins of Lost River.

I would benefit from this new apartment's bright atmosphere during the close-out phase of the operations when I would stay behind to close up everything in town, accounts, etc. I still had to ferry the helicopter to the lower 48 for upgrading to a turbine engine in place of the Lycoming turbocharged piston with its distinct sound and personality. A turbine whine just wasn't going to do it for me, although the added performance would quickly make me forget my longing for the piston's throaty roar—of that, I was sure.

Two more dramatic departures from the airstrip at Lost River still lay ahead. They would both take place before the end of the season and, luckily, I had no idea they were in my future, waiting to pounce. Both produced perilous near-misses and the specter of another wrecked airplane being added to the valley floor.

The first occurred when it was time to transport our Eskimo cook, the leftover canned goods, and, yes, his little dog to his village fifty miles away which like all villages in Alaska, had an airstrip nearby. None of the canned goods had been weighted, so before taking on the cook, I had packed them onto the Cessna as a load of unknown poundage. Scales for weight measurement were never included on a bush plane operating remotely. You just took your best guess as you hefted each case of food.

Everything was stacked forward on the cabin floor to balance the aircraft. However, this arrangement presented a problem when I attempted to situate the cook in the copilot seat upfront.

Although he was small, his 2 X 4-like leg made it awkward to position him, to say the least. Boosting him up into the seat with his legs outside the aircraft was one thing, but turning him to face forward like a normal passenger was something else.

When I attempted to place his leg under the panel, he bent at the waist like a Lego figure, his head just inches from the panel. In the end, adjusting his seat to its most rearward position was the only solution. His stiff, right leg was just inches from the panel, but at least he was safely inside.

Unfortunately for me, though, I now had to re-pack all the boxes farther aft in the cabin, where I had removed the rear seats in preparation for a large cargo situation. There were many heavy boxes left over from four months in camp, while the cook and his dog upfront were very light.

He had cheerfully requested to hold his dog during the flight. He wouldn't allow him to be taped in a box with lots of breathing holes. I couldn't turn him down; he was too cheerful. And disappointing him on this last day of our acquaintance was too painful. He had been a great cook.

Every aircraft that leaves the ground—whether a 747 or a small Piper Cub—is at its core a giant see-saw. The load on board, including the airplane's weight, must be balanced to make flight possible. Otherwise, one end or the other will want to remain on the ground. These calculations, whether guessed or computed have unwelcome consequences if figured incorrectly, just like the weight or balancing point along a see-saw. Both an aircraft's wings (lift) and its elevator (nose up or down) are designed with these limits in mind.

Pushing forward on the wheel of the Cessna to get the tail off the ground during takeoff was normal. The fact that this time we left the ground before the tail was even up was not! I immediately pushed the wheel forward with all my might to bring down the nose, but it still climbed. Like the see-saw analogy mentioned above, the airplane was too heavy in back to enable me to lower the nose, but not for lack of trying. Already at full power with the nose continuing to rise, I had no time to check airspeed, but I knew it couldn't be pretty. Right about then, the small, black and white dog jumped off the cook's lap and seemed to bounce everywhere in the cabin at once, yapping at a high pitch easily heard above the deep roar of the engine. Yikes!

As I pulled the power back, the nose leveled with the wheel full forward, but up ahead, we were out of runway. A landing from this height would put us in the tundra not far from the remains of the Fairchild. I played with the power, trying to turn back to the runway and land in the opposite direction. As soon as the runway appeared off the nose, I immediately saw that I was too high and too fast. I swooped close to ground level to see if I could do it. I couldn't.

By this time, a ragged line of spectators, consisting of the crew, drillers, geologists, and so on, had formed along the airstrip to wave goodbye to the cook. Cheerfully and with great enthusiasm, he had returned their salute as we approached my attempted landing. That same group became greatly animated when they thought I was producing a "farewell air show" for the benefit of our departing employee. The very steep climb, followed by a near wing-over turn to the airstrip and its subsequent, low-diving "buzz job" to the surface had turned them into a jumping, screaming group of revelers, no doubt recalling all the great meals at the hands of the celebrated cook now flying past them.

In return, the cook pressed his small face to the plexiglass. He was waving back at the spectators lining the gravel airstrip as if he was Santa Claus waving to crowds of children from his highly perched chair at the mall.

The details of the dog's antics while loose in the airplane— besides urinating—are not easily described. He wasn't at all happy! All I felt was terror.

I knew this next turn had to be correct because my arms were shaking badly from holding the wheel full forward, unsure of exactly where to set the power. Holding the wheel with one arm so I could use the other arm to move the throttle was almost impossible without slippage of the wheel rearward. Out the airplane's windscreen, the end of the U-shaped valley appeared, its ridges rising high above me. I turned to the right and, while flying as close to the valley wall as I dared, attempted to hug it while descending, wheel full forward. I would have a lot of runway ahead of me if I did this right, but if I came out of the turn high, I would overshoot again, and I didn't think I had it in me.

As I leveled my wings, there was the runway with its waving crowd of friends lining both sides. Thank God I was low enough to cut the power and come to earth, even though the control wheel was nowhere near its normal landing position. We rolled a fairly short distance, then I turned the airplane around and parked.

The crew along the runway deflated from celebration to puzzlement, staring at each other, unsure about what had just happened. I had an urge to shout at the dog, but it wasn't his fault. I would clean up his mess later. I exited the airplane with my knees and arms shaking, and then disembarked the confused cook, whose broad smile had waned into a sort of grimace. I assured him he would see his village before the day was out.

I turned my back on the parked Cessna and headed toward the shack where I stored the helicopter equipment. I hauled out the orange cargo net, its ropes, heavy steel fittings, and cables digging a long shallow line in the river gravel as I dragged it to a spot beside the runway. Some of the crew recognized a change of plan and came over to help. All the food went into the cargo net. The cook and dog fit nicely on the bench seat beside me in the helicopter since the big plastic bubble provided plenty of room for the cook's rigid leg.

I cranked the helicopter's engine, letting the rotors slowly idle as I warmed up the machine. Ten minutes later, we lifted to a hover and maneuvered over the loaded cargo net. One of the crew, his face blown almost flat by the rotor wash, ducked under the hovering machine to attach the net to the helicopter's belly hook. It took us longer to get to the village, but we got there. Things can be much simpler in a helicopter, but the machinery to make it happen is much more complicated. And so it goes.

Our next—and final—act at Lost River was closely run, a little desperate, and, for a short time, downright life-threatening.

The high winds boiled in from the north sometime around noon. It was our last day, and the camp had been completely closed down. After breakfast, all the rock samples had been packed and then stacked at the side of airstrip. Food, bedclothes, and personal gear were all piled next to the core samples, ready for loading onto the SkyVan (fixed-wing) scheduled out of Nome for two trips, back to back.

The wind swept over the bare hills above the camp and down the valley to the sea. Only in these latitudes had I seen the phenomena of fog formation that appeared in Lost River that day.

Rather than a shapeless cloud of gray mist blowing in from the sea, these cloud formations hugged the terrain as if they came from a giant paintbrush full of whitewash. This accumulation of soggy whiteness was being dragged across the contours of the terrain by high wind pulling the clouds unbelievably fast. Uphill, downhill, across the gullies, draws, and small canyons of this bare landscape, the topography remained barely visible beneath the white skin of this misty snake uncoiling across it.

The fog threatened Lost River with its fury. At first, it disappeared as soon as it had lapped the ridge at the head of the valley like an incoming tide, but as the foamy wavelets reached farther into the basin, they very gradually formed a solid, white ceiling above the valley floor, a canopy that fell steadily during the afternoon. The sun, shining through the thickening cloud deck, seemed to cast a golden gauze over the dingy, yellow paint and weathered planks of the abandoned cabins. Daylight left the valley much sooner than anticipated.

The SkyVan, a high-wing, twin-turbo prop airplane with a drop-down rear ramp had been chartered to evacuate the camp on this last day. It was as square as the box it had come in and was capable of lifting five thousand pounds of gear and people. We expected that just two trips would carry all the people, rock samples, drill parts, and camp gear to Nome. But they wouldn't get it all, as it turned out.

There were no low clouds the first time the airplane dropped onto the end of the gravel airstrip. Landing an empty plane into a 30-knot wind was no sweat for the two pilots on board, especially with over 4,000 feet of runway ahead of them. Even taxiing to the south end for the first trip out, its lowered flaps and the benefit of a high headwind made the takeoff toward the hills look easy.

Two hours later, the second trip in was slightly more uncomfortable. Sometime in mid-afternoon, as the air cooled, wisps of white vapor began shrouding the ridges above the camp.

This would be the last trip out for the SkyVan. It squatted on the gravel strip like a giant pod, its rear door open and resting on the brownish pebbles of the valley floor. People in twos and threes scurried in and out, feeding the beast through its sizable opening.

Anxiety began gnawing its way through the remaining group of loaders. They wanted out. Loading was hard work that took time. As they watched the threatening scene birthed by the increasing wind, everyone thought it was taking too much time.

"What about the weather?" was on everyone's mind.

Once the SkyVan was loaded, not even a flashlight or blanket remained for another night's stay. Because of the deteriorating weather conditions and the SkyVan pilot's silent but highly gestured discussion near the nose of the aircraft, the crew's faith in reaching civilization at Nome began to waver.

Staying the night was the specter that began looming, in their minds, as the dark and frigid alternative. A ragged ceiling was forming along the ridges surrounding the camp. As the SkyVan took off into the wind, climbing steeply towards the hills above the camp, it was able to bypass the scud as it turned and headed out of the valley, toward the sea and Nome.

If you read or study military history, you will understand the difficult predicaments a "rear guard" may face. The last plane out—the green and yellow Cessna with two geologists and myself as the pilot—constituted the rear guard of this day's emptying of the camp and the closing down of the operation. I had already transported the helicopter to Nome on the previous day, parking it at the airport, and was now standing by with the Cessna to fly back with the most valuable samples and what was left of the camp equipment—a very full load!

After the SkyVan departed the final time, we were alone. Soon, the ceiling thickened. The boiling clouds poured over the ridges and began filling up the valley until the ceiling was solid. The golden gauze of filtered sunlight was gone having been replaced by a fierce wind.

When there is wind, there is rarely fog, but this was Lost River, and the thick white cloud, like a giant animal, was beginning to nestle itself gently into the valley. The geologists scurried around, but as I stared at the sinking ceiling, they might as well have been working in cold honey. They couldn't move fast enough for me. They seemed to have a hundred things to do. Why, inevitably, do the remaining tasks expand to fill the remaining time? One of life's many unsolved mysteries.

By the time I had finally loaded the Cessna with people and rock samples—we would never know how heavy we were—we had everything. The ceiling had fallen to three hundred feet, or maybe even two hundred feet; who was there to tell me otherwise? The point was that it was solid. Looking towards the ocean was like staring at a target from inside a rifle barrel. At the muzzle end, where a bullet would exit, we could see the dim glow of a setting sun. The valley was not yet in total darkness; it still glimmered with the strange half-light of an old horror movie. The wind howled at 30 or 40 knots, bringing with it more and more visible moisture into the narrow gun barrel that now defined the valley of Lost River.

With such a high wind pouring over the hills at the head of the valley, I couldn't imagine attempting a departure toward the sea. During such an endeavor, the speed of the airplane at takeoff would have to match the tailwind velocity of 30 or 40 knots before the airplane could even begin to accumulate the airspeed needed for flight. Thus, 40 knots of tailwind to overcome plus an additional 60 knots to fly, would require a total speed of at least 90 knots across the rough gravel runway before we could lift off.

I taxied toward the ocean at the south end of the runway, a long and difficult journey. The tailwind from behind us gusted and hammered at the rudder, making it difficult to keep the nose straight. I marched left-right-left on the rudder pedals as if I were in a parade. The rudder's metallic banging grievously increased my anxiety, as the sense of time we desperately needed seemed to be slipping away. The Cessna's weight caused it to waddle side to side like a goose, rocking the wings sharply. The growing darkness brought a grim mood to the cabin. The prolonged taxi to the far end of the runway had brought the clock ticking in my head almost to a stop. The top of the hourglass was almost out of sand.

I reached the far end of the runway. I would need every inch. I pushed in the throttle and held the right wing against the powerful crosswind to complete a 180 degree turn. I reduced the throttle. The nose of the airplane pointed upslope into the blistering wind and toward the now darkening buildings and invisible hillsides. The ceiling was now even lower. I squinted through the windshield at the threatening scene ahead. My gut told me there was no way I'd be able to make a 180 degree turn below that solid layer of white cotton in such dim light and with a tailwind to boot. That chance had passed. The most earnest prayer was not going to lift the solid blanket of fog now filling the bowl above the runway.

Looking through the back window of the Cessna, I could still glimpse the light literally at the end of the tunnel, a small, yet promising circle of green seawater. Although the ceiling was solid, it had maintained the same height above the airstrip all the way to the ocean. Plus, since I could see water, the air had to be clear along the coast. At least the visibility there would be good—no mist. Hopefully we wouldn't have to run under a low ceiling all the way to Nome. I decided that our last chance would be to taxi back to the head of the valley and attempt the unthinkable—a downwind takeoff.

I pushed in the throttle to start the airplane rolling forward on another long taxi. The aircraft shuddered and the wings rocked back and forth as we continued along the airstrip and past the camp to the very uphill end against the sloping hills, and then turned our tail to the menacing wind once more. Before bringing the engine to full power, I glimpsed through the slow-turning prop to see a tiny patch of light that was our only exit from what was fast becoming the closing lid of a coffin.

I could barely see in the dim light of late afternoon. However, I left the landing light off. My eyes were accustomed to the dark forms around me, and I feared the effects and consequences of a sudden blaze of light. The illumination I wanted to stay in touch with was the one shining along the edge of the coffin lid three miles ahead.

Halfway down the rough runway, with the murderous tailwind driving us, we were really moving. The Cessna's tail however, was still on the gravel, which meant we weren't even close to flying speed. The aircraft twitched like a stalk of grain in the high tailwind, but every effort to push down the nose and raise the tail failed. And whenever the tail wheel rose at all, it immediately dropped heavily back to the rocky surface.

When the tail finally rose, there wasn't much on the airspeed indicator to promise flight. The wreck I had landed by when I first came to Lost River, the Fairchild, was just up ahead somewhere on the tundra. If we achieved lift off, we would fly very low over its carcass; if we didn't lift off, we would crash just short of its resting place.

There was no stopping. I was deeply entangled in all the variations and combinations of this moment. Stopping or changing my mind was no longer a viable alternative.

This certainly was not a great or even heroic aviation moment. I wanted and needed to get us out of here, and this is what I was willing to put together to get it done. My two companions trusted that we would fly, because that is how it always worked for them. They would have preferred, however, any other option, including walking to Nome, to the possibility of sudden contact with the soggy tundra ahead if they had any clue as to what was happening.

We didn't walk to Nome that night, but neither did we lift off the end of that airstrip in any honest flight configuration you would recognize. We basically ran out of runway, but a drop of almost ten feet of piled up gravel at the end when combined with the downslope of the valley beyond enabled us to drop towards the shore as we struggled into the air. At last freed to accelerate, we zoomed across the airplane wrecks just below the end of the airstrip. With bated breath, I fervently urged the Cessna toward the narrowing circle of light still visible ahead.

Minutes later, we burst through what remained of the closing circle of light and out over the beach where the sea shimmered before the setting sun. The skies were clear with the first stars appearing. We climbed high until we could see the lights of Nome in the distance. Thirty minutes later, as we slid down our final approach in the darkness of a gentle evening, I felt like I had returned to Earth from a strange galactic voyage.

To this day, I can still hear that singular screech of both landing wheels as they touched down onto the concrete runway at Nome. That memorable sound was like the sudden closing of a zippered duffel, the one closing the story of my summer in Alaska, working near the Bering Straits. The baggage tag on the duffel was labeled "Lost River—Caution! Possible danger! Do not open!"

Chapter 8

SHOW ME THE WOOD

Some years later, once again surrounded by aircraft wreckage from a more modern era, I hunched over the steering wheel of my pickup gazing up through the windshield at towering piles of wrecked helicopters painted in various combinations of red, white, and blue. The stacks lined a large graveled area behind the main offices of a small helicopter company near the Olympia, Washington airport. The receptionist had told me to "drive around back" and park my vehicle.

I eased the truck across the gravel lot, trying to resist scrutinizing the walls of wrecked helicopters and crates of surplus parts. I needed the job, but the discouraging scene was taking the edge off my commitment to apply. I quit looking around and concentrated on avoiding as many rain-filled potholes as possible to reach the parking area.

Flying logs with helicopters was known to be dangerous. And while this was only my second try at it, the short tour of the bone yard was not reassuring. They must have needed me, though, because it was one of those "fill out the paperwork, the helicopter is parked out back, you're burning daylight" kind of interviews.

Working a "long line" is the pinnacle of a helicopter pilot's skill set. This level of mastery can be more easily appreciated by imagining the following scenario. DO NOT ATTEMPT! Using the top roof of a twelve-story building, buy a ball of string long enough to reach the ground. Tie a heavy weight, say an ice-filled bucket, to the end of the string and lower it to just four feet above the pavement.

In order to simulate actual long-line work, climb aboard a motorcycle on the wide edge of that twelve-story roof and accelerate to 80 mph, holding your string with its attached bucket at arm's length over the side of the building. Take into account that it will lag behind you due to your forward speed. As you approach your ground target, slow the bike so that it comes to a stop at the same moment that the ice bucket stops over your ground-level target.

Keeping the motorcycle on the roof is your first priority, although you never take your eyes off of the ice bucket. The second priority is bringing the bucket to a standstill about four feet above the target while maintaining full control of the motorcycle on its twelfth-floor perch, being sure not to follow the bucket to the ground.

There you have the basic mechanics of good long-line hook technique: flying a 200-foot cable attached to the belly hook of a helicopter with another heavy hook dangling at the end of the cable, which can be remotely triggered from the cockpit to release the load.

Bell 204—Pulling Logs

I was first introduced to long-line work on the Olympic Peninsula in Washington State. Old, first-growth cedar, cut in blocks then split into house shingles, became a mini-gold rush not long after Vietnam ended. Smaller helicopters that could lift a thousand pounds of cedar shakes descended on the area. There were lots of hungry helicopter pilots from the war to take on the required treetop flying.

Crews on the ground would unearth ancient cedar (it doesn't rot), harvest the wood by cutting it into 20-inch blocks, and then stack them like firewood and encompass them with a rope. Each pile weighed about 1000 pounds. When finished, the crews called in the helicopter to lift dozens or hundreds of these pre-bundled cedar "bolts" out of the rough terrain and onto the nearest road. They were then hand-loaded onto flatbed trucks.

Often, the cedar was located in dense groves more than one hundred feet high or at the bottom of deep ravines in old riverbeds. Helicopters littered the peninsula after the two-year mini-gold rush. In the end, only a couple of companies remained, finding steady but competitive work flying out bolts worth $300-$400 apiece.

I hired on with one of these companies to do utility-type flying, but soon found myself with a 200-foot steel cable coiled in the back of the helicopter and directions to a large forested area to pull out cedar blocks. Again, no one drew it out on a blackboard or shared tips with the novice over lunch. You were at the controls of a very expensive machine, but the fact that you could hover and fly it seemed to be all the qualifications required. However, the helicopter was never the core issue; it was the techniques involved. The ground crews had limits of patience and tolerance, and their fuses were short, making the initial efforts painful, very frustrating, and often embarrassing.

The company had bid this particular job and needed it completed; no one had the time or money to spend on training. If they could just keep the customers relatively happy, then mission accomplished. Threading the hook at the end of the whipping cable into unseen holes in the 150-foot tree canopy to unseen men waiting with unseen loads was humbling to say the least.

In areas where old fires had burned out clearings, only 25 or 50 feet of cable were needed, making it much faster and easier to get the feel of the hanging line. I would have much preferred starting out on the short end rather than the slower and more difficult long end, which was humiliating to boot. The production money, however, was in the "short line," so the boss gave that work to the senior pilots. The new guy had to learn

the hard way.

My friend Clint Burke lost his helicopter mast during one of these operations. A hidden crack from a previous "wire strike"(helicopter flying into a wire midair) before the company bought the Hughes 500D had not been reported to the new owner. The main rotor left the helicopter at 50 feet (Clint was flying a short line, thank God!). The helicopter crashed on the passenger side, saving Clint. This was hard, hazardous flying for reasons other than the obvious.

The owner of the company once had an engine quit just as he was pulling straight up out of the trees with a load at the end of a 200 foot cable. He was headed upside down into the trees before he even knew what had happened or could release the load. The inverted helicopter with its attached load snagged a giant branch on a passing Douglas fir, jerking to a stop ten feet from the ground, upside down like a giant swing. The owner/pilot got scratched up hanging and then dropping from the suspended helicopter, but nothing else. He bought his wife a new car with the insurance money.

Helicopter logging was not cedar-bolt flying, but they both had very long steel cables and heavy hooks to manage. I was laid off for a lack of work on the foggy, wet, and cold Olympic Peninsula just before Christmas (again). After the holidays in early January, Clint called and said there was a temporary alder logging job available that would probably get me through the winter if I was interested.

The job was in Oregon during its rainy and predictably dreary coastal winter. Alder is plentiful in the Pacific Northwest, growing fast in the damp, soggy ground. Clint had flown this same job the previous summer with the same company now looking for a pilot. They owned a French Lama helicopter, which was well known for its dependability and lifting aptitude.

After my company checkout (a barrel of cement suspended on a 150 ft line, a load I moved gingerly through a course of large tires), the company declared me employable and sent me to the job.

I commuted from Gig Harbor, Washington, to the Oregon job a hundred miles south of Portland on a Suzuki 650 motorcycle, bundled in layers of clothing for warmth and a rain suit shell to protect against the constant drizzle.

Alder is a peculiar wood. It grows in wet climates because it is a sponge! When dry, it is nice to split and burn, but that means it needs to sit three to six months, depending on the time of year, before it is truly dry and light.

The ground crew I had been assigned to had worked under Clint's helicopter the summer before. The alder grove was large and on a high plateau with a steep drop to the log-landing, where a log chipper was parked in the middle of the large, muddy circle.

The chipper was there to convert whole logs into chips for the paper mill, thus saving the time and money required to deliver whole logs directly to the mill. Normally, a wheeled skidder would be used to drag the logs from the log-landing area to the chipper. This logging company thought that eliminating the "skidder" was cost-effective (fewer people on the landing, less maintenance, and less diesel fuel). Their idea was to use the helicopter pilot to fly the logs within reach of the chipper's "grapple arm"(the part that reached out to grab the logs and push them through the chipper), thus saving time and money. It seemed simple to the man running things from the pickup truck, but it had its perils for everyone else.

This new strategy meant landing the logs directly in front of the chipper, where its operator would use the grapple to place a log in the chute that led into the grinding machinery below the glassed-in cab. The chips would then fly out into a large chip van on the opposite side of the device. Once filled, this large van was then moved into a line of other loaded vans. Eighteen-wheelers would later show up, hook onto the laden vans, and transport the chips to the distant paper mill.

My first day on the job was a nightmare! Every log load was too heavy. You were constantly laying down the load and waiting while the hooker came in to unhook one log and then moved well clear of the load to see if it would fly. If not, he disconnected another log and so on, one at a time, until you could fly away. You can imagine what joyful work this was for the hooker in wet, slippery, brush. Nothing wanted to fly!

Even more, aiming at a human in a glass cage with logs that had a mind of their own, so to speak, was unsettling to say the least. The logs had to be placed just so and merely feet from the chipper cab. They had to be lined up in such a way that they could be easily grabbed by the grapple arm and pushed straight into the chute. The operation was all new to me and was very disconcerting.

French Lama—Logging Alder Wood

This would not be the only time in my logging career such an arrangement would be employed, but this was my first time. A year later, I might even be good at it, but that was not now.

I called Clint that first night from the motel. "Clint, they say you were snatching five or six logs off the hill in each load, no problem. I'm lucky to stand up two. What do you think the problem is?"

Assuming that it was technique since I was the new guy, Clint tried to encourage me.

"You'll get the hang of it. I didn't really have any problem—is the aircraft running okay?"

Clint is a smart guy, but we both missed the obvious. Alder green is not alder dry. Like I said, it is a sponge, and water is heavy. I am not a forester or a botanist, but my best guess is that a green Alder log weighs up to four times more than a dry one. Clint flew in the summer months after the trees had been cut and lying on the ground for four months. Me? I was flying wood that had been freshly cut in the middle of the winter—go figure!

I was still the new guy and new at logging, so any complaint or observation on my part was not only un-welcomed, but also highly suspect as an excuse, which was considered the worst response among hard-hitting loggers.

They had no idea what a log weighed when freshly cut and lying in the rain. I was foggy on what the aircraft could really lift. Swimming along in this combined ignorance was potential disaster, and I skirted its edge every day until my break came. Thanksgiving, I believe. I got on my motorcycle and headed north for dinner with the family.

They didn't call me back, not even to say don't come back. They just never called. It may have been the complaints of the hookers that I couldn't lift loads the way Clint had, or it may have been the chipper operator who didn't appreciate the occasional logs falling around his cab. Or perhaps it grew out of the day I broke out his window and cracked the other one as he sat frozen in his revolving chair, his gaping mouth likely emitting notes of terror that were likely drowned out by the already solid wall of noise from the chipper, helicopter, and breaking glass.

Of course they didn't know about my cockpit struggles to take the heaviest load I could to the landing each time or the repressed panic I felt maneuvering an aircraft—heavily loaded with logs dangling wildly below the machine—to a position just short of a living human being.

I also doubt they fully appreciated my raw talent (not counting the broken window), for preventing absolute disaster during my brief but hardy efforts. That would include the day I stood up a very long, fat, single log and prepared to launch it over the cliff to the landing below when the log's butt slipped over the rocky edge of the cliff. Suddenly, despite all the power I could pull, the log was taking me down to the landing, not the other way around. I could not arrest the downward velocity. It was not a free fall, since the helicopter rotors were still moving air, but it was an aerial tug-of-war where I was on the losing end.

The weight scale was sitting at close to 4000 pounds, almost twice the maximum load for the Lama I was flying. Punching off the load, if the hook would even work, meant the likelihood of a rebounding cable going straight up into the rotor blades, which would be fatal.

The ride down seemed very long because I had a good idea of what might happen at the bottom—lots of noise—but I wasn't positive. When the log struck the ground and the helicopter continued to fall, I did not back off the pitch (power). Then, the helicopter entered the soft but firm forces of "ground effect" (the air cushion created by the descending rotor wash striking the ground at about fifteen feet). It hesitated, stopped, and then began to go upward. I punched off the load from the hook at the end of the cable and then just held a high hover, trying to gather my wits before I started the process again.

If a pilot has a chance of making it at all when carrying logs swinging many stories below the aircraft, then up the hill is the only choice—not lunch, not a quick rest, a smoke, or a call home to mama. Everyone is waiting, so point the nose up the hill and go there.

My first serious experience with helicopter logging began with a phone call from the West Coast. At the time of the call, I was helicopter crop dusting on the East Coast (potatoes, gypsy moth, river work, etc.) and living in Pennsylvania. The call was, again, from my friend Clint. I had come to his mind when another opportunity broke several years later.

Clint explained that they needed a two-man crew to fly a recently overhauled Bell 214B on a logging project out of Susanville, California. He had already been hired, but was I interested? I really liked Clint. He was a good guy and a highly skilled long-line pilot. The owner had a bad reputation, as did his 214B, and he was having a hard time finding the required pilots. For Clint, joining this crew was a chance to move into bigger equipment, while for me, it was a chance to get into serious logging. The salary potential was supposed to get to six figures if you got with the right outfit. I had a family, so it sounded like a worthy goal to me. I would later get into the airlines with those same elusive six figures running through in my mind. It didn't really work out that way, but a lot of airline pilots and logging pilots got there, so why not me? I was game!

This had not been a firm job offer per se. It was more like "It's here if you want it. Come out, and we'll see if you can stick it out." On the first day, I sat for eight hours on a canvas seat against the back wall of the helicopter while the pilots ripped, lifted, and tore logs off the steep mountainsides with teeth-rattling jerks on the long cable hanging below the aircraft.

Later that night, I sat in the motel and wrote my wife a letter, a kind of will so to speak and what to say to the kids if I didn't come home. I sealed it in an envelope and left it on the blanket in the motel room I shared with another pilot, of course due to cost control. I put it there every day for the first thirty days I was logging. I figured I had at least a 50/50 shot of coming back. Anything above 50% was good in aviation; below that, you could be considered "reckless."

I didn't throw up, and I didn't scream, so I got a chance at the job after a week of holding on for dear life as an observer. Was this an opportunity or an invitation for disaster? At this point, I still wasn't sure.

In Vietnam, I had learned to fly in combat with my pilot seat all the way down and all the way back for obvious reasons. Some pilots liked it forward and high because they had learned to fly in a small helicopter or their body type fit the cockpit in a way that it worked better for them with the seat high. The seat position was a personal preference for any number of reasons, not the least being confident aircraft control.

On the day of my "test," one of the logging pilots pulled me aside and told me the key to success was to put the seat all the way up so I could get a better view of the long, vertical cable hanging from the helicopter's belly, so I tried it. It was like learning to fly all over again! The high seat position increased the difficulty of my already strained attempt at controlling the remote 100-lb hook dangling at the end of the 200-foot cable. Somehow, I managed to keep it off the ground and level with the "hooker," so they put me in the right seat as a copilot and added my name to the payroll. My wallet was about empty by then.

In a helicopter, the Pilot in Command (PIC) sits in the right seat, unlike the left PIC seat in an airplane. There are four controls required to fly a helicopter, each independent of the other. The control stick between the pilot's legs, the rudder or tail rotor control pedals under each foot, and the collective (a longish, pipe-like lever attached to the floor at one end, so it can pivot up and down). A rotating grip (engine throttle) is located at the top end of the collective. Although there is a collective, minus the switches and buttons available to the copilot on the left, if required, the manufacturer places the command collective control between the seats mainly or entry. Most single-engine helicopters, but not all, are flown single pilot.

On the other hand when helicopter logging with a long-line it greatly helps if the pilot flying (always the PIC in a two-pilot operation) sits in the left seat so the simplified collective can be reached by bending only at the waist. From this position the pilot has a much clearer view of the hook painted a bright orange he is maneuvering as it oscillates 150 feet, 200 feet, or sometimes 300 feet below the aircraft.

In addition, the important engine and power instruments are duplicated in the doorframe or outside the left door for easier viewing as the pilot looks down. This adjusted arrangement places the PIC in the left seat and the copilot in the Captain's seat during a two-pilot operation. However, even single-pilot operators prefer and use the left seat when flying solo.

The Swiss for some reason prefer the right side, perhaps dictated by the "command seat" position. Their long-line pilots who fly from the right seat must rotate their upper body to the right and look even farther back and down as they lean toward the door. At the same time, they must stretch their left arm to manage the main power controls between the seats. It is a strained and awkward position.

All French-manufactured helicopters were built and certified that way until only recently, so I have spent many flight hours in that tortured position. It hurts! However, the French machines hover right side low, which helps, but I prefer the left, always.

Large logging helicopters require two pilots. The right-seater may be just a "sandbag" who keeps the paperwork straight and his mouth shut, but most FAA airframe certifications require a human presence in the command seat on the right. The right-seater, though, will not be lifting logs and will do very little flying. No matter how large the helicopter, lifting logs is a one-man show.

Helicopters are expensive to operate. During logging operations, they only make money when wood hangs below them on the way to the landing area for eventual move down the mountain to the mills. It is a serious, no-nonsense production effort where even ten seconds wasted is lost money. Every load is slightly different, but always challenging. And the guys on the ground who fasten the logs to the helicopter's remote hook must know exactly what they are doing to avoid being hurt or killed in the process.

These "hookers" move against and through heavy brush and uneven ground, over limbs and fallen trees while preparing a load. First, they drag the heavy "chokers" (steel cables) and snake them under and around the logs like a lasso. Then, they must hold up the ends of the chokers with one hand while grabbing the heavy airborne hook, up to 150 pounds, and swinging it over with the other hand. As the hook swings by, they must slip the choker's looped ends over its curved tip and then run through waist-high brush and over wet logs to clear the area before the pilot can begin his "pull."

A good long-line pilot, twelve or fourteen stories above, can place the heavy hook at a dead stop just an arm's length from the hooker on the ground.

This skill level doesn't happen overnight. They say it takes 10,000 repetitions to be an expert at anything, including putting a logging hook in the hands of a hooker far below the helicopter. That sounds about right. At least two to three years of constant effort will get you there if the hookers don't hunt you down and kill you for all the extra running, ducking, and bruising they suffer through during your struggle toward expertise at managing a logging hook.

That's why a pilot starts out in the right seat to learn the game and then gets a job flying solo on a surplus Huey (Vietnam type). Hopefully, the helicopter has been well maintained, but it's a lot to expect from a machine never intended for such use, basically being torn apart as it flies the heavy loads. Thus the "new" logging pilot begins his apprenticeship on the hook.

Hours, days, and months of wildly swinging hooks ensue, with the poor "hooker" diving for cover, or even worse chasing and chasing the galloping orange monster around in circles. It's awful, but there are no shortcuts, and no one is going to give you a pointer or two. This is straight learn-as-you-go. Logging with a long-line is an art form when it finally comes together, but until that day everyone hates you down below. We are talking hundreds and hundreds of flying hours here.

For the operation to make financial sense, the hookers must combine logs or send single logs that are as close as possible to the maximum weight the helicopter can lift. It costs the same in time and money to take a single, light log or a full, maximum load down the mountain. Bigger load, bigger money! The statistics are checked constantly: What was the average load? How many loads are there? What was the total at the end of the day? Low numbers, low pay. Or no pay because you no longer have a job.

The men that worked the brush and hooked the logs, hookers, were nomads in the truest sense of the word. Generally, all they owned was in the duffel they carried from job to job. They lived in motels, usually with a long rough ride each morning and each night to the woods and back. They were tough, lean, and worked a daily grind in all weather, including deep snow.

When I arrived for my copilot apprenticeship, it was the fourth of July, and the loggers were having a barbecue. Later that night, I called my wife to tell her about the great food and the all-day party with the hookers. Words have meaning. It took me awhile to convince her of the difference between the two types of hookers. Looking back, I can understand how my explanation sounded far-fetched and suspect. She may have had lingering doubts until she'd heard the reference a hundred or more times over the next several months.

On occasion, a hooker would have a home and family in the area. One hooker had his wife and their family of six small children living in a travel trailer less than fifteen feet long. The family tagged along with the dad from job to job, where he simply parked the trailer in the woods within walking distance of the logging site. He always had to borrow a company pickup to relocate his trailer when the job moved elsewhere, since he didn't own one.

That is an extreme scenario, to be sure, but it gives an idea of the rough edge of humanity who filled these physically difficult and dangerous jobs.

Hard jobs by hard men in America have always included hard drinking, no matter what the century. This situation was no different. At the end of even a 14-hour day, the logging crew still had to squeeze in a beer run and the bar.

Their clothes were not North Face or Eddie Bauer. A good set of spiked logging boots for sure, to survive on slippery logs, but beyond that, they were dressed in assorted shabby shirts, coats of all colors, and pants that were cut off high above the ankle. This was the uniform of their day.

These hookers considered themselves the toughest men alive, at least within fifty miles of the job. That kind of bluster, mixed with booze, got them in plenty of scrapes, including my crew. When they took on a biker crowd in the coastal region of California, they lost big time.

Missing teeth, broken limbs, and lots of blood were donated to the cause of "I'm the toughest guy here."

The hooker that was pitched off the upper, outside deck of the bar fared the worst injuries and couldn't work for weeks. A second hooker, a young, likable kid who had just started with us the month before was shot dead by a local antagonist who went home for his gun and came back with a vengeance.

The pilot on these single-pilot, one-helicopter operations was considered the Sergeant Major over the hooker crew. Working short-handed on the hill was tough on everyone, and the pilot did anything possible to keep them rounded up every morning and moving up the mountain towards the fallen trees to put together their loads.

The head office expected it, and it was an unwritten responsibility. It was vital that they work well with you under such demanding circumstances, but if they turned against you for whatever reason, every day became unpleasant, difficult, and unproductive, a situation that couldn't last long, or else everything stopped.

When my experience as a copilot qualified me for single-pilot operation, establishing trust with my crew of hookers was a top priority.

On rare occasions, when it was doable because of a favorable job location, I flew McDonald cheeseburgers and even French fries to the hookers on the end of the hook far below. They were ice cold by the time they reached the guys on the ground, but it was the thought that counted. Other than those kind of infrequent opportunities, you did the best job you could with the hook, pulling the load of logs out and off the hill without endangering the crew below or making their task more difficult.

It was also important to keep a reality check on yourself from your perspective 12 or 14 stories above them. They scurried around like ants below, while you sat in a dry helicopter on a semi-soft seat.

It would have been stupid to watch them scamper here and there through heavy brush without appreciating what a request from you to move farther or faster or do something extra meant to them physically. Every three months or so, instead of going back home immediately on my two week rotation when the replacement pilot arrived, I would join them on the ground in the woods working under the helicopter for a day. I wanted to make sure I stayed connected to their reality.

About four or five years into my work in single-pilot logging operations, the aircraft industry introduced a helicopter that had been updated to maximize its unique ability to lift external loads.

The KMAX was an old/new helicopter. The rotor system had been produced on the Kaman Husky in the 1950s, but the airframe was newly designed. It was three feet wide like a Cobra Gunship, but with just one pilot seat. It was able to lift 1,000 pounds more than its own weight, which made it an extraordinary flying machine.

Through good fortune, I stumbled into the chance to be among the first ten pilots checked out at the factory in Connecticut. I would be flying it on a daily basis to bring logs down the mountain as part of its first-conceived design purpose. It was the first machine I had flown with a capability of lifting logs every day and all year long without self-destructing. It was strong, but ungainly, and its controls required large displacements like an airplane.

The rotor system was also unique. A standard helicopter with one main rotor (two blades) causes the fuselage to rotate the opposite direction (torque). Thus, a tail rotor to keep it going straight is standard. In the KMAX, though, two rotor masts canted to the side, each carrying two rotor blades. These four blades intermesh like beaters on the mixer in your grandma's kitchen, so to speak. Each set of double blades turned in opposite directions, nullifying the torque effect, so no tail rotor was required, the key to the KMAX's lifting ability.

Kaman KMax with Long Line—Headed for the Wood

Tail rotors take a lot of power in a standard helicopter, especially at high power settings. The more lift a helicopter requires at the main rotor, the more torque it produces, and the harder the tail rotor must bite to keep the fuselage from spinning around and around in the opposite direction.

Without a tail rotor, the KMAX directed all its lifting power with the main blades only. The net result was 6,000 pounds of wood or water (fire-fighting bucket) at almost any altitude. Even at high altitudes or on hot days, it could out-lift much larger helicopters by virtue of this unique design.

Since the KMAX was new, its first operational pilots indirectly became "test pilots" for the concept of a long-line only helicopter lifting heavy loads.

There are many stories related to these unintended test pilot experiences, such as cracked rotor blades, failed rotor head bearings, and unfamiliar flight techniques, most of them best suited for technical manual explanation, but two encounters I had with equipment failure illustrate how normal flight operations can, in an instant, turn deadly.

My first such experience came while I was descending a steep mountainside along a narrow canyon near on the way to the log landing with a full load. The sound and vibration of the whirring rotor blades began decreasing—engine failure! Or so it seemed at that moment. Not good!

I couldn't crash into the small landing full of men and equipment below. I held what power I had, punched off the load against a line of trees just beyond the landing, and then continued down the hillside to where it ended just short of a spreading lake. Touching down on the steep embankment would mean a rollover, but better that than a free fall from my present position into the trees.

The Kaman had a huge green rotor rpm arc compared to any other helicopter. This meant it could stay airborne even when the main rotor turned much slower than the 95% rotor rpm required in other machines. Although the bottom of the green rpm arc was 50%, I couldn't look. The sound and difficulty of controlling the aircraft already told me I was near the bottom of the rpm limit for flight of any kind. I was probably just short of free fall.

As it turned out, continuing to maintain the collective position throughout this grueling descent, instead of lowering it all the way to the stop, may have saved my bacon. I was running on pure instinct as I attempted to keep the aircraft aloft as long as possible.

Before trying to settle onto the steep meadow below, I pulled back on the stick to lose forward airspeed. I turned the helicopter's nose to parallel the slope, planning to drop vertically the last twenty feet. This was not going to be pretty, but with any luck, I would not roll to the edge of the lake and into its deep water.

As I began dropping vertically, a great shake in the aircraft suddenly changed my focus. The engine screamed a high-pitched whine into my very bones. I was stunned. Still dealing with my initial terror, I had braced to roll downhill amid twisting metal and crashing rotor blades.

But the engine, for whatever possible reason, had come to life with no help from me. The KMAX came to a normal, powered hover above the meadow, its drooping nose now pointed out towards the water where the sun reflected an afternoon shimmer. I hovered there, trying desperately to orient myself and prepare for a possible third surprise. Should I land nearby? Would the engine continue to hold me? The meadow filled with what suddenly seemed to be especially bright and beautiful flowers. What was next?

I hovered there, taking in the normal sounds of rotors turning and the powerful turbine running. I scanned the instruments again and again, looking for some hint of malfunction or the subtle warning of a gauge or a blinking light. Nothing.

Slowly, I moved the Kaman forward into flight, then climbed as fast as I could across the broad lake to where the mechanic and shop trailer were located. I tried not to look at the blue water passing slowly beneath me. Five minutes later, I landed in my normal spot near the fuel truck and quickly shut down the engine.

"What happened?" asked the mechanic, surprised at my sudden appearance.

"I have no idea!" I muttered, "No idea at all!" I then relayed the events as I understood them.

The mechanic unlatched the cowls and began searching and poking for failures or signs of malfunctions. Nothing. We eventually decided it could only be a mysterious tantrum of some kind on the part of the Lycoming turbine, somewhere deep in its complex assembly of parts. The engine must have momentarily lost power. We reached the owner and ordered a replacement engine.

Several days later, the replacement engine was installed. A Sprague Clutch mounted to the transmission up front where the drive shaft connects will disengage in case of engine failure, so the main blades can freely turn in an auto-rotational descent. Otherwise, the dead engine would drag the rotor to a near stop, causing the helicopter to cease flying and turn into a brick, resulting in a fatal plunge to the earth.

When the mechanic had turned the clutch housing to line up the engine drive shaft, he heard what sounded like a can of marbles clanging and dropping. This was not good. There should be no noise, only the smooth turning of fine bearings.

In the end, it was determined that the Sprague Clutch had, in fact, partially failed, consequently jamming the engine drive shaft. The powerful engine had been straining to turn the rotors, but could not. Then suddenly the engine power had overcome the jumbled metal parts in the clutch and come to life just as I had increased power to cushion my landing.

After this first event, the KMAX suffered numerous other incidents from the same cause, at least one fatal. The company I was flying for at the time later lost another helicopter that crashed into the log-landing during a repeat failure of the Sprague Clutch. Thankfully, that pilot survived.

The last clutch failure I was closely associated with occurred at another company where I was flying the KMAX. It happened to the pilot flying opposite me the day after I left the job for my two-week break. The aircraft was destroyed, and the pilot who had taken my place never flew again. At a later date, Kaman finally came to grip with the source of the failures and changed its manufacturing process, a solution too late for some.

My second experience with a self-induced KMAX failure is somewhat complicated by my disagreements with a supervisor over the recommended length of the long line. Most large logging helicopters use a 200-foot long line regardless of their ground clearance and because of their high-velocity rotor wash (down wash) and large fuselages. The longer the line, the slower the work, so I had proposed a fifty feet shorter line for the KMAX, which had minimal rotor wash and no tail rotor to factor in.

We were working a logging area that was basically a clear-cut with average rolling hills, not super steep mountainsides. I was confident that the fifty feet difference would speed up the logging production at this site due to the bushy nature of the timber and the distance to the landing area.

Reluctantly, my supervisor agreed, so we cut the line down to 150 feet just before I left for my two-week break. To this day, I can still hear that single-grinding cut of the cable chop saw removing that fifty feet of wire cable. There would be consequences.

As it turned out, a "bad spot" had developed on the logging unit in my absence, which the crew had come to call the "bedpost." There was timber to be recovered around of an uncut "seed tree" more than 150 feet high. A tall, skinny snag was located across from this seed tree and slightly downhill, which easily blended in with the surrounding terrain due to its color and size when compared to the looming evergreen nearby.

I didn't get briefed on "the bedpost" when I returned, and I failed to see the picture as I slid into the first pick-up of my shift. I assumed that I had plenty of surrounding ground and obstacle clearance with my 150-foot long line, except for the towering seed tree. Wrong!

On the first "pull," I had already been overloaded with trees heavily covered in dead, bushy limbs. Chokers from every direction seemed to merge into a central web when I attempted to fly upward to gather the load of wood, tighten the cable, and then launch back downhill.

After several attempts, it was obvious the KMAX wasn't going to fly, so I lowered the aircraft to slacken the cable. However, before the load had stabilized enough for the chokers to settle to the ground, the hooker had also leaped forward to release some of the load and reduce the weight.

Of course, this happened all at once. And the one hundred plus pound remote hook was swinging downhill at its own blinding pace. Upon reaching the end of its slack, it would snap the cables taut, which would most likely injure the hooker or cut him in half.

I dove the helicopter ahead, attempting to offset the swinging hook in time to stop its forward motion in order to save the hooker. But moving downhill to arrest the hook brought me into contact with the bedpost.

Crack! The rotor blade contacted solid wood, sounding like a shotgun going off! I froze the controls and looked to the right just as the second blade came around and shattered against the top of the cement-like snag. Not rotten like most snags, it had petrified into a stone!

Time became slow motion. Pieces of rotor blade and wood splinters mixed and exploded, the fragments seeming like the spots on a first grader's picture of an Army shell blowing up his stick figures. The speed of each piece seemed like inches, not feet, per second.

More than four feet of rotor blade had disappeared in those first few microseconds, three during the first strike and one during the second, both on the right rotor system. The hardened bedpost had sliced off the blade just inches short of its control-surface hinges. The situation was like having a bullet barely miss your artery to lodge in a bone. One millimeter to the left, and you'd have been dead.

The helicopter began shaking so violently that the gauges blurred, and the canopy of forest beyond the windscreen was a haze of green and brown. I hit the control button to release the 150-foot cable below me, along with its heavy hook. This was no time for trolling. Reaching the log landing was my sole focus.

It felt like trying to stand on a basketball. It was an extreme balancing act where any sudden movement of the control stick would flip me off and upside down in a second. I could hardly take a deep breath for fear of losing what precious little equilibrium I was somehow maintaining.

The aircraft was pointed toward the log landing across the small valley. Just three-quarters of a mile away, it seemed more like a hundred miles at that moment. A forceful voice came over the radio requesting that the log landing be cleared of people and vehicles so I could attempt a landing. I felt a twinge of relief that I was not alone. Someone else was helping.

Struggling to stay upright, with the helicopter shaking so badly, I worried that my head might fall off, but I continued towards the log landing, the only cleared or level place I knew of on the property.

Although I was aiming at a round brown spot, I couldn't recognize detail—only colors—because the vibration was too intense, to focus. The helicopter gradually turned left, since the left set of blades was doing most of the pulling. As a result, I ended at a slow hover downhill from my landing target. I was desperate trying not to bypass the log landing, but I had no idea if I could successfully make such a radical course change, or if I could even stay airborne much longer.

From a path between two large trees where I could see the landing farther uphill, I had to decide whether to land in the trees straight ahead or attempt the 90-degree turn needed to fly uphill between the two trees and land at the landing area. I had no time to consider whether or not the helicopter would fit, but it seemed the best option, and the piece of dirt I so badly wanted my landing wheels to occupy was right there.

I used deliberate moves to try to maintain some sort of control in the hover. I did not want to compound the situation by losing control altogether just before landing. The helicopter still shook violently, but the touchdown was not a hard landing.

As soon as the landing wheels settled to the ground, the helicopter's extreme side-to-side vibrations twisted the tail boom into a pretzel, like wringing out a towel full of water. I quickly shut everything off and pulled the big rotor brake. The rotors stopped abruptly. In less than a minute, I unbuckled my seatbelt, killed the switches, and climbed out. I didn't start shaking until I stepped to the ground and tried to walk.

Looking up at the damaged rotors seemed like something out of a dream. How had I stayed in the air? In fact, engineers at Kaman later published an industry article that questioned such an aerodynamic possibility. And, yes, as I was told by the ground crew afterwards—including the saved hooker— that helpful voice that had thought to get the landing area cleared before my arrival, hadn't been someone else's—it had been mine!

Chapter 9

FLYING THE LINE

At this late hour, I was flying hundreds, not thousands of feet above the dark waves, their white tops glowing in the dark. I was close enough to see each wave shed its foam on the backs of wind gusts that tore at their crests. I was alone, squinting into the black night, looking for shore lights.

I urged the single-engine Cessna along between the tumbling swells below and the low ceiling above. It seemed like the gloomy disposition of both elements had combined to slow the already rocking plane as it strained toward its destination—on the north coastline of Washington State where it snaked along the Straights of Juan de Fuca. I frequently checked the fuel gauge. It registered more than an adequate amount, but my mood was to check it again.

Many of the airline's pilots had limited experience in this size aircraft, or else felt they had graduated to twin-engine aircrafts and saw no point in going backward into a single engine for whatever reason. They strongly objected to navigating such a "tight rope" home each night, much preferring the larger, more powerful twin-engine Cessna 402C that the airline operated.

However, this nightly tying up of pilot loose ends by moving them around in a self-flown, single-engine Cessna was a money saver for the company. It avoided the costly ferrying of empty, larger aircrafts in order to position them for flights the next day. Keep in mind that other than the roar of the engine, constant whining is the loudest noise you hear around an airline.

I approached TexasGulf about purchasing the helicopter I had flown for them in Alaska. The company had recently suffered a horrific, fixed-wing accident when their four-engine corporate jet crashed during a heavy weather approach into Westchester, New York, killing all on board. The Chief Pilot had been flying, and his copilot was the friendly pilot who found me on the ramp in North Carolina and offered me the ferry flight job to Alaska (see chapter six). The company had been subsequently sold, and the helicopter was idle. I hoped to fly cedar bolts with it if they'd sell it.

I hadn't been able to break into the competitive market on the Olympic Peninsula and gave up on trying to find another steady helicopter job near home. I decided to try breaking into the airline business, which I hoped would bring steady work and a regular schedule.

It had been awhile since I had flown airplanes, and I knew my instrument skills were weak. I borrowed money from my dad to rent an instructor and an airplane at the local airfield. He was a good sport to bankroll this latest aviation effort, as my family was still growing.

A small regional airline, San Juan, operated about eighty miles north of my home in Gig Harbor, Washington. It was based out of Port Angeles, a logging port city at the top of the Peninsula. Its routes took passengers, mail, and some freight in and out of the San Juan Islands, as well as back and forth to Seattle and the Canadian cities that bordered the Puget Sound.

It is well known that western Washington is very rainy most of the year, so piloting for San Juan meant lots of weather flying. The airline flew with a single pilot in the cockpit, so most of the time, the routes were demanding and challenging—the experience I needed to begin an airline career.

After my tour of duty as a helicopter pilot in Vietnam, the Army had enrolled me in a civilian flight school to get my fixed-wing training using my GI Bill education credits. The Army's plan was to transition me later into the Army fixed-wing training program and have me militarily qualified as an airplane pilot. To me, this welcome assignment after serving in Vietnam meant living at home, avoiding military duties for six months, and wearing jeans to work.

The program had worked out well, and at its conclusion, my new orders sent me to Ft. Rucker, Alabama, for training as an Advanced Instrument Instructor pilot on Huey helicopters. Transitioning into the Army Fixed-Wing program had been dropped by Training Command, but I still had my FAA Commercial Fixed Wing license, and that worked for me.

On an "early out" due to strength reduction in Vietnam, I was honorably discharged from the Army with a Commercial ticket—both helicopter and fixed-wing—along with almost 1500 hours of flight time, and all I had given Uncle Sam was two years and nine months of an almost seven-year commitment. I held in my pocket what I needed to fly for a living in the civilian world, and it had cost me, but not financially.

After the Army, I flew helicopters in the Arctic, worked for a large timber company in the South, and crop dusted in airplanes before getting into long-line work. Wherever I could find regular work flying either aircraft, I went. I eventually got my ATP (Airline Transport Rating) in both types. I never stopped looking for the perfect flying job, an elusive ideal to say the least, but when you are young and crazy about what you do, it seems possible.

I had been in helicopters for a while, flying cedar bolts and chasing torpedoes on the Olympic Peninsula when I took a leap at applying for a pilot position at San Juan Airlines. Getting back in the "slot" with my newly refreshed instrument skills had worked out well and restored my confidence while flying in the gray, rainy weather of the Pacific Northwest.

San Juan Airlines required a flying check in a flight simulator and then an interview if the "sim test" went well. The next step was to buy time in a T33 (an early Air Force jet trainer) simulator, the one used for my check ride. Alaska Airlines also used this simulator to evaluate their pilot applicants.

At this point, more than thirty years after the T33 first flew, this particular simulator had probably been acquired at an Air Force garage sale to rent out by the hour for advanced training. Private, single-engine jet simulators were somewhat rare—if they existed at all. Anyone who appreciates or has seen a modern "full-motion" simulator may have a hard time envisioning this monster, employed to torture new Air Force "would-be pilots" in the early days of the jet age.

My only flight simulator experience to date had been the little blue simulators with stubby, yellow wings. Looking like toy airplanes, they sat on movable pedestals three feet off the ground. These toy-like devices had filled large hangars during WWII as a conveyer belt training system that taught Army pilots the skills required for blind flying.

The Army had converted what Army Air Force trainees knew as the Link Trainer into helicopter simulators for the mass training of helicopter pilots during the Vietnam War, of which I had been one. They had converted them from airplanes (the original design) into helicopters by cobbling in a helicopter control (a collective) for up and down movement, along with a throttle. Now that was a strange aircraft! It had motion, but nothing else any pilot would recognize.

Before the Army resurrected and modified these unique, simulated flight devices, they were most likely stored with boxes of C-rations, bomb sites, and pup tents, all leftovers from World War II.

The Air Force, organized after the Second World War as a separate branch of service, had gone on to new types of flight simulators. One of those jet simulators loomed in my future—a device I would have to master in order to qualify for my first airline interview—the antique T33 jet simulator.

The sight of the enormous, nondescript object that lay like a beached whale in one of many "rent-a-workshop" buildings near the SeaTac International Airport was terrifying! The only feature that had said airplane was a T33-type hinged, glass canopy somewhere near the midsection of the massive aluminum structure. There were no wings, not even pretend ones. Multiple holes and vents and the outline of dozens and dozens of access doors all screamed, "Complicated machinery beneath." I briefly thought this might be the entrance to hell, so tightly attached to the earth and so very ugly and menacing.

It was this massive pile of metal that would carry me to an interview at San Juan Airlines—hopefully!

"If I could just figure out how it works!" yelled the Wizard of Oz in a momentary flashback to his frantic waving to the crowds below his ascending hot air balloon as it climbed away from the Emerald city, "Good-bye folks!"

I now recognized that level of distress, as I, likewise, had never flown—or even been in the cockpit of—a jet. There was no real briefing about how, only spoken directions to take-off, fly a radial, enter holding, come back, and land.

Really, I thought. Me? Alone? Now? Wow!

I am still unsure about why I never passed out because I cannot remember taking a single breath during the entire experience. Do stress measurements even go that high? My face must have turned red from such a massive spike in blood pressure!

Climb out at 250mph! Rocket blast-off came to mind. I had never seen an airspeed indicator go higher than 190mph, and that had been during a dive. I felt strapped to a buzz bomb with no idea how to manage it.

I will spare you the frantic feelings and hair-raising details of aiming for a holding pattern at 350mph while watching the airspeed needle bump up against the indicator's redline on a regular basis.

The only good thing about that day was my good sense to pay for the session out of my own pocket. It was a practice session only. The simulator instructor (or in my case a witness to a startling example of an uncontrolled, Nazi V-1 rocket flight from Europe to England) promised to give no information to the airline until the airline paid for the time slot.

Clearly, one practice session wasn't going to do it for me. These sessions were plenty pricey (about $500 each), and I needed cash for one more attempt. So I went back to my dad.

He wasn't made out of money, but he believed in me, even though he couldn't have possibly imagined what I was facing in trying to qualify for an airline interview.

During my next practice session, I asked a lot of questions and carefully reviewed every minute from my recent catastrophe with the instructor. Appreciation of the slippery nature of a jet's fuselage, airspeed control, and altitude awareness were a few of the key components of aircraft management that would benefit my next attempt. I was finally ready for the check ride.

Maybe the bar was low. Maybe the instructor thought I had made sufficient progress on this third attempt. Just like the blue and yellow wooden simulators the Army had used, I figured out that this one did not fly like the aircraft either. Instead, it was more like an early version of Packman. I got the interview. Now I was flying for San Juan Airlines. I had done a month of initial training and had been flying the line for several months as a single pilot captain.

Alone on this windy night, I found myself returning to base with no passengers or other crew. It had been a very long day. It was a relief to catch the first glimmer of the city this far out and flying so low over the water.

The shore lights on the horizon of Port Angeles, Washington, brought a certain feeling of reassurance, so I quit looking at the fuel gauge every five minutes. I lined up the aircraft for an approach parallel to the shoreline. The flood of light from below felt safe rather than tentative like the white caps rolling and frothing unevenly before disappearing into darkness.

It was hard to slow the Cessna 172 to a correct landing speed after a day in a larger twin-engine airplane that landed thirty mph faster. It also didn't help that I was anxious to get on the ground and go home. The wind was right down the runway, but I landed carrying too much airspeed anyway.

I stepped out through the pilot door and huddled under the Cessna's high wing where I was sheltered from the misty rain as I put on my raincoat. I tied down the aircraft then walked across the wet ramp, leaning into the blustery wind and skirting the larger puddles. I opened the glass doors of the FBO building, the bright, well-lit room shocking my senses. Without pausing, I pushed through the exit door and quickly passed into the half light of the company parking lot.

Pulling on my rain pants, I swung into the wet saddle of my motorcycle for the thirty-minute ride along dark, wet roads to the John Wayne Marina in Sequim, a small town southeast of Port Angeles on a bay next to the straits. There, tied snugly to the wharf, lay my 28-foot Newport sailboat—Colonel Mustard— my somewhat rustic home away from home when I was flying the line.

Hot showers in the new clubhouse made the sailboat a somewhat civilized abode and even tolerable if you could manage to retain the warmth from the hot water during the dash along the dock back to the covers in your bunk. An even greater challenge when high winds blew in from the straits, as they did on that particular evening.

San Juan Airlines had an excellent staff running things, but it was an aviation sweatshop. If you put in 260 hours a month—and I don't mean flight hours—you might take home somewhere in the neighborhood of $1000.

They trained their pilots on a tabletop simulator inside a closet painted black, and they were deadly serious. It was a procedure trainer really, but it worked well because of the trainer's attitudes. They were all business.

After reaching the flight line and flying the routes at San Juan Airlines for just under a year, I was holding a bag of well-earned tools. It was time to move on, as pilots do.

Pilots are always looking for a better-performing aircraft, as well as a faster path to rank and a salary increase, even if they love what they are doing at the moment. I had entered the airline industry at the regional level where highly motivated young men and women sacrificed by living in groups to meet expenses and getting by on minimal sleep while waiting for that big airline interview. In the meantime, they were rewarded with opportunities to build significant flight time. At the majors—if hired—they hoped to finally get a life, as well as a job with real money. This program didn't really suit a married man with children, but I was here, even if a little late, and made a calculated decision to move on early in search of that "better job" on a bigger plane.

Jetstream Airlines out of Dayton, Ohio (affiliated with Piedmont Airlines), was desperate for Captains. The siren call of rank, bright new airplanes, and a flight pay at least greater than what I was currently making still beckoned. I had a lot of baggage, including children and pets. Dayton, Ohio, was a long way from Gig Harbor, Washington, but I was on the ladder now, and up was the only direction I intended to go. We would have to sell the sailboat if we got the job; however, even that tragic requirement did not dissuade me.

I flew out to Dayton to interview with JetStream—no flight simulators involved this time! Instead just one man, the Chief Pilot, asked questions from behind a dark, wooden desk. Not a committee of some kind or a group of pilot administrators, etc., but just one man. As I said earlier, they were desperate for Captains, so I assumed that one man could cull out the dead wood a lot faster than six.

The walls of his office were void of pictures or certificates. Painted an institutional green, the room gave off a feeling of industrial strength conversations, perhaps even interrogation-type exchanges.

He was much older than the green pilots working for him, an old pelican brought in to keep things straight. He wasn't in uniform, and his style of rumbled gray suit and dark shirt leant itself to the interrogation feeling in the room. Even his tie was somber.

Stepping from behind the desk, he shook my hand firmly and took an extra second to stare into my face. He didn't mention his name, but I stuttered out mine and put on my best grin. He motioned for me to sit, and I stepped sideways to a chair with a stiff, metal frame covered in black vinyl that faced the desk. I eased into the chair.

He returned to his large, worn executive chair, which let out a loud squeak as it rocked backward. Leaning forward and placing his elbows on the desk, he blurted out his main concern—no small talk first!

"These damn young pilots are burning up our turbine engines faster than we can put them back on the airplanes. How much turbine time have you got?" he said, fixing me with an intent gaze meant to unmask any tendency toward a less than honest answer.

"About 8,000 hours," I said, then hesitated. "Mostly on helicopters," I added with a hint of apology in my voice.

I waited for the usual rolled eyes and glazed look of an airplane pilot whenever the phrase "helicopter experience" was mentioned.

"Doesn't matter," he said, waving his hand in a dismissive gesture. "Can you be here for a BA3100 (twin-turbine, pressurized cabin, fast!) class starting on—" He mentioned a date and time in the very near future.

I had no idea if it could be managed, but I had only one answer: "Yes, sir!"

I left the interview and walked through the ground-level corridor of the Dayton terminal building. Just outside the floor-to-ceiling observation window sat one of the brand-new British Aerospace JetStream 3100 aircrafts I had just been hired to fly.

I caught my breath! The sheer excitement of that first glance was stunning. I turned away, unable to look again, the vision too much to take in all at once. Sometimes just one piece of cake—even if it's your favorite—is enough!

There was no way I could manage returning with the family and belongings in time to begin the ground school. My wife was an elementary school teacher, and the kids were in school, the youngest not quite two and the oldest ready to leave home.

BA 3100 JetStream—Captain, Piedmont Commuter

I called the head of a Dayton branch of the church we attended to ask about a possible room to rent for a month or so. This was a strange request from a married man, I suppose, but I explained the schedule for my approaching training classes at JetStream, as well as the plan to move my family to Dayton right afterwards.

They seemed uncomfortable about such an arrangement, but after some calling around, a local member graciously invited me to share the upper floor of a large, clapboard house. My very young roommate—a somewhat obsessed musician—had no apparent means of support other than an expensive keyboard and guitar to hock, if required. His room looked like his life: confused.

After completing the ground school and initial training on the airplane—the British love their hydraulics and spigots—I was assigned to the line as a First Officer. I hopped a flight back to Washington. I had five days left before I was due to report at 7:00 am for my first flight. Two days to pack, three days to drive.

My wife thought we would have wonderful, one-on-one chats while driving together on a UHAUL to Ohio. Not really! She suggested we each drive two hours and then switch. I drove two hours, she drove two hours; I drove two hours, she drove an hour. I drove the rest of the way, while she slept. The truck heater was stuck wide open—in August! But there was no time to stop for repairs. We arrived in Dayton just an hour before my "show time." I parked the UHAUL at the airport, changed into my uniform, and reported for duty.

My wife left the truck at the airport and caught a flight back to the West Coast. The kids were still in Washington. She then drove our vinyl-topped green Dodge Dart back across the country—with all four daughters—sharing the driving with our oldest daughter.

The weather was good that first day, and so was the Captain on my flight. I fought unconscious-like fatigue during the entire shift. The Captain, a previous C-141 pilot, carried the cockpit almost on his own with patience and a generous amount of tolerance for my state of exhaustion.

Small amounts of money, large amounts of time, and continual sleep deprivation had combined to place me in the First Officer's seat at this moment. I felt a certain relief to be standing on the next rung of the ladder and hoped such sustained effort would at last lead to the ultimate flying job.

JetStream left me in the right seat for three days before informing me that I would be assigned to the Captain course in Oklahoma City. Fast track! That worked for me.

Before my wife and kids arrived from the Coast, I attempted to have an apartment ready for them, but I had a hard time qualifying as a tenant in the apartment complex I found. My wife was not yet present, nor employed, and the apartment manager had doubts that we could pay the $450.00 rent with a gross monthly income of just $900.00. It didn't fit his formula. The $600.00 salary raise for a Captain's position was just in time to justify the considerable begging required to sign the necessary rental agreement.

Having overcome the major obstacle of obtaining a place to live, I felt hopeful about the family's prospects in the neighborhood. The complex was relatively close to the airport and safe. My wife had a good chance of employment with her experience in education. Fingers crossed that it would help fatten up the monthly income needed for living expenses for the six of us.

None of the new JetStream 3100 aircraft had autopilots. By the time I finished at JetStream a couple of years later, I would feel that even flying the Space Shuttle would be no problem. And working a "weather day" that had three or four approaches was downright exhilarating. Our level of competency was right up there, day in and day out. This was aviation at its best, except for the pay, but the flying was hands-on. When you were in the airplane, though, you didn't think about the low pay. That worry was for when you were driving home, figuring out if there was enough cash for gas.

Our first Christmas Eve in Dayton was a stormy one. The rain was heavy, but as I had predicted, the passenger load was light for the last flight of the day, bound for a smallish, midwestern college town. In an irrational way, I had determined to bring my family with me to overnight in the hotel and force a normal-like Christmas Eve. I was trying to be creative and not be away from them on yet another holiday.

Since our Christmas Eve traditions included a late evening meal, a couple of coolers were included in the family luggage. As the last flight of the day, the midwinter darkness was already well established by the time we pulled up the wheels after takeoff and began the 45-minute flight to our destination.

The loading of passengers had gone well with enough spare seating for the family. It was the copilot's leg. I could look back through the cockpit door and see my family seated in the rear portion of the nineteen passenger turboprop. They happily played as if on their way to a picnic in the back of our old, blue station wagon on a summer afternoon. Some college boys—football player types—were seated nearby, an added bonus that would keep my teenage girls in good spirits during the short flight.

We flew though turbulence and driving rain the whole way. The forecast would require an ILS approach down to almost minimums. This is an approach that brings you down to two hundred feet (rarely higher) before you breakout of the cloud deck. My copilot was a cheerful, blonde kid, young and bright and fun to fly with. You could always count on him.

As we did our pre-landing check list and set up for a precision approach in the dimly lit cockpit, a torrent of water struck the windscreen. Everything looked good; the radios checked out. We doubled checked the frequencies and were cleared for the approach by air traffic control (ATC). There was no tower at the airfield of this sleepy, college town some distance from any large airport.

We began the ILS approach. The gage for this approach contains two needles that cross in the middle, a "plus sign," so to speak—one vertical (center line of runway) and one horizontal that shows if you are on the correct glide angle to the end of the runway. They both need to be centered in the "plus sign" configuration for a safe approach. At first, the glide path seemed normal. My copilot had done a workman-like job of capturing the needle as we started down. I dropped the gear and set the flaps. We were on the center line of the runway ahead. Quickly, however, the glide slope indicator began to rise sharply. The copilot pulled back gently on the control yoke until he stabilized the needle's indication, but then, just as quickly, the needle rose suddenly and in an instant buried itself in the bottom of the gauge.

Our approach was beginning to destabilize. The copilot, who was flying the approach, gave me a sudden glance of dismay and bewilderment. His control movements began to get erratic as he struggled to capture the wily needle. It was very windy, so we bounced hard on our way down.

Of course, the closer we got to the ground, the more sensitive the needle became. This was not good. It suggested a malfunction, probably in our receiver. I ordered a go-around. The copilot advanced the throttles, and we climbed to an assigned altitude. Rather than request a second approach, I requested a course for a return to Dayton. I made the announcement on the PA. I couldn't hear the collective sigh of the passengers, but I could feel it. This was the last few hours before Christmas, and everyone wanted to be in a warm bed waiting to share the morning with those they loved.

Shortly afterward, during the return cruise, I cracked the cabin door (pre 911) to check on my family in the back. They looked like the last candle burning on a birthday cake, still cheerful and animated, while the rest of the passengers looked like caged animals wanting to be elsewhere.

It was still raining at base, but the ceiling was higher. We easily navigated a VOR approach and taxied to the ramp. It was late by now, and everyone just wanted this whole effort over. Most likely the dances with sugar plums had left the passengers' imaginations somewhere during the return trip. When they were reloaded onto a second aircraft an hour later, any lingering Christmas joy had been obliterated.

Weather conditions were the same for the return flight, but on this approach, the copilot nailed the ILS, and we exited the clouds at 300 feet, landing in a virtual river on the runway amid strong, gusty winds.

I wished everyone a "Merry Christmas" on the PA, but I am not sure it helped, even though they were safely down. We taxied to parking, where everyone got wet running for the open door of the small terminal.

The family and I plus my copilot squeezed into the taxi waiting forlornly in the pouring rain outside the terminal. He had been waiting for a crew of two on this stormy Christmas Eve and was no doubt pleasantly surprised to see Christmas spirit glowing among the four additional passengers as we all clambered inside.

The taxi's trunk bulged with coolers and bags of gifts. During our ride to the hotel, the girls told me that the college boys seated ahead of them had been grabbing the seats in front of them with both hands during that alarming first approach, and one had even looked tearful. They couldn't understand it.

We had a rather stark Christmas Eve since the hotel room was devoid of decorations, but like the Cratchits in Dickens's "A Christmas Carol," we enjoyed every minute of being together late into the night, even if all the food was cold.

It may have been that same wet turbulent night that gremlins began crowding into that particular BAE 3100, causing all-around mischief as well as dangerous avionics issues. Two weeks later, that same airframe inverted at 300 feet during a training accident. All perished.

After nine months in Dayton, JetStream opened a base in Baltimore, Maryland. I applied for assistant chief pilot at the new base, and we made another move, this one to York, Pennsylvania, just 60 miles north of Baltimore. The company paid for that move, and we ended up renting a house with a large yard—a step towards a normal family living situation.

I had flown the line all over the Midwest, including Detroit. From the new base in Baltimore, JetStream operated into Connecticut and as far south as Virginia and westward to Kentucky. These destinations were all new to me, and it was challenging flying the crowded East Coast corridor, but building valuable experience was always a plus in this business.

One small city runway seemed only six feet wider than our main landing gear. It was located in Kentucky, close to a military base. We often flew in and out of that small, local airfield, heavily loaded with soldiers going back and forth on leave or transfers, the luggage bin stuffed with their duffel bags.

It was dark and rainy when we arrived over the VOR late one evening, during the copilot's leg. Navigation fixes are usually lined up with the runway and much closer to the airport, but for this airport, the navigation fix was twelve miles from the field and the starting point for a bad weather approach to landing. Its radio signals guided pilots to the airport's traffic pattern and brought them out of the clouds at ninety degrees to the runway's centerline.

That night, the bottom of the cloud deck over the airport was reported as the exact altitude necessary to proceed with a landing, so there was no margin for error. If the cloud layer got lower, we wouldn't be able to attempt the landing. This weather approach was going to demand timing and careful, precise altitude control.

The copilot, however, kept bouncing off his altitude, one hundred and fifty to two hundred feet, not lower than specified, but higher. The bottom of the cloud layer was somewhat ragged, so we caught occasional glimpses of the airport through the cockpit windows as we approached the field. The copilot's tendency was to pull back on the yoke when he saw the ground nine hundred feet below, which took us back up into the soggy drizzle, the airport disappeared from view.

It was quickly evident that we would not be able to finish this approach. Nothing was really coming together in the copilot's hands, nor were his planning efforts competent. All sightings of the airport runway lights had disappeared into the rainy darkness. We did a go-around and told ATC we were headed back to the VOR.

I took control of the aircraft as we headed back. We'd make one more try before leaving for the alternate airport. Normally, this second approach would belong to the copilot, but his skittish control inputs and inexperience with this unusual approach profile would not lead to a successful outcome. We would not have enough fuel for a third try.

I worked at nailing each part of the second approach. We glimpsed the runway lights just as we descended to our final altitude. We flew over the middle of the runway and turned ninety degrees to parallel the airstrip, now in view out of my left cockpit window. I established a downwind leg, but hanging screens of "scud" convinced the copilot we'd probably have to "go around" again. He had the radio ready for such an announcement to ATC. His concerns were not ignored, but I felt we had everything we needed to proceed.

I called for gear and flaps and started a base-to-final calling for full flaps. The copilot thought not. I repeated my request with certain authoritative urgency. He hesitated, but complied. The JetStream felt totally in control, with just the right sink rate as we lined up on final approach. We landed in the touchdown zone and taxied to the ramp.

Later, as we secured the aircraft, an older gentleman approached, perhaps the airfield manager, who must have observed both the approach and landing. His rain slicker sparkled in the overhead lights as the misty rain still fell.

He touched my shoulder and leaned in, firmly declaring in a low gravelly voice, "I will fly with you anytime, day or night."

I have had just two or three such compliments in my career, and each one is a small treasure. Rather than ego feeders, they are the sincere acknowledgement that you have successfully combined the elements of flight in the proper order and at the proper time to return to earth as intended, with no regrets.

Crash! Books hit the floor, the hard jolt rattling my teeth! The simulator went dead. The instructor choked out an undecipherable slur and then declared the session over. It was just after midnight, which made it seem even worse.

Suddenly, we were through, but I had no idea what had just happened. The instructor unlatched the small door of the simulator and stomped off down the corridor without a word.

I caught a ride home with a pilot I had met earlier that night during the simulator session. Luckily for me, he had flown LearJets and realized exactly what had gone wrong. It was 2:30 in the morning, the streets were deserted. We talked.

He explained, reassuringly and with good technical skills, why you landed a jet differently than a prop plane. Full-stall landings were out.

"As you parallel the runway," he said from behind the wheel of his black Ford Thunderbird, "back off the throttles, and let the aircraft settle. Don't let it stop flying."

The DC-9 simulator had predictably settled violently as I attempted a full-stall landing about twenty feet above the virtual surface. Ouch! That hurt. It didn't happen again, not like that anyway. When I flew the line later, I had more than my share of bad landings, but they happened while trying to do it just right, not from falling vertically without a clue.

I was in Miami, having been hired by Eastern Airlines and assigned to the DC-9 course. The school lasted almost four months, and during most of that time, other students could be observed on a fairly regular basis exiting the living quarters with a suitcase in hand. They had been dismissed from the program and the company.

The course was demanding, and Eastern expected your potential to shine through no matter what part of the course you were in. Because of the high failure rate, the company decided that requiring a simulator test earlier in the program might improve outcomes. Oh no! A repeat of the T33 simulator experience haunted—no, terrified—me!

I came very close to being one of the guys walking down the hall with a suitcase. My evaluation "sim ride" didn't go so well. Afterwards, I was led to the chief pilot's office where only a single lamp burned dimly in the far corner. It felt like a funeral parlor. The instructor and the Chief Pilot were in another room—no doubt—brightly lit discussing the advisability of my remaining in the course.

I waited in the darkened office, filled with fear and "what ifs" and "what do I do now" kinds of thoughts. It was painful. After what seemed at least an hour, but was more likely thirty minutes, the Chief Pilot came in and sat behind his desk. If I wasn't wringing my hands, I was probably clenching my fists. This was the moment of truth—go or stay.

The Chief Pilot, a short, stocky man with thinning hair and unlike the instructor (nicknamed "Darth Vader" by the students, for the number of us he had flushed out of the program), had a friendly air. He leaned forward in the soft light, a stern smile crossed his face.

"Mr. Fulton," he said, "your performance was thin in the hold entry, but we like your attitude and believe in the end you'll do well. Be here for classes in the morning."

Luckily, I was sitting at the time; otherwise, my legs would never have held me up. To this day, I value the Chief Pilot's signature on the graduation certificate hanging on my wall.

Weeks later near the end of the course, I passed the four-hour plus, standing oral exam on the DC-9 systems, in front of Darth Vader of all people. When I flew the airplane for the first time just before graduation, as soon as the wheels left the ground, I was back in my element, one I could really sink my teeth into. After four months in classrooms and simulators, I was really flying again.

That day, my single engine, (the other engine remains at idle to simulate failure) ILS approach into MIA (Miami International Airport) was close to perfect, and I give the instructor lots of credit for literally shouting encouragement all the way down the glide slope. I still have the t-shirt I wore during that flight, wrapped in a plastic bag and tucked in the back of an old dresser drawer. Whenever I glance at it, it still seems to fondly glow from that singular triumph in my flight career.

I loved flying the DC-9! Its niche at Eastern was similar to the small commuters I had flown at JetStream. Back and forth to the main hub on legs no greater than two hours and in and out of the hub at least twice a day. Lots of hand flying at low altitudes, but of course, because of speed and performance, much more technical to manage and fly. Smaller city airports offered a wide diversity of challenges to a high performance jet. Wilkes Barre-Scranton Airport was a good example.

It had been a very short hop from Allentown to the Wilkes Barre-Scranton Airport, both in Pennsylvania. ATC had issues with their area radar, so this was going to be a full approach into a 6,000-foot runway (we would have preferred at least 7,000 feet) on the side of a mountain, during falling snow with a three-degree, centerline offset, meaning we would approach the runway at an angle when we came out of the clouds.

We were given clearance by ATC for an ILS approach to the northeast. The weather was just above minimums. At 1,000 feet, the wind was in excess of 100 knots and, yes, it was bumpy! The winds reported at the surface were almost exactly the crosswind limitation for a DC-9, 39 knots. This unrelenting and forceful airflow blew at a 90-degree angle to the runway.

The Appalachian ridges in this part of Pennsylvania are about 2,000 feet high—long, even stone walls with no peaks, as if sawed off by nature straight across the top like a giant washboard suddenly thrust up in the countryside.

You can imagine a 100-knot wind ripping across the rows of ancient mountains: giant speed bumps, stirring the wind into vertical leaps that shook the aircraft like a car crossing them at high speed.

The DC-9 jerked and rolled hard in this rushing and plunging stream of air, like a raft rising and falling on the Colorado River's white water rapids. No doubt the passengers were terrified!

They knew we were close to the earth. Besides, no passenger likes turbulence when riding in a jet. It's not expected, not like this anyway and certainly not for as long.

This night, our approach was prolonged because of radar issues. We were shooting the whole long procedure across several ridges, not simply being vectored up the valley for a straight-in landing.

A shorter approach would have halved the level of abject fear rising in the cabin with each jarring bang. We all felt trapped inside a giant cocktail shaker that no one would set on the bar anytime soon!

This approach was my leg to fly. The Captain was new. No doubt a more experienced Captain would have taken the controls on this one, but new Captains were recently First Officers, and they remember having wanted their turn to fly a leg to be their turn, period.

Several weeks before, I had flown into this airport on another rough night with a Senior Captain at the controls. The winds had been at least 30% less severe, and we had been vectored to the shorter approach. We had not experienced the sustained turbulence of this night, and the crosswind then had not been even close to the airplane's limits. To me, though, it had been a dress rehearsal of sorts.

I did not want to re-experience this night's turbulent chaos by messing up this first approach. By focusing on the headings and altitudes of the approach, I was able to keep my growing concern at bay.

In a crosswind, the pilot must allow the aircraft to crab into the wind as he lines up with the runway centerline. He then descends just short of the end of the runway to the landing zone, aligning the aircraft with the runway with only the rudder, while at the same time lowering the upwind wing into the crosswind to keep from being blown sideways. This maneuver lands the airplane on one wheel with the upwind wing low to the ground. Upon touchdown, the pilot must continue to hold the aircraft straight ahead to prevent any sideways movement as the other wheel drops onto the runway. Once the aircraft has been lowered onto both wheels, it can then be steered normally using the brakes and the nose wheel. The control wheel will remain rotated and held in the direction of the crosswind until the aircraft slows.

I had initiated this maneuver, but as we descended from a broken layer of clouds, I squinted through snow flurries, startled to discover that my crab angle was so extreme that I had to look out the side window behind the Captain's head to see the runway lights. To this day, I cannot recall that moment without seeing the Captain's profile as an integral part of my landing sight picture.

The aircraft, of course, continued to buck and sway as we approached the runway. Once its nose lined up with the centerline of the runway and I had pitched the wing down into the blustering 90-degree crosswind, behold, just like the book says, the airplane stayed lined up with the runway's centerline. We did not move sideways, and the DC-9 settled onto the pavement with the wind's velocity at the aircraft's limits on its one, upwind landing gear.

In an airliner, you want every landing to be a great one, and sometimes they are. You may even get almost a week of them, but then a month passes when you can't even buy a smooth one.

The solution to that mystery was never revealed to me during my relatively short airline career.

It had taken so much effort and so many teeth-jarring bumps to get to this point that I put everything I could into making a smooth touchdown instead of a predictably final jolt at the end of this miserable ride. And I must say that on that night, it was good—not great—but enough to qualify as smooth under the circumstances. Everything is relative.

After we taxied to the gate and the aircraft was shut down, the Captain insisted that I stand in the cramped opening just beyond the cockpit door for the standard farewell to the passengers. There were about fifteen or twenty left after our stop in Allentown, a broad mix of ages. Not one passed me without giving me a hearty hug. I think the heartiness was out of gratitude for being alive, not because they thought I had done anything special.

On that night, while walking through the airport to the waiting taxi, I had that workman-like feeling of a job well done. One of those few nuggets of memorable aviation moments when all the instruction, experience, and seat-of-the-pants skills combine into a performance solid enough to face down a serious challenge.

The taxi was a limo waiting at the curb of the airport. The hotel in town was in a remodeled railway station, the Lackawanna. It was a beautiful place to stay. However, we had a problem. The flight attendants refused to join us in the limo. They were furious about the rough flight they had just suffered through, imagining that the prolonged cocktail shaker approach had somehow been our fault, so we certainly did not merit or deserve their company. I imagine the atmosphere would have been very icy anyway, even if they had managed to choke down their ire. They took another cab, and we didn't see them until the next morning. They were still devoid of smiles or cheerful chatter.

Two years later, Eastern Airlines went bankrupt, first struggling through a strike, and then hitting the wall definitively and finally during the winter of the Gulf War, when fuel prices soared for no reason other than fear in the marketplace. Those prices sucked the remaining cash from an airline that thought they'd have enough to make it through the winter, but suddenly didn't.

As crews checked out of the hotels on the morning of the shutdown, they were greeted with a terse message from dispatch, "Bring the plane back to Atlanta, empty."

Who could forget the gaggle of empty planes jamming Eastern's ramps that day at Atlanta? All of us were on our own finding rides home.

That was a sad and dreary day for all the employees, of course, but if you had been a pilot all your career without a plan B, such as a side business doing taxes or a brother-in-law in the pool business, you were suddenly haunted with specters of selling used cars or going door-to-door peddling garage door openers. Prior income, perks, and free travel would soon be a distant memory for most of Eastern's pilots; there were even rumors of the isolated suicide. It was an abrupt finish, but especially for those with sincere—but uninformed—hope.

Eastern Airlines had once been the largest airline in the world. Eddie Rickenbacker—the famous race car driver and WWI ace—had been at its helm for many years. It was all about legacy and history and the story of aviation. Other airlines eventually suffered the same fate in the changing world of competition and deregulation: PanAm, TWA, and others. They were not bought out. They just ceased to exist.

I don't know how many pilots went to other airlines, but many did. Me, I was in my forties with children in high school. Taking my place at the bottom of another seniority list and then waiting five or more years for enough seniority to just bid weekends off seemed like a dismal prospect. Instead, I opted to return to the helicopter world, where a relatively new industry was emerging in the medical field. Best of all, I would be home every night, even if some of those nights would be short ones.

Chapter 10

WIRE DREAMS

Wire dreams are real. While in them you are flying a helicopter over cities and towns and countryside where you cannot, for the life of you, find enough clear space to ascend out and over the wires that constantly block your way. Your initial feeling of fear soon dissolves into constant frustration and then a certain desperation. You are forced to continue your flight low to the ground, unable to soar into clear and unobstructed flight.

String after string of wire lines stretch endlessly across the landscape—some the heavy ones sagging between high-tension towers, others the small-diameter utility lines strung between wooden poles. From a distance, the spaces between them seem wide enough for you to pass through, but upon approach, it never really works out. So you continue with your low-altitude flight. The view below changes, but not the scene overhead. You feel the vibration, hear the engine, and sense growing fatigue, even though this flight lives only in your subconscious.

That is the wire dream. Packed with emotion across a journey that never resolves. Perhaps the circumstances or the color or the size of the aircraft are different for each pilot, but the story is the same—endless flying with no way up. This recurring dream sometimes seems so real that it keeps haunting you long after you awaken.

For years, I thought it was a dream I alone experienced. I was shocked when I mentioned it to another helicopter pilot who immediately recognized the dream. Casual inquiries of other pilots revealed that such dreams were widespread, if not universal. And they all referred to it as the "wire dream."

In general, helicopters operate in a world far removed and much lower in altitude than the A to B-type missions flown with fixed-wing aircraft. Except, of course, for crop-dusters. But any aircraft flown below 1,000 feet—even in remote areas—enters the world of wires and its continual risks of wire strikes.

This reality was forcefully brought home to me while ferrying a helicopter across the remote Southwestern desert. A hundred miles from the nearest town, while flying at 300 feet to break the monotony of a long, solo flight, I crossed a slope strewn with boulders and devoid of any plant life. Bright flashes suddenly sparked in the blue sky ahead. With a sharp pull on the stick, I cleared a thin wire strung up a hillside. Uninsulated, it had reflected the sun's rays just in time to warn me. It stretched from a lone trailer below to a TV antenna located at the crest of the hill whose face I was now crossing—go figure! Flying low means wires, period! Be vigilant!

Striking a wire is never good, of course, but an airplane hitting a phone wire, for example, is survivable. A crop-dusting friend of mine had once done just that, safely bringing 300 feet of phone line back to the airstrip, hanging from his fixed landing gear.

But when a helicopter strikes a wire, it never ends well—too many moving parts. Either the machine is thrown to the ground with the swiftly turning rotor blades severed instantly, or else the wire will wrap around the rotating mast and squeeze the control rods leading to the rotor head, immediately making aircraft control impossible.

The world of EMS helicopter flight (Life Flight) is rife with wire dangers. The pilot's area of operation almost never involves an airport or an air traffic route structure. Landing options include cities and the highways leading to them, empty rural roads, and isolated hospitals located in the midst of small towns. Travel routes are punctuated with thousand-foot radio towers, often in clusters supported by thick cables anchored to the ground at one end and secured at the other end near the top of the tower, thus supporting its vertical position.

No official "shutdown time" exists in an EMS helicopter's 24-hour schedule. Only occasional bad weather that cannot be navigated may interrupt flight activity. Standard operating procedures for nighttime flight—with all its limitations and dangers—must be strictly observed by any low-flying aircraft and crew attempting to accomplish their mission.

Wires can be hard to see and at times even invisible, so pilots often rely on others to identify their location. Unfortunately, the perspective from the ground does not match the perspective from the air. Different background entirely. Wrong information inadvertently relayed can prove fatal unless pilots triple-check it with their own eyes as well as the observations of others onboard, coupled with a cautious approach to the landing site.

Nationwide start-ups of private and public helicopter EMS operations right after Vietnam meant that most available pilots were Army veterans who had either been flying in remote areas or else not flying at all. These emerging helicopter enterprises, despite their expense, included small, local fire stations as well as large medical universities, cities, and sheriff's departments. For pilots working as far away as the Arctic or in the world's jungles, the opportunity to sleep in their own beds at night seemed like a dream that just might be doable despite the low pay. And for those looking to break into civilian work, why not Medevac? Many had already done it while under gunfire, so how hard could it be as an everyday chore?

A more confining airspace due to wires and other civilian hazards was not fully appreciated at first by war veterans used to flying any mission they had been asked or ordered to fly. Bullets and weather while flying in remote regions were not the same challenges as wires and weather in the middle of civilization.

My own desire to once again have a home life by flying EMS had put me in the pilot seat of a fast, medium-size helicopter now barreling through the dark. As I carefully navigated the scattered thunderstorms, the four large rotor blades caught the flashes from our red, blinking beacon and reflected them back into the inky blackness. Two medical crew members—a nurse and a paramedic—accompanied me, all of us enclosed in the dimly lit cabin of the helicopter, 2,000 feet in the air. This was a hospital transfer mission, urgent, but not a mystery, since the patient waited under competent care in a distant hospital.

The paramedic rode in the copilot seat beside me. Since he was not needed in the medical bay in back during this outbound leg to pick up the patient, he proved to be an extra lookout for conflicting air traffic.

Tonight was significant. We were moving toward a small hospital where I had never landed. It had the reputation of being among the most difficult—meaning dangerous—helipads to get in and out of in Michigan. I had never seen it in daylight or at night. And it was surrounded by wires.

During orientation, it had been on the initial list of helipads for practicing touch-and-go landings, but on the day of my checkout, the instructor had been in a hurry to umpire a baseball game after work. Since this particular landing site was well out of our way, he had decided to skip it, thinking it would make us late. We could always tell when it was "game day." "It must be Tuesday" became the standard joke among the flight crew whenever he left work early or called in sick.

The paramedic with me that night was familiar with the physical layout around the hospital pad, including its dangers. It would be a complicated approach to landing. As we flew into the stormy night, the city's bright lights faded into a countryside dotted with small towns. We left the city behind, occasional lightning flashes sparking the sky. With no moon, it was very dark.

We were headed for the waterway that flowed between Lake Huron and Lake Erie and divided the United States from Canada. The small, country hospital near its banks shared the neighborhood with a very large, coal-fired power plant, an important landmark for us. The paramedic described the plant as he remembered it, sprawling south of the hospital. Its piles of coal, moving trucks, transformers, and web of wires fed the city as well as the countryside and even Canada across the river. Each of its triple smokestacks—overly tall and striped in red and white—were marked with a bright-white, vertical line of strobe lights.

The strobes were an issue. Besides those on the smokestacks, a 300-foot tower at the edge of the canal also had strobe lights marking its wires and overall structure. At our first sighting of strobe lights, the paramedic misjudged them as the high wires north of the hospital. He struggled to orient himself, but his explanation remained confusing. I wasn't convinced. Did they belong to the high-wire strobes, or were they just signaling a warning about the stacks?

The tower alongside the canal was high for two reasons. First, it served as an anchor on the U.S. side for the high-tension cables—shared with Canada—that spanned the river to another, similar tower on the Canadian side. Second, its cables had to be high enough to accommodate the large, ocean-going vessels that regularly passed beneath its massive wires.

Strobe lights marked the cables spanning the river as well as the high towers that supported them. It was critical to know this because of their proximity to our destination hospital. One can only imagine the wire nightmare extending in every direction from both the power plant and the giant tower.

When the smokestacks came into view on the horizon, it was obvious they were well marked by the flashing lights. As we flew closer, the paramedic tried to explain from memory what these lights meant and their exact location in relation to the helipad.

We weren't worried about the smokestacks. We were worried about the tower with its high-tension wires.

The confusion of that moment originated from only three sets of strobe lights. Were they indicating the stacks or the wires? The paramedic decided that they were marking the high-tension cables that crossed the river, so we were okay. Me, I couldn't picture the overall relationship without a micro map of the immediate area. Being on a mission, we did not circle at 1,000 feet to further clarify the situation, but instead flew on. The med crew had been here before.

Out of caution, though, I made a tight circling approach from above the hospital, still unsure of what was out there. The bright lights from the single-story building and its grounds formed a white funnel that rose straight up into the sky. Its edges marked the sharp border between the light and the blackness beyond. I confined my approach to its lighted interior since nothing could be seen beyond the white curtain of its boundary.

As we departed the helicopter after shutdown and walked through the double doors of the ER, it was like walking into a brightly lit stadium. The crew immediately went to the patient to begin their evaluations. He was a large man, youngish, wrapped in blankets. Due to his unique medical condition, a specialized nurse joined us to attend to him en route to our home university hospital across the city.

This was going to be a full load. Takeoff from the small helipad would require an almost vertical departure due to the bright circle of light and its potential to obscure obstacles around the building, parking lot, and bordering grounds.

I helped the crew with their bags as they rolled the gurney out through the double glass doors of the ER and down the walkway to where the blue and yellow bird quietly sat on the painted pad. Bathed in bright light, it seemed to await our boarding before being beamed up into the belly of its mother ship.

After the patient was loaded and the extra nurse briefed on emergency procedures, I walked around the machine as a final check. I stared hard in the direction of our planned departure, but I could not penetrate the curtain of light. It would get very dark the minute we parted that curtain. I felt uneasy, like I was about to jump off a too-high diving board.

I finished my walk around, opened the right-hand door, and dropped into the command seat. The outside lights lit up the interior cockpit. The crew was in the rear cabin, busily hooking up the ceiling-mounted monitors to the patient and performing, with haste, other last-minute medical preparations before they could strap in for departure.

I set the throttle on the collective and started the first engine. The heavy main rotor blades, still drooping slightly, slowly began to turn. Soon, all four blurred into a rush of motion, each blade quickly merging into a single disc.

Setting the second throttle for start, I looked at the voltage gauge. These engines seriously drew down the battery during start-up, so there was a minute or two lag before enough "juice" (electrical power) was available to start the second engine. With both engines running, I went through final checks and set the cockpit lights as dimly as possible, still uneasy about a departure into total obstacle-ignorance. I finished a double-check of critical items and then switched on the landing light, which was hardly visible within the surrounding brightness. The machine—now filled with life and purpose—was ready for flight.

I brought in power until the aircraft was light on its skids, then glanced at the torque (power) gauge to ensure there was enough remaining power for a vertical departure. I would need all fourteen-hundred horsepower and then some to climb vertically, at least initially. The power was adequate, but just barely. I steadily pulled the collective up to the power limit without pausing to hover. We left the cement pad and accelerated upward, the climb rate gradually decreasing the higher we rose.

As the vertical rate of climb slowed, I pushed the nose over to begin forward flight. The aircraft staggered slightly at low speed when we cut through the bright curtain of light and were instantly immersed in the inky night beyond. Unsure of what was ahead, I kept the helicopter's forward motion at low speed rather than rushing off into the unknown. We had passed through transitional lift (when the aircraft's forward speed is sufficient for power to be reduced), so I decreased the power without a glance at the gauges. My focus was 100% outside.

Peering intently into the area where the landing light's cone of radiance dissolved into murky darkness, I gradually accelerated. Abruptly, a horizontal line appeared—faint, but terrifying—at the far reaches of the cone's fuzzy edges. In just a split second, it was much closer. Not even a microsecond existed to consider actions or consequences or plan an escape.

I pulled the stick into my lap! The nose of the aircraft went almost vertical, the tail sliding back toward solid ground (we were only 300 feet in the air). From this nearly vertical position, I stabbed the right rudder pedal (for tail rotor pitch), rotating the nose straight toward the ground. I had never practiced this maneuver, and as I learned later, this helicopter wasn't built for it.

As the ground rushed up, filling the windscreen, I again pulled the stick all the way back, coming to a low hover over a meadow. My landing light revealed rolling grass, beaten down hard by the whirling rotors. I held the hover and just sat there. Evading the wire had taken mere seconds, but it was possible and even likely that our rotor disc had briefly overlapped the thick, unlit wires, spanning the river.

The strobe lights on the large towers as well as the oversized wires that crossed the canal were off—out—gone! Electrical failure? Lightning damage? I will never know. Those towers and wires had been waiting quietly in the black void as we approached. Unimaginable current coursed through the cables without a kilowatt to spare for their illumination. The crew later insisted that the strobes had always defined those structures whenever they had taken this route over the years. They were amazed!

I hovered in the meadow for a time, turning the aircraft slowly, left and right, then up and down. I felt no unusual vibrations or feedback, so I decided to continue. Against the distant glow of the large city, I could discern the shorter poles and towers ahead as I put the nose down and flew west.

Fortunately, we had been barely into the flight when the wire appeared. The crew had still been strapped in and the was patient strapped to a stretcher secured to the aircraft's table. Although the nurse reported that they were "good in the back," I could hear a slight tremble in her voice. We would talk about it later; they returned to patient care. Everything returned to normal as the helicopter rose higher into the sky, leaving all obstacles behind. The crew in back were solid professionals—only the patient mattered.

Nothing unusual happened during the balance of the flight, although we occasionally altered course to avoid scattered thunderstorms. Lightning continued to flash here and there.

The next morning, I got a call from the head mechanic.

"You tore up the rotor head. Why didn't you go back to the hospital and stay put?" he asked in an accusing tone.

Good question! He would have, given his stark black and white logic. A fine mechanical mind he possessed, but I had checked out the bird at a hover: no caution or warning lights, no unusual vibrations. It had seemed normal, so I had continued with the patient we had been sent to bring back.

Successfully retrieving a patient to gift them with a "golden hour" that drastically improves their chances of survival is a satisfaction shared by the entire crew. EMS helicopter operations nationwide, in large as well as small population areas, bring each patient the commodity most needed—time.

Life Flight missions are not all fraught with danger and derring-do, but given the mix of unpredictable call-out times, weather, rest, and the flight environment, on occasion, two or three negative elements could line up to work against you on behalf of disaster.

The helicopter medical emergency industry had matured since its beginnings, but accident issues still lingered. A policy of "Go-No-Go" decision-making had been developed over the years to give the medical crew more of a final say about whether or not a flight should depart. This procedure had mixed benefits, but it was a step in the right direction, making all crew members aware of the variables facing them on any given flight.

Sometimes, you just had to be out there. There was no crystal ball built into the aircraft's instrument panel. Flight decisions were never easy when the question was should I go or should I stay? As urgent as saving a patient might be, killing three people to attempt to rescue one makes no sense. The line, however, is fine. You are expected to give it your best shot—it's what you get paid for. Keeping the human factor out of the equation to consider your chances with detachment is the challenge all EMS pilots face on each flight. Their experience and training are not equal, nor are the machines they fly equipped in the same ways. One size cannot fit all, but those differences weigh heavily in each final decision of "Go-No-Go."

My decision to leave for the university after avoiding the wire had been based on my own experience and the need to complete the mission. Unknown to me, damage had been done to the rotor head as a result of my escape maneuver, whose severity I had not then appreciated. No gauge or vibration had defined it at the time. The mechanics and the people who pay for the parts see it one way—the patient, in the end, is oblivious to it all—except realizing they are back from the brink of death.

My father always cautioned, "Don't take unnecessary chances!" suggesting that having a Plan B or C is also important when deciding the right course of action. There are always risks, and at times, they are uncomfortably large, but as I have learned over the years, just closing your eyes and "going for it" is always a bad plan. Instead, honestly consider the elements you are weighing, devise a plan with an "out" if necessary, and then proceed if the benefits and the ability to achieve them outweigh the risks involved.

These critical decision-making elements involving medical flights were to be tested early in my EMS career. During my first job flying for a hospital, my more conservative decision-making skills were not yet fully developed.

Late one afternoon in downtown Philadelphia, I sat in the "ready-room" on the twelfth floor of the University of Pennsylvania's hospital. Philadelphia at night is charming. Flying a twin-engine helicopter low above its street lights on a foggy night—not so charming. It had been a dicey mission from the first phone call to our operations. The weather forecast had not been encouraging.

An urgent request for a medical helicopter had come from a small hospital in a small town north of the city. The request, despite its urgency, was getting turned down by other local EMS operations due to the likelihood of fog as the setting sun with its cooling winter darkness drew near.

We had no communications to alert us about the turn-downs from other services. At that time, each service operated independently. The small hospital making the request was way over its head with two critical patients and needed someone to say yes. The Vietnam curse of a civilian helicopter pilot still lingered in me—"Can do, just tell me where!"—so I naturally agreed to go. It never occurred to me not to.

That post-Vietnam willingness of pilots to take on nearly any set of circumstances had cost the emerging helicopter EMS industry almost 25% of its fleet during their first five years of operations. That loss record exceeded the Army Air Corp's losses during the 1920s cross-country flights, when the U.S. Mail was carried in open-cockpit biplanes, from bonfire to bonfire, in bad weather and at night.

Of course, it wasn't the industry's fault that I took the flight. My decision was based on the urgent need to rescue rather than the evolving idea that aviation considerations should take precedence over a patient's needs. Prioritizing critical care over safety too often resulted in fatalities for all onboard. That was one reason we all wore aviation crash helmets and NOMAX (fire-retardant) flight suits for every flight, as well as cotton underwear that wouldn't melt into your flesh if the aircraft caught fire after ground impact.

That afternoon in Philly, the light was poor from the low, gray overcast and the air already cool and damp when the short, cheerful, female nurse and the larger, more serious, male paramedic crossed the helipad to join me near the helicopter parked on top of the twelfth story of the University of Pennsylvania Hospital. We had just left a raucous group of hospital staff telling medical flub-up jokes. It was quieter here on the pad with only street noises audible below—the odd siren and occasional car horn.

Even in the defused daylight, the aircraft stood out sharply against the somber gray of concrete and sky. It squatted there silently on thick skids, its white with blue striping and the word "PENNSTAR," painted boldly along each side of the fuselage.

Once the decision had been made to launch, no time was wasted in departing. Two turbine engines powered this BK-117 helicopter, and the initial whine from those engines as the main rotor blades slowly accelerated tended to focus the entire crew on the task at hand.

BK117—Hospital Ship—Pennstar

In this particular helicopter model, patients were loaded through a clamshell door at the rear of the cabin rather than the more common side door, so the tail boom had been positioned high enough for head clearance. The aircraft itself was short and compact despite a large cabin, enabling landings in very tight locations. Even the main rotor appeared to sit flat on top of the fuselage.

Its rotor system was one of a kind—extremely responsive—making the aircraft very maneuverable. However, the downside of this design was that it became very squirrely in wind or in the hands of an inexperienced pilot.

Flying off the twelfth story above the streets of Philadelphia made you feel like Superman, glimpsing the busy traffic through the plexiglass floor (chin bubble) as you left the building and were suddenly very high above the ground. The visibility across the city was clear, but hazy in the far distance. That gray overcast lowered the mood in the aircraft. The late afternoon light grew even dimmer as the cloud deck thickened above us, and car lights came on one by one along the streets below.

We climbed past the tall buildings that dotted this large city, heading northwest up the Schuylkill River. Our immediate challenge was crossing the first ridge of low hills that rose above Philadelphia's flat river plain about ten miles ahead—where lowering weather had been forecast.

Our mission was related to two automobile accidents, most likely the result of the rain and overall nasty conditions that day. Plymouth Meeting, a suburb of Philadelphia and the scene of the unrelated accidents, was just beyond the ridge we were worried about crossing. A trauma patient from each accident site had been delivered by ambulance to the small, local hospital awaiting our arrival.

Both patients were badly injured, one from having gone through a windshield. The aircraft radio relayed these details along with each patient's list of injures and vital signs. In those days, EMS pilots could hear it all. A medical crew today—usually a nurse and paramedic—has a private channel with the hospital, so the pilot's flight decisions will not be influenced by the patient's condition, thus prioritizing overall safety.

Whenever a patient is identified as a child, all crew, no matter who they are, assume a different attitude and tone—a sense of urgency that unites them. On this mission, both patients were children, one less than a year and the other eighteen months.

As the radio crackled weakly into silence, the intensifying ingredient of "children" was added to the mix of pilot, nurse, paramedic, and airborne helicopter. Our heightened caution up to that point was not stripped away, but became noticeably reduced. And the tensions already felt from the day's gloom only magnified once we knew that two babies waited in the trauma ward below as we prepared to land.

I quickly accomplished a single, low-level circle around the helipad—located near the street and close to the hospital—to determine wires, obstacles, and wind direction. I decided on the best landing path, all things considered, then began the steep approach without hesitation.

The touchdown was firm. The engines sighed deeply as I pulled them to idle, their high-pitched whine gone as I waited the normal two minutes before closing the throttles above my head. The crew had already departed with their equipment rather than waiting, as usual, for the completed shutdown.

At last, the rotors stopped turning. I released the rotor brake, secured the aircraft cockpit, and quickly exited, striding with urgency toward the trauma room.

The small children lay foot to foot on a single table surrounded by busy hands. As I walked into the room, our energetic nurse seemed to be in three places at once, deliberate, but not rushed. She dodged artfully among the hospital staff, her yellow-striped, blue flight suit a contrast among the white uniforms. Suddenly, she was in front of me, handing me an IV bottle to hold. I had now been drawn into the care part of the mission where I didn't belong.

I stared down at the 18-month old. Lying on her back, eyes closed, she was connected to the IV I was holding. Her curly, brown hair clung to her tiny skull, pressed there by moisture—rain or sweat. Half-naked, she lay on a clean sheet that was just a little whiter than she was. The steel table beneath her stood motionless, its large, black wheels locked in place. It was the only stationary object in the entire room. A father myself, this scene struck me hard.

I glanced at my wristwatch and then at the flight nurse as she labored over the younger child with a syringe in one hand as she gently rolled the child with the other. Needing her to comprehend what I was about to say, I leaned closer.

"We need to be off the ground by 4:30," I earnestly whispered. "That's in about 20 minutes."

She heard my words, but it was hard to know if her look of concern indicated that she understood our urgency to outrace the encroaching darkness or reflected her singular focus to stabilize the children. Then, the rush inside the room intensified as more staff entered with additional equipment they set up alongside the other flashing, tube-draped boxes. Like dedicated soldiers, these machines were present for one purpose: to preserve life.

This increased activity began eroding my determination to leave ahead of the dark and its inevitable companion—fog. It was imperative that we clear the ridge before daylight vanished altogether. Beyond that crest of hills was the lower ground near the river, our landmark into the city and our "home pad."

Still holding the trickling IV, my arm ached with fatigue. Of course IV stands were available, but this scene was like being on the street. We were expecting to leave at any moment, so no one wanted to struggle with extras. When the time came, it was going to be a dash.

If I left to start the helicopter ahead of time, I would interrupt the effort, not advance it. The patients were small, but there were two of them, not one. Extra hands, arms, and legs would be required to relocate this scene into the back of the helicopter. The situation itself was delicate. I was now part of the care effort and could not be separated easily. Plus, my presence ensured that someone would keep pushing the time factor. My waiting in a helicopter that was already running would not get us out of this room as soon as we needed to be.

My heart rate kept pace with the tension ratcheting up in the medical bay. When a metal pan crashed to the floor, no one even flinched. Heads stayed down; hands never missed a beat. My ability to have us on our way seemed just beyond my grasp. "What ifs" filled my mind as I deliberated over our return route.

Leaving a well-lit town to burrow into immediate darkness would take major adjustments—adjustments that would depend heavily on ground references. If sudden fog obscured those references, our mission would be over. We would be forced to return to this small hospital, leaving our tiny patients stranded far away from the university's much higher level of pediatric care so vital to their survival.

By 4:40, the children had been transferred to the helicopter's single stretcher. The steel table, its large wheels finally unlocked, now rolled down the hallway toward the exit with only necessary and trained staff alongside to carry bags and dangling IVs. We were leaving the trauma bay to begin a journey that hopefully would end on the twelfth floor helipad and, ultimately, in the pediatric ICU at the University of Penn.

By 4:50, the crew hovered over the kids in the final preparation for flight. The rotors turned slowly as the first engine whine grew louder. Although I would have preferred an immediate takeoff, the needed seconds for preflight, start-up, and cockpit checks dragged past as if I were moving in molasses. The crew were so focused on the precarious condition of the little ones that I had to remind them to "belt in" for departure.

As we climbed up and out of the small suburb, street lights were beginning to come on. Homeward bound motorists crowded the small, shop-lined streets, their car lights encircled with halos from the moist air. I drew a deep breath and settled down for what I expected would be a difficult trip to the university, where more advanced care awaited. The two diminutive patients were now enclosed in a time machine that promised an opportunity for recovery.

The friendly street scenes faded behind us as darkness settled inside the cockpit. Lights from below were infrequent now, too dim for reflection in the plexiglass windows. Only the glow from the panel lights lit up my world.

A black curtain had been drawn behind me to protect the cockpit from the overhead lights back where the medical crew labored to keep the children stable and alive. Occasionally, though, the helicopter's vibrations would briefly separate the curtains, and sharp stabs of white light would pierce the darkened cockpit.

Across this section of Pennsylvania, lights from scattered houses dotted the fields and roads below us. The sky ahead—a blend of fading daylight and misty cloud deck—was darkening, the horizon becoming opaquer by the mile.

Thin strings of translucent fog hung from the low clouds, touching the ground in places like vague pillars of an ancient temple holding up the darkening overcast. Barely visible farm fields were already knee-deep in ground fog. It wasn't raining, but the air was sodden with moisture. Cooler temperatures—the aftermath of a setting sun—would also drastically hasten the build-up of vapor that would block our way.

Time was running out for us. We had launched too late from Plymouth Meeting to expect help from the golden orb. It was gone. The rushing helicopter had one urgent task—to reach its destination—and no other options existed except one: to land there, a commitment that would most likely determine the fate of the two injured children. Their helplessness and need to survive had launched this mission at this hour. We weren't here for a joy ride.

I still had ground contact as we headed for the ridge, but just barely. Staying fairly low to avoid entering fog or disappearing into the low ceiling, we crested the hills and descended toward the Schuylkill River. I planned to follow it into the city. Even though high ground no longer separated us from the city, its million glowing lights were unable to penetrate the thickening gloom around us. At this point, I would have welcomed even a glimmer of encouragement.

Almost all helicopter EMS operations are flown single-pilot. When patients are onboard, the crew in back are far removed from the dimly lit cockpit where the pilot's focus is vastly different from their own. A tiny, blinking, yellow light is the only signal to the pilot that they are talking with the hospital. Intercom conversations seldom occur between them and the pilot unless everything in the back is stable and conditions outside are fair. Tonight, they are neither.

With their special skills and tools, the crew are trying to save lives in the back, while the pilot uses a different skill set altogether to try to save them all, including the bird. On nights like this, he strains to connect with the world below. The oppression of growing danger envelops him—the sole decision-maker—in isolation before he even realizes it has come. The outcome of combining these skills is noteworthy—life is now possible.

Fully committed to that singular goal, I hoped to catch the river at Conshohocken, here it came from the west and made a sharp bend to the southeast. Somewhere in that area, high-tension wires were strung along the southwest bank below the highway and above the river. Large complicated towers—all rust and dark metal—carried the heavy wires. They were hardly visible in daylight, let alone at night.

During the descent, I peered into the gloom, straining for any reference light to keep the aircraft level and oriented to the ground while moving forward. As the aircraft slowed, I realized I was figuratively groping for the next ground light.

I was confident that I understood the path of the wires and their height along the steep bank leading up to the highway. I would have to stay above the wires and avoid the temptation to fly low over the river. Although I couldn't see them, knowing they crossed the river to the east near Manayunk would enable me to get closer to the water and follow it into the city.

Lower and slower now, I passed Manayunk and knew the power lines were no longer a factor. The boat houses for the various University sculling crews remained hidden in the mist below, passing behind us in the dark as we crossed Fairmont Park. We were in the built-up part of the city, and I was low above the street lights in West Philly over an avenue that I knew would lead to our destination—the Children's Hospital beside the building we had launched from earlier that afternoon. That outbound leg had taken us only fifteen minutes to reach Plymouth Meeting; this return flight was pushing forty minutes.

Driven by the thought of the two infants I had stood over in the trauma bay, watching them brought back from the edge of death, I wasn't considering failure. This flight had become an extension of my holding the life-saving IV, and I wasn't about to drop the bag and watch it burst.

Phone and electric wires crisscrossed the city, of course, but following the street lights was the only safe option. I was at a fast hover, high enough to clear obstacles and slow enough to see wires, but fog had so enveloped the city after dusk that my visibility seemed about a quarter of a mile.

For obvious reasons, this kind of flying was long gone from the current helicopter EMS industry, but in Vietnam, no one had checked the weather when we scrambled on a fire mission or were called to cover a Medevac ship. Nor had we said that it was too dark to fly or looked impossible to accomplish. Many of us still carried that attitude whenever we faced a flight task involving life or death. The response was automatic. Being so young, none of us considered death the likely outcome of our determination to complete a mission.

Today with GPS, autopilots, and IFR-equipped helicopters, many more options are available to insure a safe flight. This flight had nothing to do with being brave or proving your pilot skills to others. Instead, it was about dealing with the situation and the weather as you went along, the way you had learned in the war.

I had been flying for twenty years since leaving military service, but not in EMS. This was my first job in the industry.

I had accomplished many tasks with a helicopter, but none of the missions involved this kind of urgency—centered around a human life.

As I neared the vicinity of the side-by-side hospitals, I now realized there was no way I could reach the twelfth-floor helipad of the Children's Hospital. If I attempted a circling approach, I would immediately lose my orientation in the thick fog and crash into the nearest building. Although I was in direct communication with dispatch, located at the top of the building, the prospect of an even longer delay—while police cleared the street and secured the area from potential flying debris—seemed daunting. In fact, I never considered it. Delivering the children as quickly as possible was my all-consuming focus now that we were close.

Then as I came to a high hover in front of the hospital and noticed the lit windows of the patients' rooms, I determined to follow them up the side of the building in a kind of up-elevator strategy. However, if I flew too far out, the thick fog would block the lights, so I had to tuck in close to the brick walls. Once I passed the last row of windows, I would be at the helipad, which would be brightly lit. They knew we were coming.

Luckily for us, this type of aircraft had the horsepower to go straight up. With a more heavily loaded helicopter, that would not have been an option. Slowly, but with continuous upward motion, I finally cleared the last row of windows on the eleventh floor. Then as the aircraft popped over the edge of the helipad, I was almost blinded by the many bright lights. It was as startling as having a bucket of ice water thrown in my face! The swirling rotor separated and scattered the cloud-like moisture as I came to a hover. Somewhat disoriented, I managed to plant the skids on the pad.

A flurry of activity immediately surrounded us. Helping hands slid out the single stretcher—where both kids lay wrapped in a warm blanket—and positioned it onto a hospital gurney. The gurney, on its black, rapidly wobbling wheels, was then pushed into the waiting elevator. The doors closed against the swirling eddies of mist generated by the turning rotors of the parked helicopter. For me, it was over.

After two minutes, I closed the throttles, reached for the rotor brake, and pulled weakly on the lever, my strength suddenly draining away. As the rotors slowly came to a halt, I secured the switches and killed the battery, dropping my flight helmet onto the passenger seat before unlatching the pilot door.

I placed a foot onto the skid step, hesitating for a moment before stepping down onto the cement pad. The air was cool, and the sounds of the city were muffled by the thick fog. I drank in the utter relief of that momentary stillness after what, at the time, had seemed like hours of intense flying. Water droplets from the saturated air moved gently across my bare skin, evidence that I was at last reunited with earth, no matter how temporary.

I walked around to the clamshell doors that were still open from the medical crew's final rush into the building with their two small patients, trailed by doctors and staff. The crew had held IVs and straightened dangling tubes as they crossed the pad, everyone talking and gesturing at once. Now I was alone. A comforting silence permeated the shadows behind the helicopter, where I stood with one hand on a door.

Before I could think to close and fasten both doors, I did something I had never done after any flight. I cried. My shoulders convulsed with sobs for a full five minutes there in the darkness. I didn't know if my emotion was from relief at finally reaching the pad, from the sheer elation of safely delivering the children, or from the release of suppressed tension into the vapor around me. Perhaps it was from all three.

I couldn't really figure it out. I wiped my sleeve across my face to clear away the tears. Drifting fog blew across the helipad and swirled at the edges of the building, its moisture easing my flushed skin like a splash of cool water. I felt better. The weighty burden I had not fully realized I was carrying had vanished. I might have staggered a bit beneath its load, but I hadn't fallen.

I still wasn't quite home, though. My final destination was next door. Getting from the top of one building to the next, even though they almost touched, was going to be difficult but doable with a little planning and patience. The helipads were at different levels with bracing wires and antennas in between. The medical crew would finish up and go back to the crew quarters to write their report. I didn't have to wait for them.

I cranked the machine—all flashing and rotating lights turned off—and lifted to a hover. I didn't even switch on my landing light to avoid possible reflections from the surrounding fog. I managed to make the short hop without a scare. Shortly after landing, the aircraft again sat in total silence; all moving parts had stopped. I was back where we had started two hours earlier.

As I walked into the crew quarters, I stuck my head into dispatch, giving a wave to my friend Gaspero, sitting behind the radios. His had been the steady and reassuring voice replying to my position reports throughout the flight. He had also reported accurate conditions at the hospital when we first flew into the city. Although he had "sweated it out" with us all through the extreme weather and darkness, he hadn't allowed it into his voice. Tall with curly hair, he was always cheerful, and tonight, that positive tone over the radio had given me a sense of confidence that I would see him shortly.

He and I belonged to a Civil War Roundtable in the city and knew each other well. Glad I was back, his face reflected a certain strain along with a silent plea for more detail, but the night crew was coming on, and the place was full of boisterous laughter and backslapping. "Later," I said and continued down the hall, past the noise in the ready room to my locker.

Tonight, the night crew would be carefree. Driving to work in the lowering visibility, they knew they would be sleeping all night or be on light duty in the hospital—no flights. And once the night shift pilot had pre-flighted the chopper, he too would return to the comfort of the crew lounge, then TV and an early night to catch up on rest. I would see him again the next morning at crew change. Perhaps the mechanic would come in to look over the helicopter or pull an inspection, knowing the machine would be grounded by weather for at least twelve hours.

There was no debriefing. There were no "stress counselors" to hear your story. The emotional release had helped, but no one there would ever know it had happened—it is understood among pilots everywhere that such an admission works against the image of fearless, steely-eyed aviators. No tears—ever!

While changing out of my flight suit and into my clothes, I kept going into short trances, thinking back to the flight and savoring the normality of standing in front of my locker getting ready to leave. As I returned my flight helmet to its bag, I made a mental note to bring a clean flight suit the next morning. Then I walked to the elevator, pushed the down button, and waited.

When I opened the glass doors and stepped into the street, everything—including the sidewalks—was wet from the dew-laden fog, as if a heavy rain shower had just passed. People coming and going from the main hospital entrance behind me shook their coats before entering, or else stopped momentarily before leaving to pull their jackets closer and tighten their scarves against the penetrating, damp chill.

Aluminum food trucks, famous in Philly, were lined up in front of the building; they glittered with moisture. Rivulets of water streamed off the attached awnings that sheltered various hospital staff who huddled in the cold to buy their dinner. Nowhere in the world would a better Philly Cheese steak be placed in your hand—a hot, large bundle wrapped in foil, smelling of melted cheese and sizzling meat.

Tonight I wasn't that hungry, but I walked up to the open counter on the side of the truck to order a large Coke and a bunch of fries. I tossed my head back to take a long pull on the icy Coke. I had no idea I was so thirsty. This was probably my first drink since leaving on the mission earlier that afternoon. The ketchup thinned as I poured it over the hot fries. They burned going down, and my fingers were soon sticky from the red sauce. I gulped down the rest of them on my way to the parking garage. I pulled some napkins from my coat pocket to wipe my hands, then tossed them into a nearby trash can before turning up the collar of my flight jacket against the wet, cold air.

I found my car, climbed in, and sat for a few minutes in the quiet, its calming stillness only occasionally shattered by the odd horn or chatter of hospital workers passing by. Sitting in the driver's seat of this machine, a cockpit of sorts, was a sharp contrast to the cockpit I had just left upstairs. Decisions made on the ground were one-dimensional—you were transporting yourself, not an event. If your engine ran out of gas, you stopped along the road. There weren't a thousand feet to fall before you quit moving.

I gradually relaxed in the worn seat of that old car. I thought of the infants upstairs in the Children's ICU. No doubt by now the flurry of activity from their "golden" hour had subsided, both of them now were connected to machines and wrapped in warm blankets, being closely monitored in their separate hospital cribs.

I leaned my head against the car's steering wheel and briefly relived the intense emotion of that trip's peril, then was comforted by the realization that both babies had been oblivious to the circumstances of their journey. Somewhere in the hospital, they had begun their return from near-death. My brief prayer asked for them to live. I sighed deeply, then sat upright and turned the ignition key. I considered what I might bring for tomorrow's lunch as I pulled out of the parking garage onto the busy streets of the city.

As I drove west to my work apartment, the passing trees seemed to snag the fog in their branches. Traffic slowed as we crept through the lowering visibility along the higher elevations west of town. Oncoming headlights rebounded off the saturated atmosphere, their approach like backlighted aliens heading toward you from the ramp of their spaceship.

I walked upstairs to the attic room I rented whenever I was in Philadelphia; my home was a hundred miles west. However, tonight it didn't really matter that I was away. It was just damn good to be anywhere as long as it was out of the milky sky and on solid ground. The warm room, away from the chill at last, drained the rest of my bottled-up tension.

For several moments, I stood at the window of my small room, gazing down at the street below. The few neighborhood street lights glowed softly as the air—thick with water droplets—swirled around them coating the shiny surfaces of the tall poles that supported them. They pointed skyward, where the misty vapor that clung to them now would travel when the sun's slanting rays broke through the clouds of a new day. However, the intangible spirits of the two children would not depart with the fog, but remain here to live and to grow and to be loved.

EPILOGUE

That night in Philadelphia, as I gazed out the window at the fog swirling around the street lamps, I was completely unaware that I was already more than halfway through my flying career. Up ahead lay further variety and reinvention, a FAA float-plane rating that led to a job demonstrating and selling them on the East Coast, DC-9s at a major airline, lengthy stints at helicopter logging from British Columbia to Utah, more firefighting with a water bucket suspended above the flames, and an eventual return to helicopter EMS.

I would never have a real opportunity to build on anything for more than a few years before some kind of disaster suddenly vaulted into the midst of an operation and destroyed it. Fatal crashes with management aboard, company bankruptcy, owner divorces, mergers, and arbitrary or uninformed decisions often doomed long-term opportunities at any current job.

A wheel of fortune seemed to accompanied my years in the air labeled with categories such as "Safe," "Good Salary," "Difficult Crew," "Seniority, If you're Lucky," "Land if You Can," "The Brass Ring," "Try Harder," "Retirement and Benefits—Maybe!" Generally, I spun the wheel with vigor and often a short prayer, attempting to insure that the needle stopped where I needed it. Sometimes I pulled with trepidation, but more often, I spun it with eyes closed and a figuratively trembling hand. The outcome could be joyful, irrelevant, or downright miserable, given the consequences attached.

Losses along the way of close friends and acquaintances, whose remains disappeared within tangled piles of metal, smoking holes, or trackless geography, were constant reminders of the perils of moving a machine across the sky or of conducting a complicated task above a dangling cable and hook in a single engine helicopter at an altitude that offered no options for survival if the power stopped suddenly or something broke.

I have seen marvelous sights with my own eyes while looking down from a cockpit—Beluga whales, snaking nose to tail along a mile of gravelly Arctic shoreline barely twenty yards into the lapping waves; perfect circles of musk ox surrounding their young; wolves tracking a herd of moose through the snow. I have been chased by a hundred curious caribou while dashing toward my parked aircraft and have watched pure white wolves creep toward the running helicopter until they were beneath the spinning rotors. I have seen cougars in their dens and waterfalls of epic beauty rarely visited by humans.

I have even seen every version of grizzly and black bear charging through the brush and across streams, briefly closing in on them so the geologist in the seat beside me could see their fangs and the foam streaming from the edges of their mouths. It was a measure of any man or woman if they were still willing to step out onto the tundra for their daily exploration task after such a sighting.

I have found broken wooden propellers and the broken airplanes they came from, as well as farm houses and Arctic camps with well preserved, rustic buildings that sat void of human habitation for decades. It seems they were suddenly abandoned, leaving behind tables already set for a meal, tickets to a county fair, school books opened for study, laundry still in washers, and walls covered with *Playboy* pinups from its earliest days of publication. Weather, disease, fear, or an imagined catastrophe propelled the inhabitants of these structures from their comforts during a moment in time that demanded action—no hint of the reason was present.

I have looked down on red, faded Russian stars painted on the broken wing of a P-39 fighter plane lying in the tundra. It had once wended its way across Alaska toward Mother Russia to join her fight against the Germans, the plane once gifted from the US government during the days of Lend-Lease. I have viewed the tail of a helicopter sticking up out of a shallow lake, crashed there by a pilot I never knew before yesterday when he landed beside me to borrow gas for his ship. Dripping oil and streaks of soot disfigured the blue and white paint on his machine. After refueling, he flew away to the south and the end of his life.

I have carried a legally blind artist and his daughter to an abandoned native village far into the mountains—the scene he drew there he painted and framed out of gratitude; it still hangs on my wall. I have met extraordinary people, unforgettable personalities, and unusual men and woman I will never forget. I have flown into remote valleys where gold miners labored for an owner who lived not in a log cabin, but in a home that could have been lifted straight out of a Seattle neighborhood—bricks, porch, and all.

Once while flying high in the Arctic, I spotted an aging cairn. I landed with my crew of technicians. Hidden under the stones at the top of the pyramid was a metal pipe secured at each end with a threaded cap. Its contents revealed that a Canadian Mounted Policeman had passed this way with a dog team posting hunting placards. The Mountie's name and the date he had stopped there—1902—were still legible on the back of the yellowed paper. We had been the only ones to open the two-inch lead pipe in all the decades since then. We added our message to a scrap of paper torn from the back of the flight manual, wrote the date, the tail number of the helicopter, and then signed all our names. After slipping it into the tube, we screwed the caps back on and returned it to its resting place beneath a mossy stone at the top of the pile and then flew on.

These highlights and many, many more are the lasting memories of an aviator who sometimes against his will, but always to his benefit, was gifted a solid thread to follow throughout his career. A thread you could follow or hang onto, it never led to the end, but only just over the next horizon.

I wore a leather flight jacket for more than half of my flying hours. Indestructible and tough, only the leather collar and shoulder loops showed any wear, although I did replace the trim at least twice as it had worn into tatters. I finally quit wearing it when a young pilot asked if I had been lifting weights—a backhanded dig about the broad expanse of my chest that showed through an opening I could no longer cover by closing the zipper.

Like my career, I had picked a jacket size with no idea that I might one day have an increasing girth, symbolic of my youthful disregard for whatever the future might bring. My younger self always savored the satisfaction of the moment—leather jacket with the collar up and a cool car (that didn't happen)—but at least I was flying something. You always wished for a bigger and more complex aircraft, a more challenging assignment, and more money, but having a current seat (a flying job) was all that really mattered in the early years.

The end to my flying career came suddenly. One day, I was in my office running a county EMS helicopter operation and the next morning I was in HR with the rest of the pilots being handed a severance package—the program had been shut down. I had recently invested four million dollars of public funds to purchase a previously owned, IFR, high-performance machine, along with refurbishing our "smaller, back-up helicopter." Both paint jobs were new and spectacular!

We had moved into a new hangar, built just for us, and I had completed a project establishing a series of GPS approaches for recovering patients from the coastal islands on foggy nights. However, the "earthling" county employees involved strove for just two things daily—retirement and eliminating competition—they were now responsible for pulling down a service thirty years in the making. Too obtuse to comprehend the long-term implications for county residents, their main talent was the ability to excel at shortsightedness.

But it was time. Only in my late sixties, I had never contemplated being grounded. Like the flight jacket I had outgrown, I remained oblivious to this similar dilemma; it needed to be mentioned. I adapted. It was like facing an aircraft's sudden failure when at the last moment, fate again swung to my side of the scale, landing me safely one last time, but just a little short. The long tread of my career had finally brought me over the last horizon and fastened me loosely to the ground.

Regrets, very few. Sorrows, yes, still. Faces and places remembered, beyond count.